138 HAN
The wisdom of your
child's face : discover y
Haner, Jean, 1953-
853987

SO SEP 2010
RU Aug 12
NA MAY 2013
Su May 15
WK NOV 2015
SC MR 2018
VE DEC 2018

THE
WISDOM OF
YOUR CHILD'S FACE

D0207481

Also by Jean Haner

THE WISDOM OF YOUR FACE:
Change Your Life with Chinese Face Reading!

◎ ◎ ◎

Hay House Titles of Related Interest

YOU CAN HEAL YOUR LIFE, the movie, starring Louise L. Hay &
Friends (available as a 1-DVD program and an expanded 2-DVD set)
Watch the trailer at: **www.LouiseHayMovie.com**

THE SHIFT, the movie, starring Dr. Wayne W. Dyer
(available as a 1-DVD program and an expanded 2-DVD set)
Watch the trailer at: **www.DyerMovie.com**

◎ ◎ ◎

HEAL YOUR BODY: The Mental Causes for Physical Illness and the
Metaphysical Way to Overcome Them, by Louise L. Hay

THE INDIGO CHILDREN TEN YEARS LATER: What's Happening
with the Indigo Teenagers! by Lee Carroll and Jan Tober

THE INTUITIVE SPARK: Bring Intuition Home to Your Child,
Your Family, and You, by Sonia Choquette

SEVEN SECRETS TO RAISING A HAPPY AND HEALTHY CHILD:
The Ayurvedic Approach to Parenting, by Joyce Golden Seyburn

THE THREE SISTERS OF THE TAO: Essential Conversations with
Chinese Medicine, I Ching, and Feng Shui, by Terah Kathryn Collins

WHAT THEY KNOW ABOUT . . . PARENTING! Celebrity Moms
and Dads Give Us Their Take on Having Kids, by Cindy Pearlman;
edited by Jill Kramer

All of the above are available at your local bookstore,
or may be ordered by visiting:

Hay House USA: **www.hayhouse.com**®
Hay House Australia: **www.hayhouse.com.au**
Hay House UK: **www.hayhouse.co.uk**
Hay House South Africa: **www.hayhouse.co.za**
Hay House India: **www.hayhouse.co.in**

THE
WIS D⊙M OF
YOUR CHILD'S FACE

Discover Your Child's True Nature
with Chinese Face Reading

JEAN HANER

HAY HOUSE, INC.
Carlsbad, California • New York City
London • Sydney • Johannesburg
Vancouver • Hong Kong • New Delhi

Copyright © 2010 by Jean Haner

Published and distributed in the United States by: Hay House, Inc.: www.hay house.com • *Published and distributed in Australia by:* Hay House Australia Pty. Ltd.: www.hayhouse.com.au • *Published and distributed in the United Kingdom by:* Hay House UK, Ltd.: www.hayhouse.co.uk • *Published and distributed in the Republic of South Africa by:* Hay House SA (Pty), Ltd.: www.hayhouse.co.za • *Distributed in Canada by:* Raincoast: www.raincoast.com • *Published in India by:* Hay House Publishers India: www.hayhouse.co.in

The following image numbers are from **iStockphoto.com**: 28, 30, 35, 37, 51, 59, 66, 72, 82, 83, 85, 89, and 92. All other photos were taken by Brian Hartman, Seattle, Washington. Figures 1 and 2 were created by Jean Haner. Figures 91, 93, 94, 95, 96, 97, 102, and 103 were created by Stephanie McWilliams, San Diego, California.

The quotation by Elisabeth Kübler-Ross on page 121 is being used with grateful permission from the Elisabeth Kübler-Ross Foundation.

Project editor: Patrick Gabrysiak

All rights reserved. No part of this book may be reproduced by any mechanical, photographic, or electronic process, or in the form of a phonographic recording; nor may it be stored in a retrieval system, transmitted, or otherwise be copied for public or private use—other than for "fair use" as brief quotations embodied in articles and reviews—without prior written permission of the publisher.

The author of this book does not dispense medical advice or prescribe the use of any technique as a form of treatment for physical, emotional, or medical problems without the advice of a physician, either directly or indirectly. The intent of the author is only to offer information of a general nature to help you in your quest for emotional and spiritual well-being. In the event you use any of the information in this book for yourself, which is your constitutional right, the author and the publisher assume no responsibility for your actions.

Library of Congress Cataloging-in-Publication Data

Haner, Jean.
  The wisdom of your child's face : discover your child's true nature with Chinese face reading / Jean Haner. -- 1st ed.
    p. cm.
  Includes bibliographical references.
  ISBN 978-1-4019-2534-5 (tradepaper : alk. paper) 1. Physiognomy--China. 2. Children--Psychology. 3. Character. 4. Personality. I. Title.
  BF851.H277 2010
  138--dc22

                              2009047647

ISBN: 978-1-4019-2534-5

13 12 11 10   4 3 2 1
1st edition, June 2010

Printed in the United States of America

THIS BOOK
IS DEDICATED
TO THE POWER
OF A WOMAN'S HEART
TO CHANGE THE
WORLD.

CONTENTS

Editor's Note: In order to avoid awkward "he/she," "him/her" references, in some cases we have opted to use either masculine or feminine pronouns for certain examples, alternating between the two. The same information pertains universally to both boys and girls. Additionally, where we have chosen to use the word "children," this also applies to parents with one child.

"For nothing is fixed, forever, forever, forever,
it is not fixed;
the earth is always shifting,
the light is always changing,
the sea does not cease to grind down the rock.
Generations do not cease to be born,
and we are responsible to them because we
are the only witnesses they have.
The sea rises, the light fails, lovers cling to each other,
and children cling to us.
The moment we cease to hold each other,
the moment we break faith with one another,
the sea engulfs us and the light goes out."

— JAMES BALDWIN

INTRODUCTION

I was still in a state of awe as I lay my newborn son down in the shiny wooden crib for the very first time. Even though he was a normal-sized baby, he seemed *sooo* small, and the bed looked enormous in comparison. Unable to bear him looking so tiny on that large mattress, I finally laid him crosswise at the head of his bed! And then I sat down to gaze at his tiny sleeping face, searching for the messages I'd been trained to read. *Such a full mouth!* I thought. This would be a very cuddly guy, a young boy who would revel in family gatherings but have a hard time with change. As a teenager, he would never neglect to visit his grandmother, but might become a bit too much of a pleaser. *His ears lie close to his head,* I noticed with a relieved sigh . . . and I hoped they'd stay that way and not start to stick out later on. This meant that he wouldn't be an obstinate child. *Thank goodness!* But he might need extra encouragement to go after what he wanted in life. What his nose would reveal would have to wait awhile—that wouldn't start to grow into its true size and shape for a few years. His hair was red, which made me laugh out loud. My son is half Chinese, so everyone fully expected him to be born with black hair and no hint of my own strawberry blonde. When she first saw him, my sweet Chinese mother-in-law had hastened to assure me that it would soon change to black, as if red hair were a misfortune! As he grew, his hair did darken to brown, though with red highlights, and I have to admit I'm still tickled that his looks reflect a balance of both sides of his lineage.

Discovering Face Reading

When I married into a Chinese family seven years before, I never dreamed it would open a doorway for me to discover that someone's inner nature could be understood by reading the features of his or her face, let alone understand my own baby on such a deep level right from the start. It was my very traditional mother-in-law who first introduced me to Chinese face reading, pointing out that a certain person wasn't someone to *ever* do business with, and that another would have no trouble attracting a mate, based on just looking at their faces. This all seemed rather "woo-woo" to me, and incredibly judgmental on top of that. How on earth could the shape of people's eyes or the creases in their cheeks have anything to do with their temperament or potential in life? And what a harsh thing to reject or accept others based strictly on appearance. If you were born with one kind of nose, was that the end of it for you—that is, no one would want to hire you or marry you? But if you happened to have a different sort of nose, would everyone then want to be your best friend? Initially, this was just a bunch of superstitious folklore, as far as I was concerned.

However, what *did* intrigue me was the advice my mother-in-law shared with me when her son and I were searching for a home right after we got married. What she was saying made intuitive sense to me and confirmed my own reactions to various properties; although up to that point, I had no logical explanation for why one house just didn't seem right and another was winking and wiggling its hips at me!

My husband's mother talked about this very strange thing called "fung soo-ey," which back in the late 1970s was barely known in the West, though we know of it today as *feng shui*. The rest of the Chinese side of the family was quite embarrassed by this, insisting I shouldn't listen to her and that she was just being superstitious. But unlike her face-reading advice, this information regarding the energy of environments made distinct sense to me, and I paid close attention to what she was saying. But she usually wasn't able to explain the "whys" of her knowledge, and it was important for my analytical mind to understand the logic underlying this system. I went on to seek out many teachers over the years to learn the deeper meaning behind the set of odd rules that my mother-in-law followed, and eventually ended up teaching feng shui and doing consulting work based on its principles all over the world.

It was my work with feng shui that brought me back to Chinese face reading. After learning about its ancient foundations, I began to reexamine my initial negative reaction to it. Perhaps it too was more than it had seemed at first. What really convinced me to reconsider its validity was the thought that if I could know more about my clients' inner thoughts and feelings, I could be more effective for them. But what I discovered was so much more than that, and it changed my life forever. Certainly being able to know my feng shui clients on a deeper level based on the powerful messages their faces revealed was revolutionary for my work, but it was seeing how this wisdom could help all people finally feel comfortable in their own skin—and as a result understand their life journey for the first time—that made me aware I had to bring this information to the world in a more accessible way.

So after years of teaching and consulting, I wrote my first book, *The Wisdom of Your Face*, in order to help people read the "sacred calligraphy" of their features and learn to love themselves and others in a much more spacious way. The outpouring of excitement and gratitude I've received in response to that book has been breathtaking, and the international community carrying its message of compassion and awareness has continued to grow exponentially. In every city where I speak or teach, people come up to me and share the personal revelations this work has brought them. And so many of the stories have had to do with parents understanding their children better, thus preventing or healing conflicts; *or* them understanding their own parents better, which allowed them to resolve old issues that had kept them tethered to the past. It soon became obvious that a book about children was the logical next step in my journey.

What You Can Expect from This Book

What you hold in your hands is the accumulated knowledge from years of study and observation of parents' and children's faces, personalities, relationships, problems, and life choices. Its purpose is to present you with easy and practical ways to understand your children's behaviors better; recognize who they really are inside; and trust, honor, and support those bright young spirits so they can flourish. There have been many times in workshops and private consultations when I've been amazed by how often parents misinterpret their children's behavior because they aren't aware of what their little ones' true inner experiences really are. This can lead to misconceptions piling up, creating frustrations and reactions that only serve to make everything worse. I've worked with more than one family who was barely speaking to each other by the time they finally met with me, due to a complete misread of the real reasons behind their child's actions and attitude. While that's the extreme, even smaller everyday interactions can cause so much needless stress—something that we all have too much of already.

On top of that, it's natural for parents to project onto their children certain expectations, hopes, or dreams for who they want them to be. Anytime they differ from these, it can at the very least be confusing for the parents, if not discouraging, and create anxiety about how a situation should be handled. For example, if you expect your son to be as bookish as you were at his age, but instead he couldn't care less about reading, do you try to manipulate or bribe him into being interested, or worry about his ability to succeed in school and eventually in his career? Do you hold your tongue but harbor a sense of concern or disappointment that he can still feel? Wouldn't it be valuable to have the power to know if it's necessary to take action about a concern, or whether what you're experiencing is how your child's process was designed to be?

Through my work over the years, I've come to believe that each of us is born with a soul's intent: to be a certain kind of person; to learn specific lessons; and to heed an inherent calling . . . that is, we each have a special purpose to fulfill. The challenge we all encounter to one degree or another is to stay true to our inner nature and personal calling. Our job as parents is to love and support our children as they embody their unique design so they can become its fullest expression.

The messages waiting on our children's faces are our guides to who they came here to be, what they plan to learn, and where they can go with their potential. This vital information gifts us with the wisdom to know how to trust and honor their life plan and make them feel truly loved for who they are.

• • •

In Part I of this book, we'll examine Western concepts of temperament and personality, which are our culture's understanding of human nature that's most similar to that of the Chinese. We'll then discover how important faces really are to us humans, and how the practice of reading them developed in China over the millennia. In Part II, we'll learn the universal principles that are the foundation of this work, and how they appear as archetypal personalities that are observable in children's behavior and recognizable in the features and characteristics of their faces. Aside from specific guidance for parents, each section will also include thoughts for teachers who, in my opinion, are obscenely under-valued in the U.S. and should be earning the salaries of sports stars. In Part III, we'll discuss additional information that can be recognized from the different areas of anyone's face and how the facial map reveals the journey through life. Then we'll look at some faces for practice readings along with my commentary. Last, we'll see how interconnected families truly are, and how who we are—our own thoughts and feelings—influence our children far more than we might imagine.

◎ ◎ ◎

Part I

THE TERRITORY

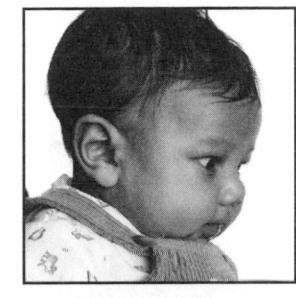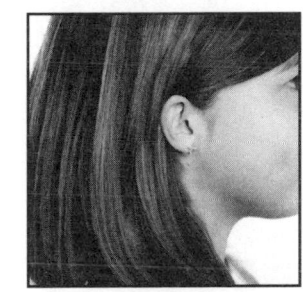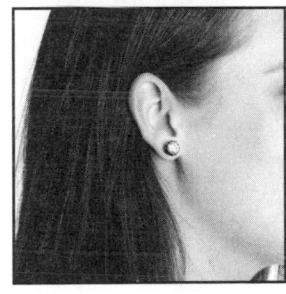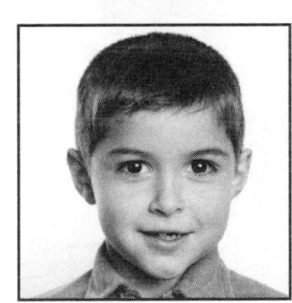

*"The worst loneliness is not to be
comfortable with yourself."*

— MARK TWAIN

TRUST

People joke that your child doesn't come with a user's manual, but they're wrong. It's written in her face, and all you have to do is learn to read it. Every aspect of your child's inner nature and personal potential is eloquently inscribed in the curve of her cheeks, the shape of her eyes, the contour of her brows; it's the unique language of her original design. The messages waiting for you there will explain who this little spirit really is—how he'll tend to think, feel, and behave; and what he needs in order to feel loved and happy. In fact, your son's or daughter's face provides you with the map you can follow as you navigate your journey of parenting; it's the best way to help them flourish and become the most powerful expression of their authentic selves.

The secret to discovering your child's true nature lies in profound and ancient knowledge that evolved in China over the millennia, but has only begun to be translated for the West in recent decades. A branch of Chinese medicine, face reading is a science that teaches that we are all born with a unique blueprint, a design that is ours and ours alone, and that this inner architecture is reflected in the patterns observable in our outer design.

Just as in nature, where each seed is predetermined to develop into a certain kind of plant, each human spirit is born with a coherent plan, a soul's intent. When a plant grows in a supportive environment—nourished with the right kind of soil, food, and light for its special needs—and isn't obstructed or damaged, it blossoms into the most complete manifestation of its potential. In the same way, if children are loved, honored, and supported to develop in alignment with *their* inner design, they can actualize that plan, physically, emotionally, and spiritually.

If you're a gardener, you have it easy; you know what you're nurturing. If you plant nasturtiums, you'll know to prepare the soil in a certain way, place the seeds to receive just the right amount of sunlight for healthy growth, and sow those seeds at the time of year that's best for them. You'll make sure to fertilize them according to their special needs and water them appropriately to yield lush blooms that will spread throughout the garden.

As a parent, you can have a different experience. Delivered into your life is a glorious but totally mysterious little being whose physical care may be relatively easy to figure out, but the deeper complexities of emotional nurturing are not so obvious. And sometimes you're expecting a nasturtium and you get a hollyhock! The sooner you realize this, the better the chances are that you can help your child thrive, because you'll know how to do exactly what's needed for him or her to grow into the most vibrant, beautiful adult possible. But if you keep treating that flower (child) like a nasturtium, you'll be in for some confusion, and that plant might struggle to fully express itself.

This is how it is with our little ones. If we're able to recognize their inner plans, for example, we can support them in ways that are in alignment with their potential. Overall, the result is a less stressful parenting experience, and children who will be comfortable in their own skins and much more likely to prosper in life.

Supporting Your Child's Journey

So much of my research for this book revealed study after study showing that the most important factor in children's emotional health and success at school is feeling a sense of connectedness with their parents. Kids who feel loved and understood at home do far better at school and in life in general than ones who don't. They actually grow more synapses in their brains, can self-regulate and manage stress more efficiently, get sick less, and establish better friendships. In fact, it's been determined that the single most powerful predictor of children's success in life is the quality of the connection they have with their parents.

Of course, virtually all mothers and fathers love their children, so how do some young ones end up feeling bereft of a strong sense of connection? Children know that they're truly loved when they feel seen, understood, and accepted for who they are. Parents may love their little ones and yet still not comprehend who these beings really are and why they're feeling or behaving in a certain manner. The result is often layers of misperceptions, leading to an undercurrent of stress for everyone involved. Despite loving behavior being projected toward them, children can still sense that something isn't quite right.

Interestingly, a study done at the University of Tennessee showed that children's satisfaction during a play session with their mothers didn't relate to how much praise the youngsters received, but instead on how much the parents "mirrored" or reflected back what their children were doing. In other words, what was most important was being understood and acknowledged. If kids don't receive this kind of acceptance, they'll struggle with their own self-acceptance, they won't feel a genuine sense of connection with their parents, and they won't feel as loved. Acclaimed author and physician Bernie Siegel talks about studies showing a one-in-four chance of illness by midlife if people felt that their parents loved them, and an approximately 90 percent chance of illness by midlife if they felt their parents didn't. This is how powerfully important the parent-child connection is.

Children come into the world with strengths, challenges, potential, tendencies, and personal qualities that are hardwired and affect their responses to what they encounter in life. All parents struggle, in varying degrees, to recognize and understand these distinct aspects of their children in order to decipher the best ways to help them succeed. If you can recognize your child's true nature, you have an open doorway to connect with and embrace him for who he is right from the start. Your experience as a parent will be more joyful and less stressful because you'll have a map to guide you on your journey. You'll be equipped to raise a child with a grounded sense of self who, as an adult, will be able to find the work that really feeds his soul instead of chasing money and ending up stuck in a job that drains his spirit. He'll attract a nurturing partner and be able to express his love in healthy ways to everyone around him; he won't react in resistance to life's challenges; he'll regain balance easily when stressed; and, most important, he'll be able to discover his calling in this lifetime and fulfill his special purpose in the world.

But how often have you met someone like that? Instead, here's how life usually works: You're born with your inner design all bright and shiny, with the vitality of a new life ready to begin the journey. But soon after you arrive, you begin to receive messages from the world around you. Your parents have expectations about how you'll think, feel, and behave; it's often assumed that you're a little version of them, with similar thoughts and emotions, and they can feel confused and stressed when you don't conform to these presumptions. To one degree or another, they'll also project onto you their own hopes, and react with disappointment, negativity, or even force if the reality of who you are is different from what was expected. Other family members will also bring their own ingredients to this soup; and then there's the experience of school, with teachers and other kids influencing how you feel about yourself. Add to this the impact of society at large—and its current definitions about what's acceptable, beautiful, and valued—and you're a child who's immersed in an atmosphere of subtle and not-so-subtle judgments about who you're supposed to be.

As a child, you're a little being who's arrived on this planet, and are just trying to learn the rules. If your parents want you to behave one way, you do your best to comply, even if it conflicts with what you're actually able to do. If you're told that you shouldn't be feeling a certain way, you'll also try to make that adjustment, though it's a bewildering experience to have your genuine emotions contradicted.

Naturally, you want to be loved, so you do your best to become the person you're told will be lovable. But this may not always match your inner self, and it can require you to try to limit, change, or suppress your true nature. Over time, you can develop a sense that there's something wrong with you, causing you to start blaming yourself for who you really are inside.

Before you're even through childhood, you're likely to have a negative talk-radio station playing in your head, telling you all the things that are wrong with you. You tend to think everything would be okay if you could just change, or may even feel a yearning toward a certain way of being but deny it in order to fit in and be loved. Over the years, you'll travel farther away from your true nature, so misdirected in your navigation that you make choices in your career and relationships that distance you even more from your authentic self until it becomes a mere whisper inside your soul.

There's a way to prevent this cycle, which is to not get so far off course in the first place. If you have a map for your journey, you're more likely to reach your destination. Just like knowing what flowers have sprouted in the garden, if you can discover your children's inner design, you can help them follow that plan to become the openhearted, clear, and compassionate people they're meant to be.

As part of my research for this book, I interviewed both children and parents. During the process I asked each adult what their own experience of childhood was like—what they thought was special about their personalities or needs in life, and if they ever felt misunderstood by their own mothers and fathers. The last question I would always ask them was: "If you could send a message back in time to your parents so they could make you feel more loved and understood, what would you say?" Time and time again I heard some version of this answer: "I just wish they would have trusted who I really was." The goal of this book is to give you the tools to discover who your child is inside and to trust that essence to guide you in every moment.

This concept of a specific inborn temperament is validated by Western science, which teaches that children aren't blank slates, but in fact arrive with individual tendencies and potentials that need to be recognized. In the next chapter, we'll explore how this can contribute to your understanding of your own children's inherent personalities and your ability to help them feel loved and connected.

◎ ◎ ◎

> *"Often people attempt to live their lives backwards:*
> *they try to have more things, or more money, in*
> *order to do more of what they want so that they will*
> *be happier. The way it actually works is the reverse.*
> *You must first be who you really are, then, do what*
> *you need to do, in order to have what you want."*
>
> — MARGARET YOUNG

 **TEMPERAMENT**

I was sitting in a sidewalk café in Seattle when a young mother walked up carrying her toddler on her hip. A woman at the table next to me called out to compliment her colorful purse, and they got into a conversation. I watched as her baby looked right into this stranger's eyes and beamed the brightest smile I've ever seen. She wasn't just gazing at the woman; she made direct eye contact in the expectation that they were going to communicate, even though the woman wasn't looking her way yet. But even beyond that, the expression on the little girl's face was of pure delight and total confidence that her experience with this new human was going to be positive. A man soon arrived to join the woman at the table, and again, the youngster beamed at him with the joyful expectation that he'd interact with her, too, and that it was going to be fun! Again and again over the next several minutes, I observed how self-assured and extroverted this child was. Some of this can certainly be attributed to wonderful parenting, but much of it is understood to be the inherent temperament of the child.

Later that day, I watched as a little boy of a similar age frantically hid between his mother's legs as a family friend attempted to say hello to him; and I observed a young girl running circles around her father, yanking at his hand and screaming when he stood still one moment too long for her comfort.

We've all seen these kinds of behaviors in children of very young ages, and it's an accepted fact that babies are born with a core nature, a style of being in the world, even before their first interactions with their parents. Infants are often defined as being one of a certain set of types; for instance, they're called quiet and easygoing or fussy and hypersensitive. Even from the earliest days of a baby's life, these tendencies are apparent, and it's been found that the behaviors continue throughout childhood and into adult life. A child's temperament is like the default setting in a computer. It's the place where he'll always start from and return to, and his way of experiencing everything in his world.

Nature vs. Nurture

In the West, the idea of inborn temperament dates back to ancient times, with the theories of Hippocrates in the 5th century B.C.E, who labeled humans as one of four types of dispositions: phlegmatic, melancholic, choleric, or sanguine. Early in the last century, Carl Jung's work contributed a thoughtful new understanding of personality, as well as individual levels of introversion and extroversion. But with the horrors of the Holocaust during WWII—the murder of millions of people justified on the basis of their inherited nature—the world turned away from a focus on people's inborn tendencies. In the 1960s, this was compounded by our culture finally striving to eliminate racial and sexual discrimination. Any theories about our inherent traits seemed too intertwined with the concept of our personal worth or abilities. Instead of looking at inner "nature," psychologists emphasized the examination of the impact of "nurture," such as parental influences, to explain human behavior.

It wasn't until the '70s that these theories of innate personality reemerged with psychological studies of young children. The results of this research revealed a complex range of inborn temperaments, including how physically active kids will naturally be, how adaptable to change they are, their tolerance of frustration, their level of distractibility, and their sensitivity to sensory experiences. The studies showed that babies arrive with unique dispositions that existed *before* mothers and fathers began to add their nurturing to the mix.

As a parent, you most likely don't need a study to tell you that you had nothing to do with the fact that your son is slow to warm up to a new group of kids while your daughter jumps right in; or that one youngster gets distracted if a bird flies by, and another can sit and read for hours. But aside from establishing scientific validation for your personal experiences, the research also showed that these aren't just temporary childhood phases; the traits continue to define people as adults.

Core nature stays as true to its original design as ever. For instance, many kids who were determined to be hypersensitive and extremely shy when they were little matured into socially adept adolescents, so it was assumed that they'd outgrown their shyness. However, when scientists used functional MRIs to view the brains of these young adults, they found that those who had originally been recorded as shy in infancy still showed the same strong responses of hypersensitivity in their brains. In other words, they were shy then, and they were still shy at maturity. Interestingly, when these teens were interviewed, the feelings they described having inside didn't match their outer behavior. While they *ap-*

peared poised and outgoing, they actually reported feeling overly sensitive and tense, being uncomfortable with direct human contact, and experiencing anxiety or depression that interfered with sleep and normal life choices much more than the less-sensitive subjects. So even as we all learn to cope and move through life in new ways, in our hearts we're still the same as the moment we entered this world.

Additionally, over the last few decades, studies of twins began to contribute astonishing results to the whole idea of nature versus nurture. You may have heard stories of identical twins who were separated at birth, grew up in entirely different families in distant parts of the country, and only rediscovered each other later in life. Once reunited, these sets of brothers or sisters found that they shared so many characteristics—down to the career they chose, the toothpaste they favored, how they organized their sock drawers, and even in the names they gave their children—that mere coincidence couldn't have been the only factor involved. What researchers found was that identical twins who grew up in different households were as similar in personality as identical twins who had spent every day together since birth. Further, when they tested identical twins who had been adopted and raised with nonbiological siblings, they noticed that they were nothing like their adoptive brothers and sisters. In other words, a twin, separated from her biological family, who was adopted and spent her entire childhood under the same roof with the same parents, education, food, and life experiences as her adoptive brothers and sisters, ended up being as different from them as a random stranger pulled off the street!

These days, research into temperament is exploding with the advent of behavioral molecular genetics. Scientists are now examining specific genes associated with individual human traits and tendencies that are built into our disposition before birth. They've identified genes that give us more potential to be shy, for instance, or risk seeking, extroverted, distractible, or optimistic. Through a new understanding of genomic imprinting, they can even discern which traits were inherited from our mother's DNA and which came from our father's.

It's important to realize that this doesn't mean your personality and destiny are carved in stone. Each one of us is a richly complex being, and these genes don't cause a certain trait outright; however, they enhance the possibility of it appearing and create tendencies toward certain states of mind and patterns of feelings or behavior. If you had the opportunity to know ahead of time that your son is inherently distractible, and that this may explain why he keeps slipping out of his chair at meals and running around the room, how much frustration or blame (for yourself or him) would that knowledge save you in dealing with the issue?

But this evolution in understanding children's diverse dispositions has barely affected the status quo. We live in a culture where boys and girls with different learning styles are expected to adhere to rigid educational systems and can be labeled as having learning disabilities if their individual needs don't fit the mold. We feel the weight of social trends that value certain personality types more than others and the pressure to involve our little ones in nonstop activities. Even judgments from extended family members about how we're raising our children can create extra stress, not to mention the subtle but insidious influences that have us believing that success means external achievement in the world—to earn money and fame and own more stuff than anyone else. It's extremely difficult to follow our own inner principles without at least some sense of worry that our children will be socially rejected or feel like failures if we don't pay attention to this "consensus reality."

The One Important Question

You do the best you can to figure out how to raise your children, remembering how your parents did it, asking friends or family for advice, and probably getting lost in scads of parenting books and Websites. When my son was born, my own family lived 2,000 miles away. My mother-in-law lived nearby but was little help—as it sometimes happened in Chinese families of her day, her children were actually raised by her own mother-in-law while she worked outside the home. She had never even changed a diaper! I was so grateful to have a guide in parenting my son: this ancient Taoist system of face reading that I could use to comprehend who he really was inside and what he needed from me as his mother. Certainly I made plenty of mistakes all the same, but there was so much that I did right because of what I knew. The less you understand from the start, the greater the likelihood that you'll miss important clues that could make life so much easier for you and the whole family.

It's also important to keep in mind that parents have their own personalities and tendencies to perceive life and other people in ways that may be different from their children's. When any two people are in a relationship, there's an energetic exchange between them: one reacting to the other, who reacts to that reaction, and so forth. If you're going into the situation blind, there's a much greater chance for misunderstanding why your children are behaving as they are, and you may respond in a way that only gets you all further off course. I've worked with many mothers and fathers in workshops and private consultations who berate their children for things that they aren't able to change about themselves, but the parents judge their kids as if they just *won't* change. This creates an entirely different dynamic, one with harmful results for everyone involved.

With the dizzying amount of information available today, it's easy to lose sight of the right questions to ask, but no matter what the situation or problem is, the first and most important question has to be: "Who is *my* child?" The true nature of your child is a powerful guide for you. The more you understand it, the more on course you'll be regardless of the circumstances; the more you successfully nurture all her inherent strengths, the better equipped you'll be to help her with her inborn challenges. These unique patterns are your navigational tools that provide a parenting plan like no other—one designed for your child's individual needs that will help her live a joyful and fulfilling life.

◎ ◎ ◎

"God has given you one face and
you make yourself another."

— WILLIAM SHAKESPEARE

FACE VALUE

While the West has only recently been studying temperament in depth, the Chinese have been researching similar concepts for thousands of years. As a result, their understanding of the human spirit has grown to a far more sophisticated level. One of the foundations of Chinese medicine is that you can observe patterns in any part of a system that you're studying to gain valuable information about how it functions as a whole. This is the concept of the microcosm revealing the macrocosm; that in examining any one small part of something, you can discover the truth of the entire system.

Under these principles, Chinese medical facial diagnosis evolved. As physicians in ancient China researched human health, they began to notice certain types of features and characteristics of people's faces that were consistent with different aspects of their physiology. From this they developed the ability to diagnose illness by analyzing patients' faces. As doctors worked to deepen their knowledge of this visible information, they began to realize that along with revealing the condition of the body, these clues on the face also divulged amazingly accurate details about personality. These early scientists knew what we in the West have only come to understand in the last few decades: that our physical, mental, emotional, and spiritual selves are exquisitely connected and exist in a constant cycle of interaction, each part of our being affecting and reacting to the others.

Out of this study came Chinese face reading, which is a method of recognizing how people will tend to think, feel, and behave, and what they need in order to be happy in life. Texts about the subject date back to 600 B.C.E., and its origins are said to be from the time of Huangdi (the Yellow Emperor) between 2697 and 2597 B.C.E. The original face readers in ancient China were Taoist monks and scholars, highly educated men who acted as a combination of priests, healers, and compassionate advisors to the people of their day. In more recent times, face reading became more of a divination system among the general population and lost touch with its deeper roots. As a result, it deteriorated into what was mostly a superstitious form of fortune-telling, focused on discerning good or bad luck in terms of business deals or marriage arrangements. In addition, from the 1950s to the 1970s, Mao Tse-tung, in the name of modernization, not only tried to banish face reading and feng shui, but also stripped their source, Chinese medicine, of its psychological and spiritual depth, thus eradicating its rich power and creating an almost sterile version that was then transported to the West.

But since Chinese medicine arrived in the West, a resurgence of interest in its profound original principles has occurred. As Eastern and Western wisdoms have intermingled, we've recovered a focus on the spirit level that now offers itself as an even more powerful force in our modern lives. We'll explore this in the chapters to come, but I first want to look at how much science has discovered about the importance of faces in our lives.

Face to Face

Within one-tenth of a second of seeing a new face, you've already made a judgment about what that person is like. In a flash, you know whether you trust him and what you expect your experience with him to be. Studies have found that different people come to remarkably similar conclusions when they view the same face, even if it's just for an instant.

It's well known that faces are very important to us, and scientists have mapped entire sections of the brain devoted specifically to recognizing and reacting to them. Babies only nine minutes old already prefer to look at pictures of faces rather than any other image; and 12 hours after birth, infants favor photos of their mothers to those of other mothers. Newborns even respond with a different set of facial expressions when they see a human than when they look at an object.

This emphasis doesn't disappear with maturity. In fact, we all unconsciously read and react to faces all the time without really knowing why we're having an aversion or attraction to them. There are thousands of studies that show the ways in which our appearance influences how people respond to us. In criminal court, for example, men on trial with small, more subdued features and rounder faces are more often exonerated than men who have sharp jaws or large noses. In experiments, men with full lips; wide eyes; and thinner, more curved eyebrows are selected as good choices for husbands, as they're judged to be more open to commitment and less likely to be unfaithful. Men with square jaws, large noses, and smaller or more deeply set eyes are labeled as less warm, less likely to commit, and more apt to try to dominate in romantic relationships.

The results of these studies may seem to highlight what a foolish focus on superficial appearance our culture has, but what's astonishing is that, in many cases, people's conclusions about others' personalities are accurate! For instance, in one study, photographs of CEOs with strong jaws and prominent chins were chosen by test subjects as people more likely to run a profitable company—and this is true: statistics show that CEOs with these features actually *are* more successful. Another example is that a far higher percentage of men whose faces are described as compassionate work in the caregiving professions than would be statistically expected.

In a different experiment, subjects were shown pictures of politicians in obscure elections where they didn't know the candidates or the outcome of the vote. Based on simply viewing the faces for a few seconds, these people were able to choose the winners 72 percent of the time. Now this may mean that voters are making their decisions just from physical appearance (yikes!), *or* it could indicate that people are responding to information on the candidates' faces that accurately conveys who they really are.

It was interesting for me to watch President Barack Obama's 2008 campaign for this very reason. If Chinese face reading had to provide three words to describe the message that his face communicates, they would be hope, optimism, and change. Do these sound familiar? They were the message of his campaign. Voters, unconsciously reacting to the information his face was presenting, would hear his words and feel an energetic match, which in turn would make them believe he was telling the truth and someone they could trust.

We respond to the features on people's faces—the size and shape of their noses, for instance—but also to the expressions they make and wrinkles they develop as a result. It's common to think that wrinkles are just a natural sign of aging and they don't appear in any meaningful design on the face, but this certainly isn't so. The lines that we form give us remarkably clear messages about the patterns of emotion we tend to have on a regular basis. Anytime we have a feeling, we subtly make the expression associated with it. Even if it's just for a fleeting moment, we show a tiny microexpression, and, over time, as we repeat certain feelings throughout each day, we'll slowly carve different kinds of wrinkles into our faces.

This is not a "bad" thing; there are actually certain wrinkles that you're *supposed* to get, and if you don't, it's not a good sign! For instance, the lines called "crow's-feet" in the West are called "joy lines" in Chinese face reading and are considered a reflection of an open heart. People with these lines are easily able to give and receive love. After all, you develop joy lines by smiling frequently, and you usually only smile when you're communicating with others in a loving way. It's impossible to fake the kind of smile that creates joy lines, by the way. In most people, the orbicularis oculi muscles that activate around the eyes during a genuine smile can't be moved voluntarily; they only go into motion when you're really feeling it!

Some fascinating research has been done regarding facial expressions. For example, scientists in Israel filmed blind people and their relatives as they talked about their happy and sad life experiences, worked on puzzles, listened to a gory story, and then heard a question expressed in gibberish. As participants felt various emotions, each change in expression was recorded. What they found was that the blind subjects made expressions that resembled their family members' more than those of strangers. These were blind people who had never even seen their relatives' faces; in fact, one blind subject had never even met his mother until he was 18—yet his facial expressions matched hers more than others. So again we have another instance of how our inner nature is piloting our lives from the beginning, and how it can be read on our faces.

There isn't much focus on wrinkles in this book, since it's about children's mostly wrinkle-free faces. But it's important to know that our faces are remarkably clear indicators of who we are and who we're becoming. By learning to read our little ones' expressions, we'll know more accurately how to help them deal with their emotions. In the size and shape of their features, the inherent traits and tendencies that are coloring how they perceive their experiences are visible. Such valuable information can be used for guidance on many levels.

Establishing Empathy

I've already discussed how Western science can now validate that when two people first look at each other they always make numerous conclusions in the instant of observing the other's face. What's also been recently discovered is how significant this exchange is in establishing empathy. It's been found that when you view a face—whether in person or looking at a photo—you immediately and unconsciously match its expression, usually just for an instant. However, that's not the end of it. In brain scans, scientists determined that at the precise moment your facial muscles move into mimicking another person's expression, your amygdala (the part of your brain that sends emotional signals throughout the rest of your system) suddenly activates.

In one experiment, scientists used a Botox-like drug to paralyze parts of volunteers' facial muscles and then did brain scans. When the subjects were shown photos of angry faces, their amygdalae were quieter and the usual neural communications that trigger emotions were absent. In the control group of people who weren't given the drug, their amygdalae reacted as they normally would, flooding the system with emotion. The inability to make an expression prevented the first group from empathizing with others. In other words, when you see a face, you start to feel what that person is feeling.

In another study, Harvard researchers had volunteers bite down on a pen, which caused their faces to use the same muscles as when they smiled, and found that this stimulated feelings of happiness. Just the act of making an expression causes the emotion associated with it to manifest. When we meet other people—friends or strangers—we're programmed to resonate with them, to immediately meet them in our hearts by feeling what they're feeling. We're actually designed to have empathy for each other! (This does make me wonder about the implications for those who may be "Botoxing" away their natural ability to do this, and if their relationships are suffering as a result.)

As You Use This Book

So we see how important faces are to human beings, even without any of the brilliant knowledge Chinese face reading can add to the mix! Now, as we're poised to focus on reading children's faces, there are some essential things to keep in mind. First and foremost is that of course the faces of our little ones aren't fully developed at birth. A baby's face is formed between the fourth and tenth weeks in utero, but it continues to grow throughout childhood, and different features emerge at different rates. For instance, infants are born with a very thick layer of fat under their skin, which makes their faces look very round and plump until about the age of five. After that point, the fat reserves begin to disappear and their features become more distinct. The facial bones become larger and stronger as they mature, and this also changes the shape of their faces.

Some features bloom at puberty; for instance, the brow bone and chin grow at this time in response to hormonal changes. Children's noses grow faster than the rest of their features, and their faces aren't completely developed until their mid-20s. This is why it's not a good idea for teenagers to have rhinoplasty; if they wait a few more years, the rest of their features will grow in and their noses won't look as large in comparison!

So as you begin to read your child's face, her age will determine just how much you'll be able to discern from each feature. There are things that you can immediately spot from the very beginning, and others that will appear as time goes on. For a very young child, you might also try what I call "backwards face reading," which is to observe her behavior and then identify the personality pattern you'll learn about later that will explain what other aspects of her nature this will reveal. Then you'll be able to see if you can recognize the associated feature on her face, or, if it's not developed yet, observe over time to see if it emerges!

Another thing to keep in mind as you use this book is how to judge whether certain parts of a face are large or small. You should always compare a feature to the others on *that* child's face, because on one youngster a detail can look small, while on another it can appear large. Another method is to just step back and look at your child as if for the first time to see which aspects immediately draw your attention. What's most impressive? If you think, *Wow, that forehead goes on forever!* then you're probably right that it's large. And what's least impressive? You may notice that one part in particular seems much less prominent than the others. As you'll soon learn, that will also offer you valuable information.

These are universal principles that apply to all human faces throughout the world, and they'll be true regardless of racial or ethnic background. However, always read faces within races; compare Caucasian faces to other Caucasian ones, African faces to other African ones, Asian faces to other Asian ones, and so on, as there are aspects of certain features that differ slightly from race to race. For instance, a large nose on a Caucasian face usually sticks out far off the face, while in some African and Asian faces, if a nose is large, it may be wide rather than prominent. It's possible to read mixed-race faces, by the way, but it just takes more practice.

· · ·

Often at my lectures, someone will raise his hand and say, "I have this nose because my father had this nose. It's just genetic." My answer is always a resounding, "Yes. You absolutely inherited your father's nose. You also inherited the personality characteristics associated with that kind of nose!" Considering the work I do, I tend to be more skeptical than you'd imagine, so I can understand this comment. I'm very analytical, and things need to make sense to me before I can accept them. One of the reasons I believe so strongly in this work is that it's based on science that has evolved over thousands of years and developed a deep foundation of proof over time. I also devoted myself to a long study and extensive practical application before I felt this knowledge was grounded and valid. But I always tell people that I don't expect them to believe this is true just because I say so. Try it out in your own life, with your own child, and decide for yourself.

It's important for you to know that the focus of my work is on the inner spirit. I don't have medical training, and none of the information in this book relates to the physical health of your child. Please also note that Chinese medicine often defines individual organs or body systems differently than doctors do here in the West, so if I mention a part of the body, it may not relate directly to how you understand its function physically. Nothing here is meant for use as diagnosis of illnesses, and you should of course consult your child's physician for any health concerns. I also highly recommend that you consider including a practitioner of Five Element acupuncture in your team of health-care professionals.

In this book, I'll give thorough descriptions of each feature with the disposition it reflects and examples of how this might show up in everyday life. However, each human being is a gloriously complex expression of his or her personal mixture of tendencies and potentials. There is no cookie-cutter approach to this wisdom, so please understand that the examples I've given are not the *only* ways a quality can manifest in your child's nature. I've described each energetic type in great depth to provide you with a solid base of knowledge to recognize it in your child.

It's also essential to keep in mind that you can't tell everything about your child from just one of her features. To accurately read a face, you have to weave together all of the meanings of its parts. The information one detail reveals can be modified, diminished, or enhanced by another; and if you don't take that into account, you won't get a clear understanding. For instance, a large, full mouth is an indication of a generous person, but it can also show a potential to be taken advantage of by others. You need to look at the rest of the face to know how likely this is, as there may be features that will help keep this tendency under control. Reading a face is like putting a jigsaw puzzle together; each piece gives you a different bit of information, and it's only when you put them all together that you see the beauty and meaning of the whole.

Finally, please be aware of how your own emotions may influence how you interpret this book. As a mother myself, I understand the powerful biological and emotional drive you possess to protect your children, provide only the very best for them, and prevent any suffering from reaching them. You may be afraid you're going to discover that they have a feature indicating some personal difficulty they'll struggle with. In fact, let me hasten to assure you that, yes, this is almost certain to happen! But please understand that the foundation of this work teaches that everything has a front and a back; in other words, each of your children's qualities has a positive and a negative side. On the one hand, they will have been gifted with genuine strength, but at the same time its shadow will confront them in some way. This is the truth of how life is designed, and it's nothing to resist or be afraid of. It's often in the challenging parts of your nature that you'll discover your greatest wisdom. The more awareness of your children's light and darkness you gain, the more empowered you are to help them embrace all aspects of who they are so they can move through life with an open heart toward themselves and everyone they encounter.

Now let's move on to discover the map you can use to navigate a successful journey for both you and your children!

◎ ◎ ◎

Part II

THE MAP

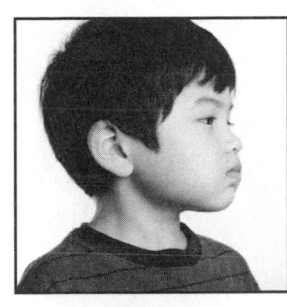
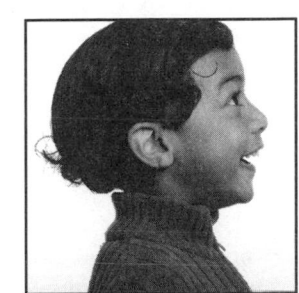
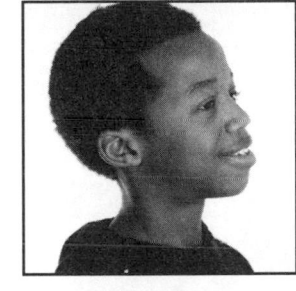
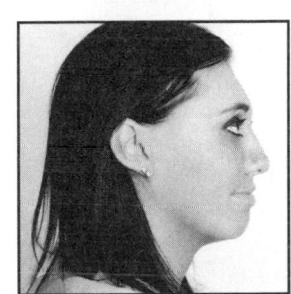
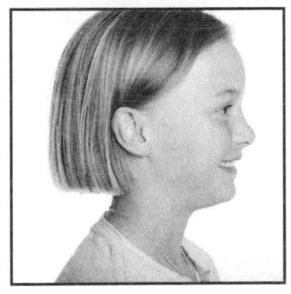
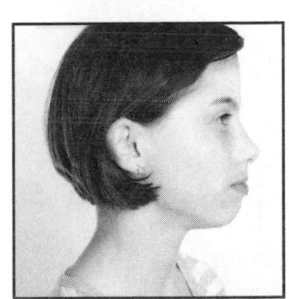

"People usually consider walking on water or in thin air a miracle. But I think the real miracle is not to walk either on water or in thin air, but to walk on earth. Every day we are engaged in a miracle which we don't even recognize: a blue sky, white clouds, green leaves, the black, curious eyes of a child—our own two eyes. All is a miracle."

— THICH NHAT HANH

THE SECRET

It's been said that the best place to hide something is in plain sight. The secret of how all life on this planet works is right before our eyes, and it always has been. It was discovered thousands of years ago in China and developed into the philosophy of Taoism, the basis for Chinese medicine, and infiltrated the culture with feng shui and face reading.

Now I'd like to share with you the secret to life on Earth:

Fig. 1: The Secret

How can this possibly mean anything important? you may be wondering. Over the centuries, ancient scientists and philosophers based their study on observing the patterns of nature around them. They watched the dance of the seasons: the cold stillness of winter transforming into the vitality of spring, the full bloom of summer moving to the abundance of the fall harvest, and then life seeming to wither and disappear again into winter, year after year. They saw the repeating cycle of how the days passed: morning moving to noon, afternoon, evening, night, and then dawn appearing once again. And they witnessed the human journey from the mother's belly to vigorous child, exultant adolescent, mellow middle-ager, declining elder, and finally death—all the natural and predictable rhythms of life on the planet. What the

Chinese came to see is elegantly and deceptively simple: everything moves in a circular rhythm, a beautifully defined passage from beginning to end and then to the beginning all over again.

As these early philosophers continued their observation of this natural flow, they noted the diverse qualities within the cycle. The energy of winter is nothing like that of the summer, and the spirit of the adolescent isn't the same as that of the frail grandparent. Similarly, the freshness of morning is a far cry from the heavy feeling of the afternoon.

Energy changes as it moves, transforming from one phase to another, with each stage of the cycle connected yet very different from the others. As early as the 3rd and 4th centuries B.C.E., the Chinese had defined five distinct phases of life and developed descriptive names for each: Water, Wood, Fire, Earth, and Metal. It's not that they thought the world was made up solely of these physical substances; rather, the names were meant to represent the type of energy present at each stage in the circle. These archetypal symbols came to be called the Five Elements, or the Five Phases, and they form the map of how everything on Earth works—the seamless and infinite choreography that all life dances to. You can watch this pattern at work in how a business meeting functions, the life span of a romance, how you eat a meal, or how you take a breath. It's the harmony of life itself, and if you live in alignment with it, you attain a coherence with the natural rhythms of the world.

The study of the Five Elements is a lifelong journey; the innocent circle belies the sophistication and complexity of the system. But despite its depth, you can easily start to apply this knowledge to your everyday life. Let's start by getting a clear sense of each Element.

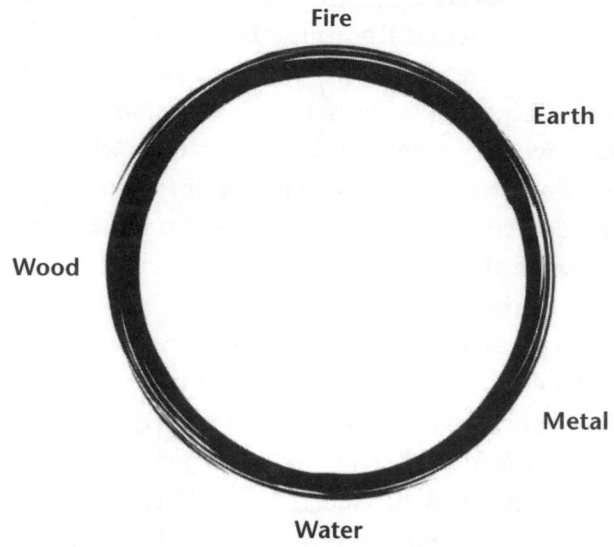

Fig. 2: The Five-Element Cycle

— **Water = night, winter, death, and prebirth.** This Element is the energy of the stillness of night, as well as the hibernation and dormancy of winter. It's the mysterious land of the afterlife, but also of the dreamtime before birth—characterized by the baby floating in the amniotic fluid and the seed germinating underground. Water is a dark, still, floating movement; yet it possesses powerful potential.

— **Wood = morning, spring, birth, and childhood.** This Element is morning at dawn when all life is stirring. Wood is the drive to be alive, the force of spring when the plants burst through the ground. It's the dynamic "push" of birth and the little child running and shouting with enthusiasm. The action that distinguishes this Element is vital, upward motion.

— **Fire = noon, summer, and the prime of life.** This Element is noon, the peak of the day, and the sun at its brightest. It's the summer when the flowers are in full bloom and we enjoy long days of fun. This is the stage of life when we're fully grown and at our greatest physical vitality. Fire's movement is upward and outward in expansion.

— **Earth = afternoon, late summer/early fall, and middle age.** This Element is afternoon, which is a slower period as the day starts to settle. It's harvest time, when food is abundant; and it's middle age, when we begin to slow down and enjoy the fruits of our labors. The energy of Earth is downward moving, consolidating, and heavier.

— **Metal = early evening, late fall, and old age.** This Element represents that time of day when we finish the last of our work and prepare to rest for the evening. It's late fall when the leaves are dropping and the trees' bare twigs are etched across the gray sky. Metal is old age, as we begin to fully appreciate the preciousness of our remaining time on Earth. Its energy is moving inward, contracting, and hardening.

This map of the Elements and how they interact is what a Chinese doctor would use to evaluate an individual's physical health and design a treatment plan. But in what ways does this cycle correlate with the inner nature? And how in the world can that show up on the face? Each Element has distinct qualities that reveal themselves in our personalities as archetypal patterns of tendencies to think, feel, and behave in certain ways—and inherent perceptions of the world around us. We all have some aspects of each of the Five Elements in our makeup, but to varying degrees, and these can be read in our faces and observed in our actions. But from birth, there's always one personality type that's home base for each of us, like a computer's default setting. I sometimes refer to it as our "home planet"—that is, it's the place where we come from and the "language" we speak.

Some children have one Element that's strongly expressed in their nature, and by recognizing it, you know nearly everything you need to about them. Others start from their home base in one main Element, but then show a second one as an additional major influence. The patterns the Elements form on their faces will reveal the intricacies of their inner designs, and once you learn to read them, their inner worlds will open to you!

In this Part of the book, there will be two chapters for each Element. The first will describe the personal nature associated with that energy, and the titles of those chapters offer three archetypal roles you often see that kind of personality play out in some way. These are meant to be descriptive and not to serve as limiting functions. The second chapter for each Element will focus on the individual features and what they mean for your children. So, let's start our exploration at the beginning of the cycle, with Water.

◎ ◎ ◎

"A man finds room in the few square inches of the face for the traits of all his ancestors; for the expression of all his history, and his wants."

— RALPH WALDO EMERSON

Chapter 5

THE WATER CHILD: ARTIST, INNOVATOR, PHILOSOPHER

Marisa

"We call her the mermaid," Marisa's father tells me. "Puddles, ponds, streams, swimming pools, the lake, the ocean . . . if it's wet, she jumps right in. She even tried to climb into our neighbor's aquarium!" As he's telling me this, I look down into this six-year-old's soulful face that already has an exotic beauty, even at this young age. Marisa has several Water features: thick, wavy hair; a domed forehead; a well-defined philtrum (the groove between the nose and the upper lip); and big, plump earlobes. "The bathtub is her favorite place in the house," her father says as he smiles. "Every night it's a fight to get her out of it." Marisa is already the classic Water child; she's not only attracted to anything that's wet, but also exhibits the dreamy personality that's the hallmark of this Element. She loves to lie in her bed any time of the day and sing to herself, gaze at the ceiling, or scribble with her markers. This youngster is slow to get going in the morning and seems to dawdle on her way to do anything. She's obviously not a "straight line" kind of girl, as her behavior already demonstrates her mind's nonlinear way of functioning. In the park, Marisa loves to wander and explore rather than climb on the playground equipment. Sometimes her parents find her staring off into space, as if she's seeing something that's invisible to them; it's like she's in touch with other worlds. People of this Element are often highly intuitive, even psychic, and it was no surprise for me to learn that after her grandfather's death earlier in the year, Marisa reassured her mother that Grandpa still played with her in her bedroom.

Water is all about darkness and what's hidden under the surface, and this is a girl who loves dark places and anywhere she can find to hide. If her family can't find Marisa, the first place they start their search is in the closets. Her mother sometimes makes blankets into a tent on her bed and lies there with her, finding patterns in the weave of the coverings. This is a highly imaginative little being who makes up complex stories and has shown an early talent for drawing, but when her art teacher tried to make her color in the lines, she cried. Tears are not a rare occurrence for Marisa. "The waterworks turn on every time her feelings get hurt," her mother says. "And her feelings seem to get hurt a *lot*. But I'm hoping that as she continues to mature, this will stop."

Dream on, I think to myself and smile. The Water personality is all about feelings and emotions, and it seems that tears are never very far away for those of this nature, even for adults. This is *not* a sign of emotional weakness, however, but of depth; Water people simply feel things far more deeply than others. But aside from dealing with a few extra tears, and having to keep a watchful eye on Marisa around bodies of water, she's a relatively easy, calm child who's able to entertain herself for long periods of time.

This little girl has already lived in two different countries during her short life due to her parents' diplomatic careers, and the family is currently packing for a move to another distant part of the world. Water people often find themselves traveling frequently or living in exotic locations, not through deliberate choice, but because this is just how their lives naturally unfold.

Daniel

Daniel, 15, is a quiet boy with a sense of mystery about him. The natural shadowing around his eyes, a distinct widow's peak in his hairline, and a prominent chin give him a look that leaves you unsure of his exact ethnic background; he projects a personal energy similar to Johnny Depp's enigmatic charm. He's obviously humoring his mother by letting me interview him, and is clearly uncomfortable with the whole situation. His room is dark with navy blue curtains pulled over the windows, and the walls are filled with Japanese anime posters. His mother smirks, saying, "He wanted to paint the whole room *black!* So instead I let him get dark curtains." Daniel's bookshelves are filled with CDs of obscure local bands, anime DVDs, and science-fiction novels. On his nightstand is a journal, where he immediately scribbles what he remembers of his dreams as soon as he wakes up. Daniel tells me he gets ideas for sketches that way, and later confides that he picks up clues about what's going to happen or what he should pay attention to from his dreams as well.

Even during our conversation, he keeps an earbud in his ear, listening to the tunes coming from the iPod in his pocket. His life revolves around music, as he plays two instruments and is in a band with his friends. Certainly he has the classic face of a musician, so it's very natural that this would show up as a major focus in his young life. Water Element has to do with the ears, listening, sound, and that altered state created by music . . . but I also noticed another sign of Water's strong creativity: piles of his drawings of fantasy scenes stacked on his desk.

Daniel loves solitude, which isn't unusual for a teenager, but this has been a lifelong requirement. His father jokes that his relationship with his son consists of talking to him through his closed bedroom door. It isn't quite that bad, but Water kids do need their desire for privacy and alone time allowed. Daniel's parents also spend what they call "silent time" with their son, where everyone lounges in the family room with no TV or conversation. In this way, they're all doing their own activities alone but together.

This boy is already showing interest in the mysteries of life. He's reading about philosophies of different cultures and informs me that he'd like to go to India to find a guru or to Peru to study shamanism. He's keeping this a secret from his parents, who he says roll their eyes whenever he brings up his fascination with the mystical. "I know what they're thinking," he adds, scowling. "And if I keep talking about it, they're just going to ground me. They think I'm crazy, and they might even try to take me to the doctor to put me on some drugs to set me straight or something."

Here's where we encounter another aspect of this Element that has the potential to cause some problems. Water is about what's silent and unspoken, what's below the surface and unseen. In terms of temperament, this can contribute to two issues: First, these kids don't easily speak about their difficult feelings and tend to keep secrets. Second, they believe that other people are doing the same thing. In other words, as we all tend to do, they think everyone is just like them—in this case, saying one thing but keeping their true feelings or plans hidden. Combine this suspiciousness with a tendency toward fantasy, and all kinds of stories will fill the Watery mind that may be quite far from the truth. Daniel has blown up his parents' mild disdain for his dreams of exotic adventures to a plot to medicate him and take away his freedom, which isn't anywhere near reality. It's often wise to realize the importance of having regular "reality checks" with these kids. We should give them opportunities to talk about their inner thoughts and emotions, but must allow them time until they feel ready to share. They're *not* open books!

Fig. 3: This boy's face shows the kind of chin, philtrum, and under-eye area associated with Water.

The Water Child's Nature

In this chapter, you'll learn about the inner nature and outer appearance of Water children, and the following chapter will detail more information about each feature associated with this Element. To begin with, the following list shows what to look for in your child's face. Please note that not *all* of these characteristics have to be present for Water to play a strong role— seeing any of these aspects means it's a factor in your child's personality. The more of them you see, the more Watery his or her nature is! Look for:

- Large ears and/or earlobes
- A widow's peak in the hairline

Fig. 4: This girl's rounded forehead and puffy under-eye area reveal her Water Element.

- A domed or rounded upper forehead
- Distinct shadowing above and/or below the eyes, or puffy under-eye area
- A well-defined philtrum
- A strong, prominent chin
- Thick or wavy, lustrous hair
- A black undertone to the complexion

Well-known adults with many of these features include Jay Leno, Will Smith, George Clooney, Reese Witherspoon, Christina Ricci, Quentin Tarantino, Jon Stewart, and Vanessa Williams.

As Your Child Grows

It's important to note that two Water features, the forehead and chin, will change as children develop. Many youngsters start out with what's called a bulbous forehead, the very rounded kind that's also a hallmark of this Element's nature. As your child matures, the forehead may slowly transform into a different shape. The meaning of a rounded forehead is covered later in this chapter, and as long as your little ones have this feature, they will possess those specific traits. If the forehead changes as they grow, you can then refer to this book and read about the emerging aspects of their personalities.

Also, all babies' chins aren't completely formed at birth, and they can remain small until later in childhood. Use the information about this feature to monitor the meaning of your youngster's chin as it develops, and then decide how Watery your little one is!

Qualities of Water Element

- *Facial features:* ears, hair, hairline, upper forehead, under-eye area, philtrum, chin

- *Other parts of the body associated with Water:* kidney, bladder, reproductive system, bones, teeth, lower back, joints

- *Strengths:* willpower, courage, wisdom

- *Challenging emotion:* fear

- *Archetype:* artist, innovator, philosopher

- *What Water feels like:* night; winter; death and prebirth; dark, floating, silent

Water is the dreamtime. It's the night when we float in an unreal world of bizarre images and fantastic experiences, unable to control what comes our way. It's winter, when life is hidden and seeds are lying deep in the cold soil, silently drinking in the rich nutrients, their immense power and potential as yet unseen. This Element represents the prebirth state, where, as babies, we're suspended in utero and immersed in fluid and darkness, knowing our universe mostly through sounds: the rushing, thumping songs of our mother's body; and some dim, muffled noises from the outside world. And it's the mystery of death, the dark abyss, and the unknowable place where we all return.

Water is about hidden power and strength. The seeds that wait below the surface of the earth give no hint that they will grow to break through solid earth and push on to great heights and extravagant blossoms. This Element also means perseverance: the continual trickle that slowly carves out a canyon over millennia and the relentless endurance of ocean waves crashing against the shore. Other aspects of Water are a calm, reflective pool; deep, dark seas; rich swamps; the blast of a geyser; and the chaos of a hurricane. This is the energy of "being," not "doing," but don't be deceived. Still waters run deep, and immense power and potential are brooding beneath the surface.

Every quality of Water can be seen in those who carry it, although its expressions can manifest in many different ways. To best understand the true spirit of this Element, and thus your little one, learn the essence of Water. What follows are the basic aspects and a few examples of how it can reveal itself in your child's behavior, emotions, needs, and perceptions.

The Spirit of Water

Just the thought of the word *water* as your child's Element may make you laugh out loud if you've already noticed a major aspect of this personality: a love of water! One family bought their son a water bed for his birthday and said it seemed like his life was now complete. Even months later, if he could have his way, he'd read, play, and eat all his meals on this magical floating mattress! This brings me to another insight regarding kids with this inherent quality: horizontal is their favorite position. In other words, they feel best if they can be in a state that's as close to floating as possible. To Water children, lying in the tub, reading in bed, stretching out on the couch to do their homework, or drifting in the pool are heavenly activities!

This dreamy energy shows up in other ways as well. You may often catch your Watery child gazing out the window, lost in her own daydreams. And most of these kids are able to amuse themselves for hours on the strength of their own imagination. Another side to this kind of fluidity is how they curve and meander rather than going in straight lines—that is, they may wander in conversation, taking forever to get to the point; or circumnavigate the store, exploring as they go, rather than heading right toward what they want to buy. And being on time? Forget it! There appear to be no clocks *or* straight lines on the planet they come from. Monitoring minutes in order to arrive somewhere at an exact time is a foreign concept; their minds have a nonlinear way of perceiving the world. Because of this, Water kids may also have a learning style that works in an associative manner—through patterns and complex interconnections rather than structured logic—resulting in quite innovative ways of thinking.

These children process their experiences differently than you might expect, so it's also helpful to know that you can't realistically rush or pressure them and expect positive results. They need time for things to "trickle" down; they'll make decisions slowly and won't spring into action in any situation. If you ambush them with rapid-fire details or try to push them into motion too quickly, they may freeze, shut down, or become resistant. And this links with another very significant factor to understand about those with this core nature: freedom and independence are of vital importance. If Watery youngsters had their way, school would start whenever they felt like it on that particular day, and they'd be able to leave when the mood strikes them. This Element flows freely, and the more restrictions these children encounter, the less they'll like it.

Water is persistent, determined, and endures over time just as slow drips carve channels into rock and the surf pounds away at coastal bluffs. These children will have an enormous wellspring of perseverance, and can be single-minded in their pursuit of whatever they want. This profound level of willpower can serve them well in life, though as a parent, you may experience more of the challenging side of this trait—stubbornness!

Night

Water people tend to come alive at night. When these children are small, they may tire on the same schedule as others, but as they get older, they'll likely perk up as it gets later and love to stay up. Once asleep, they'll tend to go deep, as these kids aren't restless sleepers and can be difficult to rouse in the morning. After all, why would anyone want to leave that beautiful floating world? And even if you succeed in waking them, they'll probably still want to linger in bed or move far more slowly than you'd like! One mother told me she literally has to lift her sleeping daughter out of bed in the morning to get her up.

Nighttime is also about darkness, and you'll find that these kids love a darkened room. Their favorite times of the day might be when they can lie in the dark listening to music or lounge on the couch watching TV with all of the lights off. This preference will even show up in their choice of clothes. Black is the color associated with Water, so don't be surprised if they prefer a black T-shirt and jeans while all their friends are wearing bright colors.

Winter

This season is about what's hidden. In winter, it looks like there's nothing happening on the surface; thick snow has turned the world silent and everything seems motionless and cold. All that's alive is deep underground. And there's a lot that's silent and unseen with these children as well; they tend to appear quiet and calm on the surface, but underneath, there's so much going on! They don't babble about every thought in their heads, and getting them to talk about what they really think or feel may be like pulling teeth. If you want to know what's going on in the heads and hearts of Water children, you'll do well to give them time to let that information travel up from the depths. Don't expect to sit down and have a quick conversation about what's really bothering them or what they need to tell you. Remember that things move more slowly in winter.

Death/Prebirth

Water Element is associated with the beginning and end in the cycle of life, the mysterious primordial sea of the process before birth and after death. Even as children, people with Water personalities seem to carry an age-old wisdom in their bones, as well as a spiritual and emotional depth far beyond their years. These are the deep thinkers who may show a special interest in philosophy; attempt to examine the furthest dimensions of the human soul; or exhibit a fascination with magic, mysticism, and people with special powers, such as gurus or shamans. The rich world inside these young ones also endows them with a talent for understanding complicated scientific processes, an ability to work with abstract concepts, and the capacity to synthesize complex information into a cohesive whole.

Don't be surprised if Water children have dreams that come true or an uncanny ability to know who's calling when the phone rings; their natural intuitive gifts are pretty much standard issue! This Element can access information from other realms, and these kids should be encouraged to practice developing this kind of intuitive intelligence.

It can also be especially important for you to consider that these children may sometimes be aware of ghosts or other kinds of things that you aren't able to perceive. You can prevent them from feeling frightened or alone if they have these experiences and help them understand that they're just better than most people at sensing hidden information in the world around them. However, there's a delicate balance between validating their experiences and getting overly excited about them, especially if you get caught up in thinking that you have a "psychic" child. I've spoken with far too many parents who've either been afraid of their children's intuitive abilities and tried to suppress them, or have gotten so thrilled about these special "gifts" that they pressure their young ones to perform at the risk of disappointing Mom or Dad. Talk about what they're sensing and explore what it might mean, but try to stay as calm and nonchalant as possible so they feel comfortable that what they're experiencing is natural.

These children have rich imaginations and are often artistically inclined in music, art, or writing. "My son gets home from school and tells me he's headed for his 'art place,' which is a big table in the basement where he works until dinnertime. I think it's like his daily vitamins," said one mother. Other kids might put on their headphones and travel off into their own special world. Since Water Element has to do with the ears and hearing, this explains why music is frequently an important part of their lives. Moreover, many kids with this nature may develop beautiful, melodious voices as they mature.

This creative sensibility leads these youngsters to think outside the box and do things in unusual ways. Medicine and finance are other fields filled with many innovative Water people, and because of this Element's inherent connection to the afterlife, they can be especially attracted to exploring genealogy, history, or anything related to ancestors or ancient times. They may also have a fascination with, or intense fear of, death.

Understanding the nature of Water as a beginning and ending place is also crucial when it comes to these children's need for solitude. Since their energy has to do with the time before we enter the world and after we leave it, their experience is more about being alone than joining in with others. This doesn't mean that they'll be antisocial or won't have friends, but they *will* need to spend time by themselves to be quiet and flow with their own thoughts and feelings. Allowing them this on a regular basis will make them feel honored and supported.

And speaking of *feelings*, well, they're a big part of what defines Water children. Those who carry this Element as their dominant one have a depth of emotion that is strong, rich, and pervasive; they see the world through their feelings and respond from an emotional base. This in no way means that Watery children are weak or fragile; in fact, just the opposite is true. These youngsters' incredible inner strength is what allows them to feel things so deeply, giving them the capacity to understand things beyond their years.

But as part of this quality, tears and crying will likely be a bigger part of who they are than other kids, and this will continue throughout their lives. Their feelings may be more easily hurt than other children, and being misunderstood or overstressed can also get the waterworks flowing. However, at the same time, these emotions won't be easily expressed in words. In fact, it's likely that the deeper the hurt, the less they'll be able to communicate and the more they'll withdraw or hide what's really going on inside. When Water children get upset, they pull back, go undercover, and become silent. You may only notice the fact that they're quieter as a clue to their internal distress. If this condition goes on too long (and it can), and they continue to sink into silence, a dark, brooding mood may materialize that disguises a geyser forming inside. You'll want to help them move through their feelings before that geyser has to blow.

Water Challenge: Fear

Every Element has one emotion that consistently arises under stress and can send the system spiraling out of balance. This challenging emotion for Water is *fear,* and it can manifest in numerous ways. One of the contributing factors for a Water child falling silent is that his energy reacts to fear by freezing. A common symptom of this will be that it's almost like he loses his voice. He's unable to communicate the depth of his feelings in words and is likely to believe that no one will understand what he's going through.

Kids of this nature crave reassurance to help diminish their fear, so your compassionate guidance will do wonders to help them cope. But if they become lost in these feelings, your words of encouragement will be useless because they won't even hear you. When Water feels overwhelmed, it's like the ears cease to function—that is, these children know you're talking, but your words are muffled by their panic.

Because this is the beginning of the Five Element cycle, and not yet connected with the outside world, children with this nature have the potential to feel cut off from others or scared that they'll be misunderstood. This kind of fear may cause them to be secretive or even deceitful when they're stressed. Aside from sometimes not expressing what they're thinking or feeling, Water children might choose to lie if it will help them hide even more. Keep in mind there's no malicious intent, and the real cause is that they're feeling unsafe.

An unfortunate consequence is that because they move through life in this mind-set, they'll assume others do, too. They perceive things a certain way, but aren't able to tell the truth about them, and they'll think that you're doing the same. This can lead them to constantly make inferences from what you say or do, to create stories about what you're thinking that may have nothing to do with reality.

Water Strength: Willpower, Courage,
and Wisdom

The salvation for Water children's struggle with fear is the power of their deep, natural wisdom. This is the essence at the core of their being, and when they can summon it, they'll discover their tremendous courage as well. Helping children explore a problem to find their intuitive understanding will transform their experience of the issue. By allowing their determined spirit to rise, you'll help them use their strong will to push through their fears.

With older children, give them a "container" for their fear to prevent it from spreading everywhere—as Water tends to do—by reassuring them and thoughtfully talking things out. If they're so immersed in their feelings that they can't even process your words, forget about having a conversation at that point. It's your strong, comforting presence that will suffice until they can listen and talk again.

With the younger ones, just wrap your arms around them and be with them, as discussed above, or you might encourage them to draw pictures of how they feel. All this can move them to a place where they'll accept some of your ideas about how to take action to resolve the situation. As you'll read next, Water children have the power of their ancestors within them and are stronger than you might think. They *will* persevere!

⊙ ⊙ ⊙

*"Time engraves our faces with all
the tears we have not shed."*

— NATALIE CLIFFORD BARNEY

READING THE WATER FEATURES

Chapter 6

Certain features on our faces have to do with Water, and the more prominent or noticeable they are, the more we possess this Element as a major part of our original nature.

However, it's important to keep in mind that we all have Water Element in our faces and personalities, just in differing amounts. The Water characteristics can be examined to determine the unique ways in which they show up in your child's design, whether or not they're predominant.

Ears

The Chinese believe that when we come into this life, we bring with us the inherited essence of our ancestors, a rich and potent energy that's a source of strength and nourishment throughout our years. They call this essence "jing"; you can think of it as being born with a fully charged battery. However, we're all born with varying sizes of "batteries": some people get large ones with lots of juice, and others arrive with smaller ones, and thus a lesser supply. The quantity of a child's inborn jing, or constitution, is revealed in the size of the ears. Kids with ample ears are said to have copious reserves of this inherent energy, while those with smaller ones don't have such an abundant supply. This doesn't mean that these youngsters aren't vital and strong, but their source of strength is of a different kind, to be discovered elsewhere in the face.

In face reading, you look at the ears to understand how your little ones may feel about taking chances in life. The concept is that if this feature is sizable, you have a large battery, and thus, energy to spare. If you take a gamble and fail, you'll lose a bit of life force, but there's plenty more where that came from! So people born with large ears will be more likely to feel comfortable with risk. Those born with small ears will know on some level that they need to conserve their energy, and as a result will be less likely to take chances in activities such as extreme sports, making speculative investments, or even gambling with their money.

How do you discern whether your child's ears are big or not? The general rule is that if you have to ask, they're not! But if people take one look and say, "Wow, get a load of those ears!" they probably *are* large ones! Another tactic is to compare the ear size with the rest of the features to see if they are one of the most noticeable aspects overall. In face reading, you compare the size of one feature to those on the rest of that particular face. It's not unusual for large ears on one child to seem small on another of the same age, but what you're looking for is what is sizable on that individual's face.

Prominent ears also have another meaning: Jing isn't only the supply of life force that children have inherited from their ancestors, but also the quantity and quality of their lifetimes of accumulated wisdom. The more of this they've been gifted with, the greater the size of this feature. At the extreme are enormous ears, which are called "Buddha ears," implying that they possess the wisdom of the Buddha. Children with this feature can seem to be wise in the ways of the world at a very early age. You may be astonished by the pearls that drop from their little mouths, or they may just give you a sense that there's a calm depth to their personalities and they're not easily ruffled.

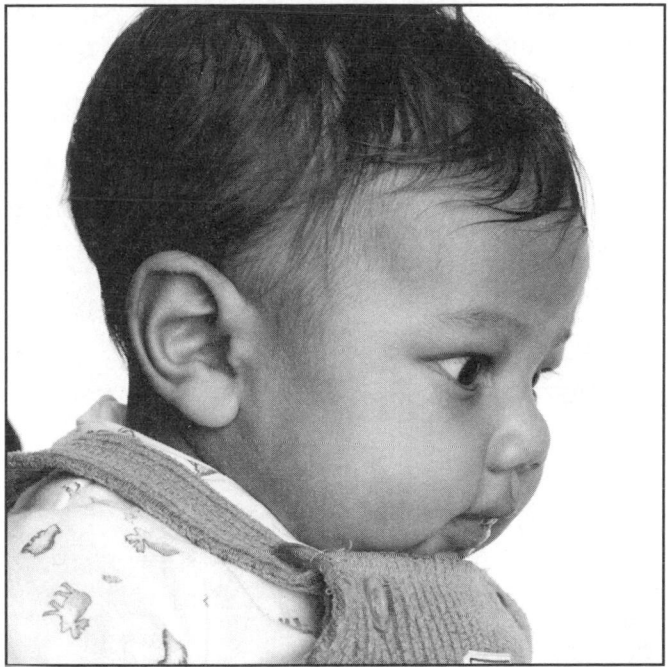

Fig. 5: A child with large ears is said to have been born with natural wisdom.

Having small ears isn't a negative thing, but unless there are other strong Water features, this kind of natural wisdom won't be a big part of who they are. For instance, there is knowledge that isn't inherited but instead is learned from life experiences. (It's important to note that I'm not talking about intelligence, but rather an inborn depth of understanding of life.) One thing to watch for, however, is that children with extremely small ears are said to be especially impacted by fear, whether due to external influences or as part of their natural temperament. It can be helpful for you as a parent to understand this perception of the world, and you may want to pay more attention to building an overall sense of safety for them than you might for other children. One father had been treating his son's fear of the dark as a weakness, and refused to give him comfort at bedtime as an attempt to toughen him up. Once Dad understood the message of this boy's very small ears, he realized that his son wasn't being immature and genuinely did need more reassurance.

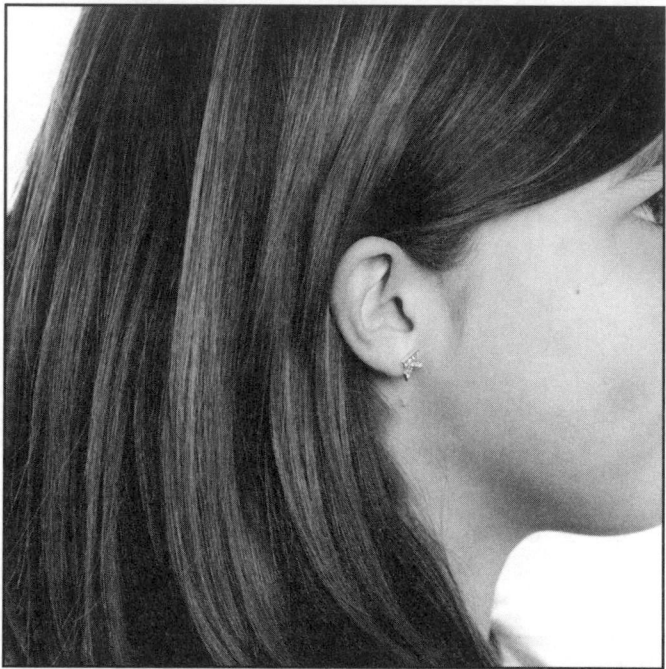

Fig. 6: Small ears show someone more influenced by fear.

It's been noted that over the last few generations, people have had smaller ears. You can certainly see evidence of this if you watch old movies from the 1940s or '50s and check out the enormous ears many of the actors had compared to what you see today! The concern is that since the size of this feature relates to strength of constitution, this implies that each generation has become weaker, possibly due to environmental pollution and a less nutritious diet. One encouraging note I've found just in my own experience is that the boys and girls I've been reading in the last few years have better-sized ears. This may be a reflection of the latest wave of parents' greater emphasis on organic food and the reduction of toxins in their homes, and I hope to continue to see bigger ears in the future!

The status of an individual's physical constitution can also be read by feeling the rims of the ears, which are made of cartilage and should feel flexible but firm. If you take the edges of your child's ear between two fingers, you should be able to bend it easily, but it shouldn't feel too delicate. You may have to practice on a few ears before you can truly know what the range of flexibility is like. (We do this in workshops, and feeling other people's ears always induces quite a bit of laughter!) But don't worry too much if you're not sure, because it's only the extremes that really matter.

If your child's ears are almost rigid and hard to bend, this indicates a very strong constitution. Also be aware that this can show a personality that tends toward obstinacy! However, if her ears are quite delicate and bendable, this can mean that she'll need to conserve her energy and not overextend herself too often. You may have already seen some hint of this, whether through her tentativeness toward life in general—as someone who seems reticent—or because she isn't as emotionally hardy as other kids.

The width of the ears can clue you in to how adventurous your little ones are. Those with broad ears are more likely to be comfortable with taking risks, while children who have particularly narrow ears will instead have a natural need to play it safe. In childhood, for instance, this can look like a tendency to hang back from new experiences, an avoidance of behaviors they think might get them in trouble, or extra care with their money.

If your child's ears stick out, you are the proud owner of a willful spirit! They indicate a highly independent nature and a personality not always inclined to do what he's told. This can be

Fig. 7: Broad ears indicate comfort with taking risks.

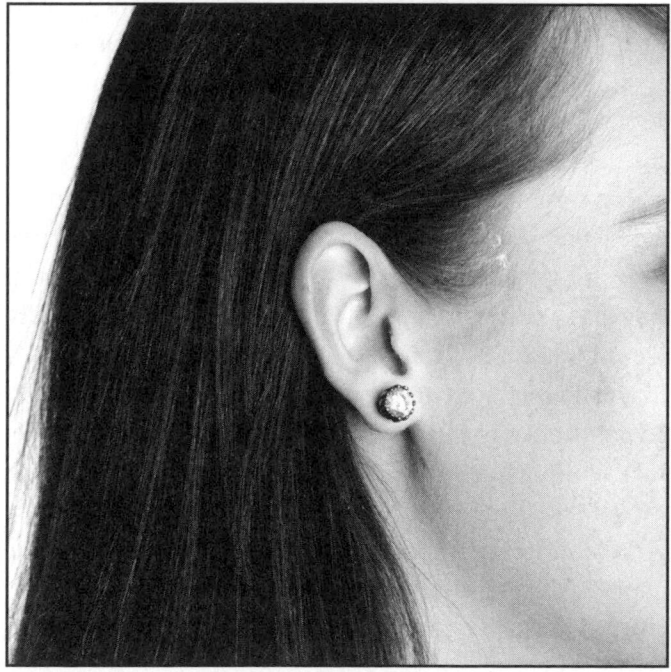

Fig. 8: Narrow ears reveal an emphasis on playing it safe.

a trial for parents, but it also means that as an adult, he won't be a pushover and will be able to think for himself. President Barack Obama has these ears, and an independent mind can certainly be a good quality for a leader!

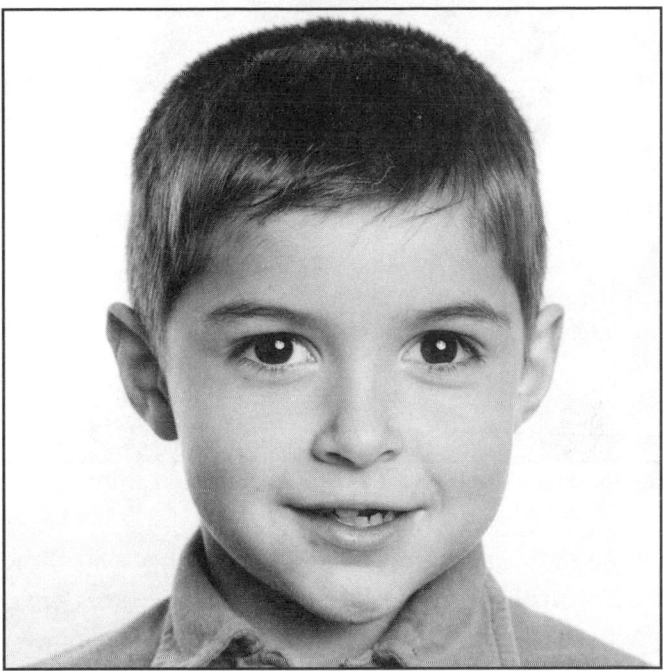

Fig. 9: Ears that stick out reveal an independent nature.

If your little one's ears stick out *and* forward, this is said to be a sign that she loves to listen to the sound of her own voice! I've noticed this trait in a few waiters during my time; they're the ones who seem to ramble on as you try to give them your order. But as with every aspect of face reading, there's a benefit here, too. People with these ears can also be excellent communicators because they pay so much attention to what they're saying and how they say it. There are many successful media professionals who have sticking-out-and-forward ears. You may not be able to tell at birth whether your child's ears stick out, but this characteristic can start to reveal itself early on.

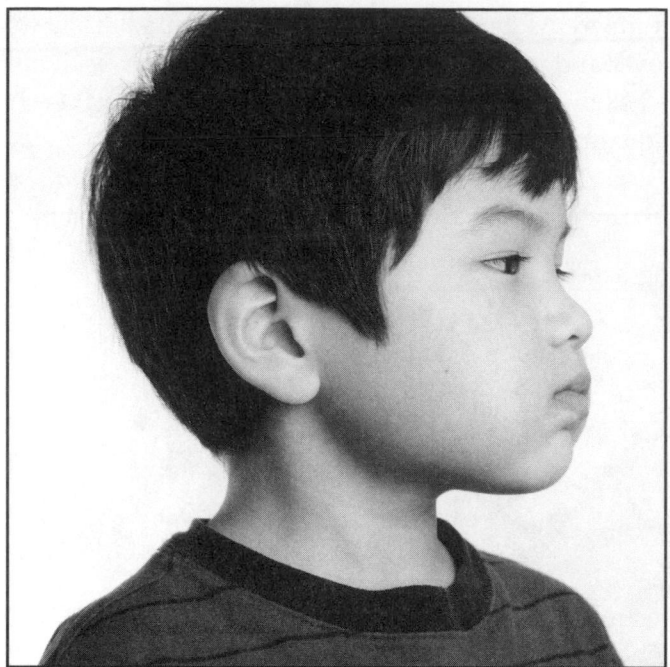

Fig. 10: Large earlobes reflect a talent for long-term planning.

Even the earlobes have messages for us. Called one of the three "reservoirs of wealth" on the face, large or long lobes are considered beneficial because they reflect wisdom with money. Basically, this means that people with sizable earlobes have a talent for long-term planning, and this relates to finances, also. With your youngsters, this can be a sign that they won't squander each week's allowance on some toy that immediately breaks, but instead may want to start a bank account or invest their cash.

Small earlobes don't indicate bad money managers, but they do indicate that they'll think more in the short term and not look too far ahead. They may need some help in this regard, but it can also mean that when they're grown, what they do in the present is what will be the most powerful for their long-term security. Remember that the earlobes are just one tiny part of the whole, which will give you complete information about how your little ones will tend to make choices in life.

You may have noticed that some earlobes seem to grow into the sides of the head or barely exist at all. Others are larger and can be pulled away from the head. These are indications of the level of connection to family. If your youngsters have "attached" earlobes, they'll maintain close connections with family throughout their lives. This can suggest that even if they move away,

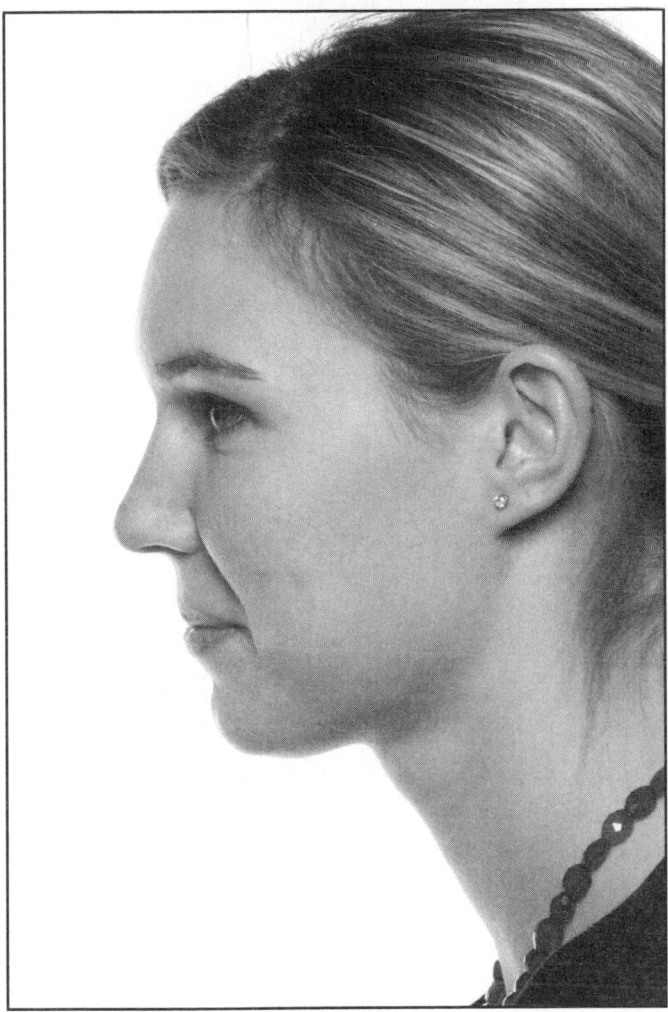

Fig. 11: Earlobes that look like they're attached to the head are a sign of lifelong attachment to family.

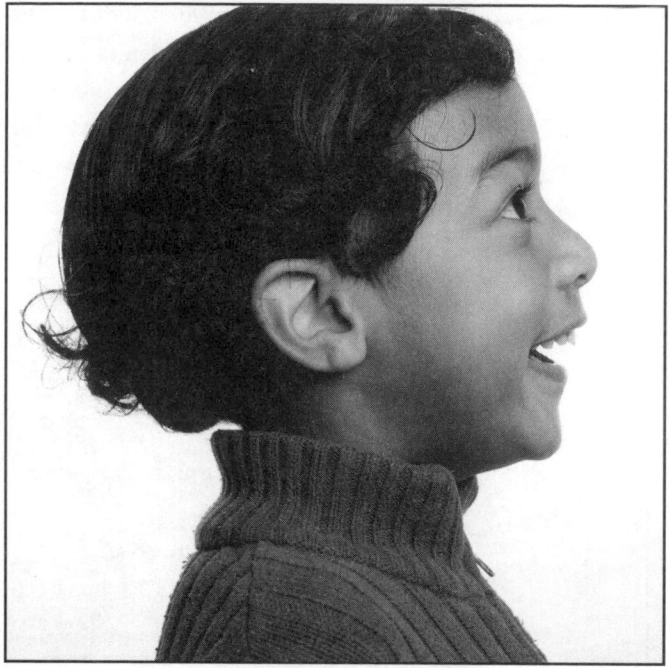

Fig. 12: Earlobes that can be pulled away from the head show the ability to separate from family at maturity.

regular visits or communication will remain an essential part of who they are. However, it might instead signify that as adults, they'll retain such a strong negative reaction to familial influence that they want *less* contact. On the other hand, children with "detached" earlobes will of course still love their families, but it will be easier for them to leave home and be independent. Please note that this isn't necessarily a result of feeling the need to escape their family.

Hair

Classic Water people will have thick, wavy hair that appears lustrous and healthy. This will usually be accompanied by other signs of this Element on the face, and it's simply considered a confirmation that its traits are in their nature. Please note that wavy hair is associated with Water, while *curly* hair belongs to Fire Element; so if your child has curly hair, read on!

Hairline

Hairlines come in many different shapes. One type looks as if the hair was drawn in a straight line across the forehead. This is the mark of a rule breaker   a rebellious child who may challenge you and always try to push the envelope. If the hairline also juts in at the temples, it's usually an indication of slightly more aggressive tendencies, which can cause stricter parenting as an attempt to deal with this rebelliousness. A straight hairline is actually a sign of a child with lots of drive, and that can be a benefit in adult life. However, as the parent, you may get to experience more of

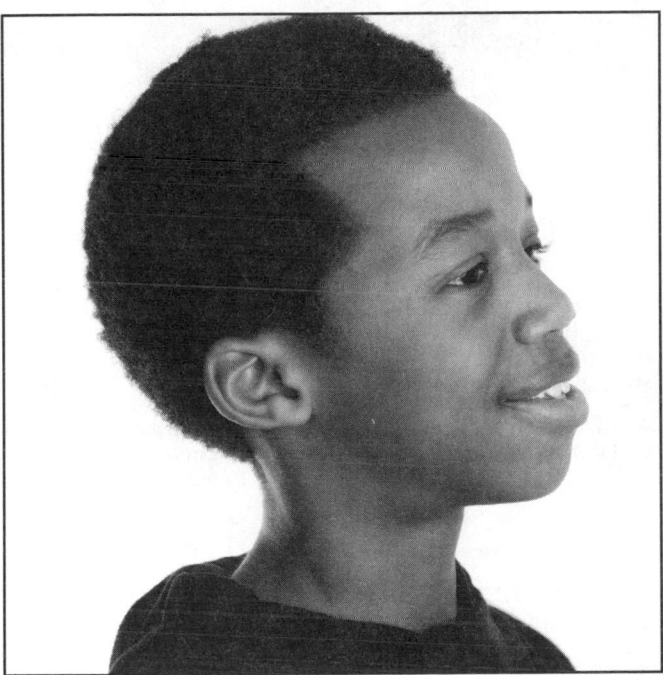

Fig. 13: A straight hairline that juts in on the sides reveals a rebellious nature and a strong drive in life.

the downside of that temperament! It can help to remember that this attitude shows his potential to evolve into a paradigm shifter, someone who can make an impact on the world and change things for the better.

A widow's peak is a little "V" of hair that dips down into the exact middle of the forehead. This is an indication of Water's creative nature, as well as seductive charm. Even during childhood, these kids can have a rather magnetic personality, and a mysterious quality that draws others' interest at first glance.

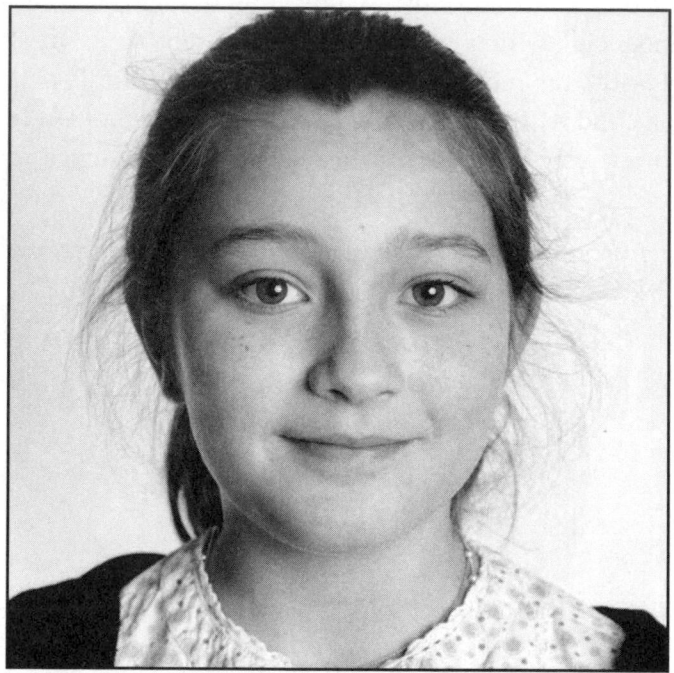

Fig. 14: A widow's peak reveals creativity and magnetic charm.

If a child's hair goes back diagonally in the corners—in other words, if it looks like he or she is balding at the right and left corners of the hairline—this is called an "expansive mind" hairline. It characterizes a youngster who will be open-minded, interested in exploring unusual ideas, and not limited by linear thinking.

These children seem to move easily between both the left and right sides of their brains, using logic and intuition simultaneously. In problem solving, for instance, they may start out using a step-by-step process, and then suddenly their instincts kick in and they leapfrog directly to the right answer without having to analyze each detail along the way.

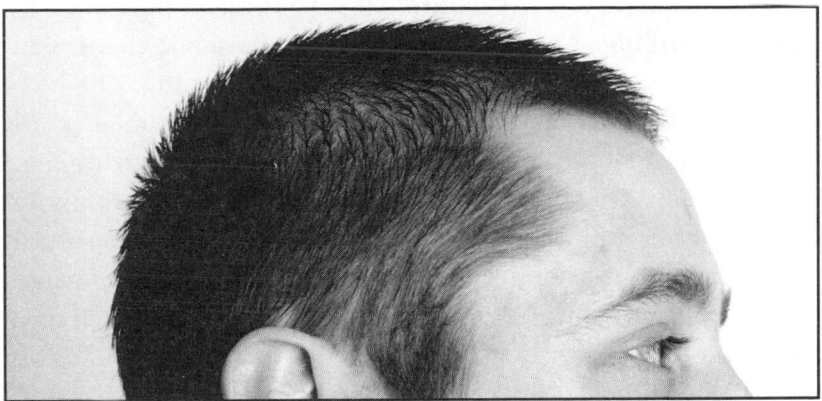

Fig. 15: A hairline that goes back in the corners signifies open-mindedness.

In Chinese face reading, the hairline is called "Mother's influence," and it gives us information about an important gift Mother is supposed to give her children, that of socialization—teaching them manners and the rules of society so that they'll be accepted and survive in the outside world. This is an important lesson, yet some mothers are too heavy of an influence. For instance, they may overdo it in controlling their kids' behavior, pile guilt on them for small misdeeds, or frighten them by giving them so many rules that they're nervous about making their own choices. The result can be adults who are pleasers or who take longer to find their place in the world, because their mothers' voices are so strong in their heads that it's hard to develop independent viewpoints or goals.

The sign of a heavy Mother's influence is a perfectly rounded, oval hairline, often with faint hairs along the entire edge. It's as if even the hairline is trying to be precisely perfect under such sharp watch. Ideally, mothers will provide their children with gentle and subtle guidance—a light hand and moderate pressure.

Upper Forehead

If the upper half of the forehead is rounded, it's a sign of a highly imaginative Water nature. Most youngsters start out with very rounded upper foreheads and, even if the shape changes later, while they're domed they still have this meaning. The more the forehead is curved, the more creative your little one may be. This can even be the case very early on, especially in creating art and music, making up stories, or just perceiving the world in unusual ways. One mother marveled at how her son found patterns everywhere, from seeing smiley faces in the placement of garage door handles to discovering maps of the world in the stucco of their house.

This feature also indicates a highly intuitive nature, maybe even psychic ability, and is considered one of the signs of spirituality in the face, although you may not recognize it as such in younger kids because they might not be capable of communicating their inner feelings in that way just yet. But if older children have rounded upper foreheads, they might show a special interest in spirituality, such as learning to meditate, reading about philosophy, or even studying magic.

A rounded upper forehead also indicates a special ancestral inheritance. These children have been gifted with traits, talents, or abilities that have been passed down through their lineages; and they'll need to be encouraged to put them to use. You may have heard that it's important to honor one's ancestors in traditional Chinese culture. This is a bit of a stereotype, yet it's also true, for the belief is that those elders continue to beam blessings to their family members after death. This is one reason why feng shui developed thousands of years ago, as it was important to bury Grandfather in the right spot so that his blessings would be

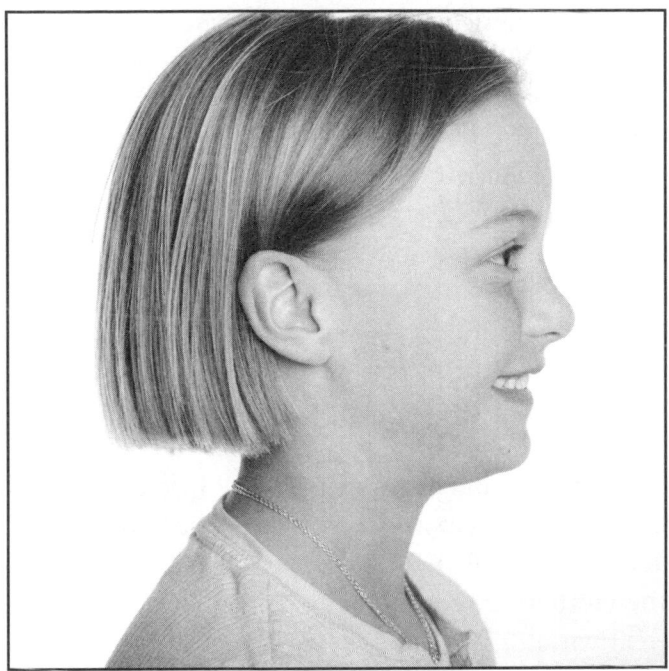

Fig. 16: A rounded forehead shows strong imagination and intuition.

accurately aimed in the direction of your house and not the neighbor's! The feng shui master was consulted in both my husband's father's and paternal grandmother's deaths to ensure that they were buried in the appropriate plots in the right cemetery. In this case, their graves ended up in entirely different locations in distant parts of town rather than being placed in a family plot, as is the Western tradition.

The main concept here is that the influence of ancestors lives on after their deaths. If children's upper foreheads are curved, their lineage is especially important in this regard. The gifts that come from this feature will be for you to explore with your kids as they grow. A child may have inherited her grandmother's talent for music; a great-great-uncle's woodworking skills; or a love of the cuisine from her family's native country, even though the family emigrated many generations ago. Another expression of this trait could be youngsters that have an unusually strong interest in maintaining relationships with older family members or exploring their family history by taking up an interest in genealogy. What's most important is that they be allowed to make use of these gifts, even if it doesn't seem logical or worthwhile for them to be spending their time in this way; somehow, there's a treasure for them to discover that will benefit them throughout their lives.

One mother came to me for a private consultation because she was very concerned about her daughter's escalating behavior problems over the past three years. When she showed me a photo of this teenager, I immediately noticed a classic Water face, including a dramatically domed forehead. We talked at length about all aspects of the girl's face and why she thought and felt as she did, as well as the reasons behind the choices she was making. I also read the mother's face in order to identify any possible conflicts between their differing natures. We made a lot of progress during the session, but something was still nagging at me. I kept feeling that this concept of lineage, and of ancestors, specifically, was essential to understanding the issue. But no matter how I tried to bring this up, I got nowhere. Finally, as if it couldn't possibly matter, the mother said to me in a very off-the-cuff way, "Oh, well, she's adopted, and for the past few years she's been very upset with me because I won't tell her anything about where she came from or let her find her birth mother." Here was a girl aching to connect with her ancestral lineage, but being totally disregarded. And it was ultimately her forehead that gave me the message of how important this was for her.

On some upper foreheads, you'll see that there's a protrusion on one side or the other. It will look like a large bump, and this is an indication that the child will be more heavily influenced by either the mother or father, or one side of the family over the other. The left side of the upper forehead is the paternal side, and the right represents the maternal. A protrusion in this region reveals a specific influence—that one parent or side of the family has more of an impact, negative or positive. A protrusion on the right side may mean that he inherited his mother's math skills or that his relationship with her will be especially positive *or* challenging. Alternatively, it can mean that his mother's side of the family is a more important factor in forming his character.

If there are protrusions on both sides of the forehead, but not in the middle, it means that both parents are influences, but in very different ways—for example, perhaps they have distinctly contrasting personalities. If a child's forehead is highly rounded in the very center, then similar traits from both sides of the family are enhancing his nature. Actor Rainn Wilson (from the TV show *The Office*) has this type of forehead, for example.

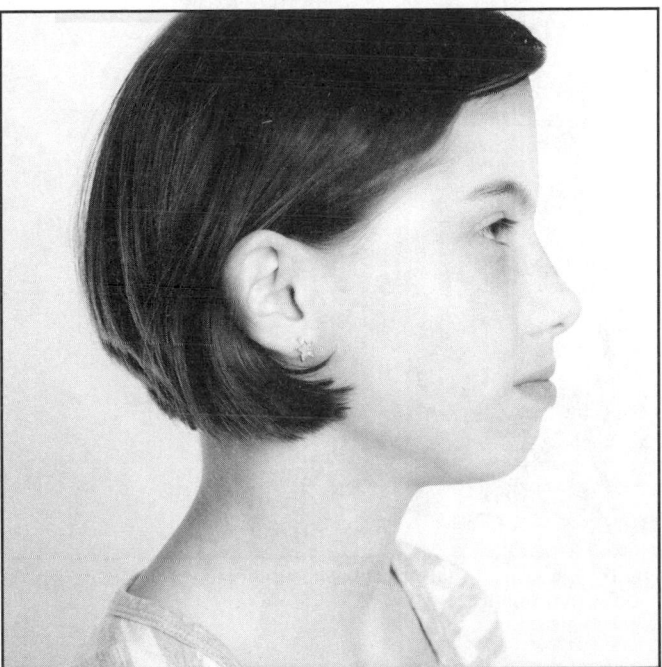

Fig. 17: A straight forehead indicates less influence from this child's lineage.

Not all kids have curved upper foreheads, of course. Or, if they do early on, you may see the shape change as they get older. Each forehead shape has a meaning, so if youngsters lose the roundness of this feature, this doesn't mean their ancestors no longer love them! It just indicates that their life purpose won't be so intertwined with their lineage. For instance, if a child develops a forehead that's more straight up and down, this is a sign that she'll pave her own way in life, not carrying forward any family karma, which can be a very good thing!

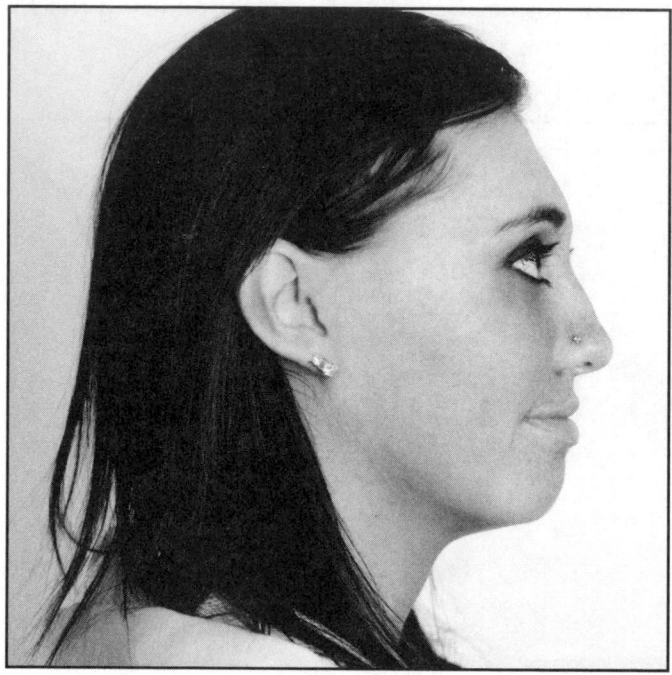

Fig. 18: A forehead that slants back is the mark of someone who's good at making deals.

In ancient China, if a forehead slanted back from the brow, it was the mark of a criminal! This is the kind of negative judgment that first put me off of face reading, and it's not true. What this feature really should be called is a "dealmaker's forehead," and it's the sign of a person who's adept at figuring out how to make things work. For example, a child with this characteristic may be able to brainstorm creative ways to make situations come together successfully or strike a deal by figuring out how to bring everyone into agreement. Many successful entrepreneurs have this forehead.

This part of the face can even give clues to preferred learning styles. In general, kids with low foreheads—that is, with a noticeably short distance between their hairline and eyebrows—will learn best in hands-on settings rather than studying books for long periods of time. If they're allowed to roll up their sleeves and dive in as teachers guide them, instead of sitting through long explanations of *how* to do something, they'll retain more while enjoying the experience.

Children with high foreheads are the opposite. They thrive in situations where they can study, analyze, and observe before attempting whatever it is they're trying to learn. For these little ones, it's best not to pressure them to try something without thoroughly explaining it first.

I want to emphasize that no aspect of the face has to do with low or high intelligence. In this case, it's about learning styles, not abilities or potential.

Under Eyes

The under-eye areas reveal what's going on emotionally. If this part of the face is naturally shadowy (that is, if the shadowing is lifelong and not temporary), this is a strong sign of Water and an indication of someone who will feel things much more deeply than others. It's important to understand that these kids will perceive life and respond to situations in a more emotional way. The official term for this trait is "unshed tears." After all, Water people have so many feelings that there will always be tears to shed! These are children for whom crying may be a near-daily occurrence—and not just because they've fallen down or gotten frustrated. There's a soulfulness to their nature and a depth where you sense that they feel everything down to the bottom of their little bodies.

As I mentioned before, this in no way means that these youngsters are emotionally fragile. In fact, they possess tremendous inner power. But know that their feelings can be more easily hurt, and harsh words or rejections by other kids can stay with them for a long time. You may have to help your child learn to develop an understanding that not everyone moves through life the way she does. For instance, reassure her that her friend didn't realize that his actions were so harmful or that her teacher only accidentally didn't give her a cookie at snack time!

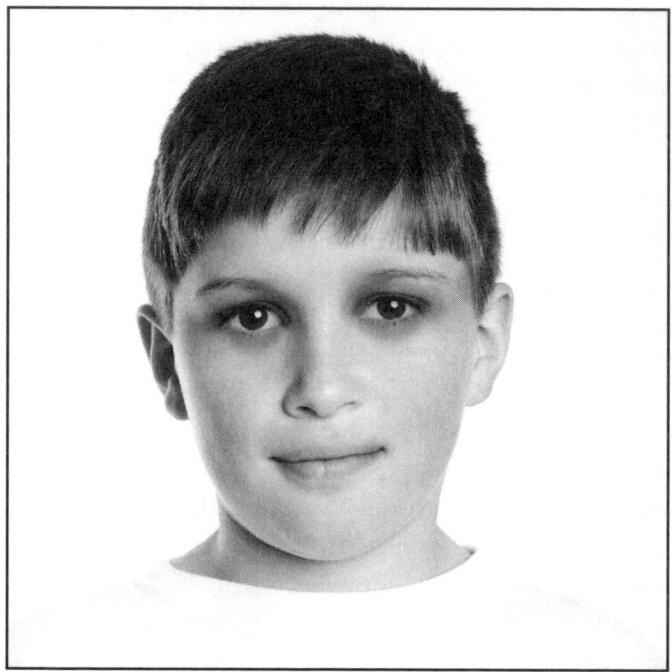

Fig. 19: A naturally shadowy under-eye area reveals someone who feels things very deeply.

The under-eye area is also the main indicator for how well hydrated and/or rested your little ones are. The skin is the thinnest in this area, so it responds quite quickly to dehydration or tiredness. If this part of the face suddenly develops shadowing or a sunken look, it may have to do with physical well-being rather than emotional nature. But these things are also associated with Water. Hydration literally has to do with water in the body, and this Element is the definition of restoration and rejuvenation. When your children haven't been sleeping well or getting enough rest, both their physical and emotional reserves are probably depleted. If their under-eye areas become dark and this isn't normal for them, determine whether or not they're overtired or dehydrated. Shadowy under-eye areas may also indicate allergies, which stress the immune system and exhaust the body.

Some kids have naturally puffy under-eye areas, and this, too, is a sign of Water nature and the "unshed tears" trait. If your little one suddenly develops this, however, you might suspect allergies again. It could also be due to a diet that's too high in salt, which causes fluid retention that's visible in this part of the face. Even drinking large quantities of mineral water could have this effect.

Any signs on the face are related to our inner nature, physical condition, or both. Chinese medicine discovered the mind-body link thousands of years ago, and as I've previously mentioned, this is something the West has only begun to accept in the last few decades. Our emotions are linked to our physical health; we are a beautiful, complex, and totally interconnected system of reactions and counterreactions. Thus, physical imbalances can begin as emotional issues that aren't successfully dealt with, and over time they'll manifest in the body in some way.

Philtrum

The philtrum is the vertical groove below your nose and above your upper lip. Some are highly defined, while others are vague and barely visible. This feature is the major indicator of creativity on many levels. First, it reveals creative health in terms of physical fertility, since the reproductive organs are represented in this part of the face. If the philtrum is large or has a deep groove, the Chinese would say that this child will have many little ones of her own one day! However, if the philtrum isn't a well-distinguished feature, this doesn't mean she'll have fertility challenges; it just shows that this aspect of Water is not a major part of her nature.

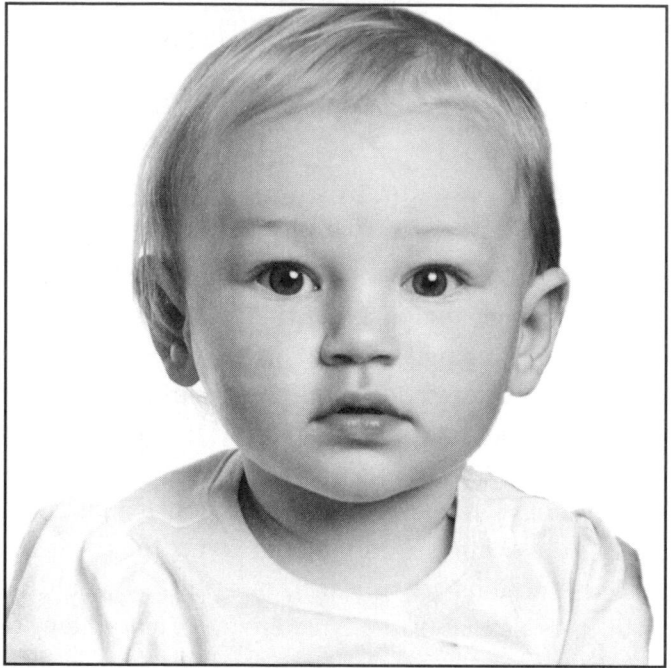

Fig. 20: A well-defined philtrum shows a highly creative child.

You'll see many artists, actors, and highly imaginative people who have strong philtrums; it's the telltale sign of an artistic nature. Youngsters with this trait should be allowed to have plenty of creative outlets in their lives; and since a quality of Water is perseverance, you may have no choice—just stand back and let them go for it!

Chin

The final Water feature reveals the strength of your child's willpower and tenacity. This aspect of the face is reflective of the will to live; it's that energy that keeps people pushing forward in single-minded determination no matter what. Sometimes Water flows around obstacles, but sometimes it overcomes them in order to get where it wants to go! The chin shows the quality of that latter tendency. The larger it is, the greater the supply of this strong will. Big chins usually stick out quite far, and this may be most noticeable from the side. Chins that are prominent show tremendous potential to not give up when times get tough. Once these kids have set their minds on something, they won't quit till they get there. And it also shows a very stubborn nature! If there's something they *don't* want to do, they'll dig in their heels and be very hard to budge.

Fig. 21: The larger the chin, the greater the amount of willpower.

Some kids have receding chins that barely seem to be there at all. (Remember, however, that very small children have yet to grow their true chins.) This can mean they don't feel that they're able to be stubborn, stand up for their needs, or refuse to do what they don't want to do. Not being allowed to exert their willpower may be a reflection of feeling oppressed in some way. If your child has this kind of chin, examine how you can help him learn to be more powerful, including perhaps giving him more real opportunities to be steadfast and say no.

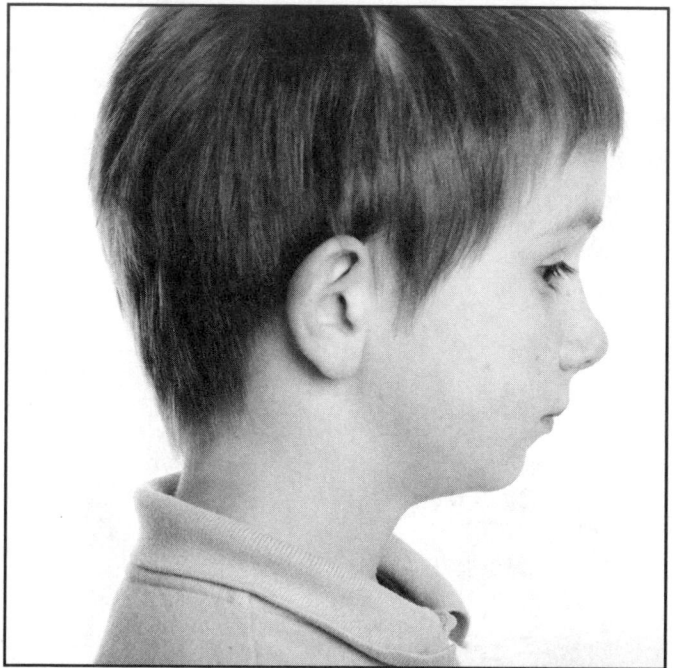

Fig. 22: A receding chin is often seen in people who feel that they can't exert their will.

Chins have different shapes, and each one has a distinct meaning. A pointed chin, especially if it's long *and* pointed, marks a bit of an indecisive nature. It may indicate a youngster who can be too easily influenced by others. If a chin is rounded, however, this is a sign of a caring disposition. If she's going to be stubborn, she'll at least try to be nice about it! A squared-off chin, meaning that the bottom is more of a straight line rather than rounded or pointed, reveals an attitude with an extra touch of practicality.

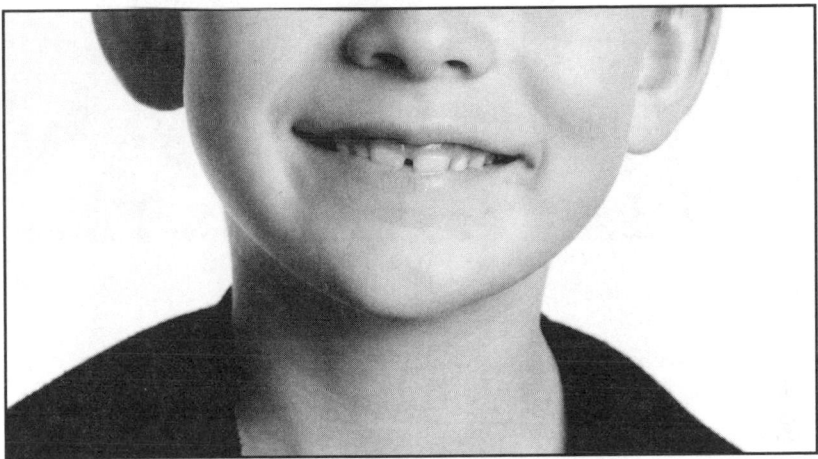

Fig. 23: A pointed chin reflects an indecisive nature.

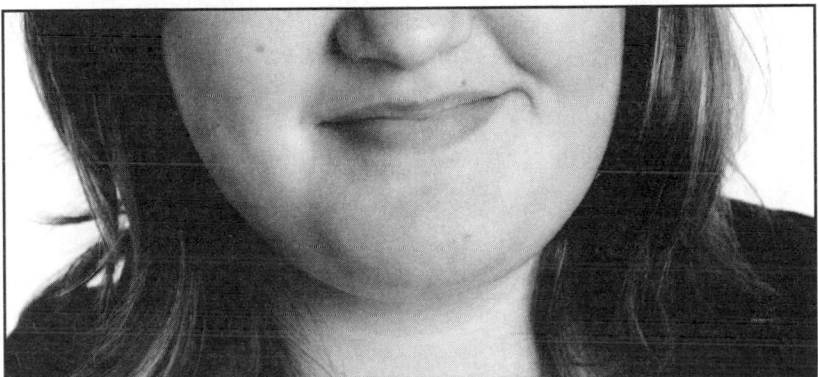

Fig. 24: A rounded chin shows some kindness despite stubbornness.

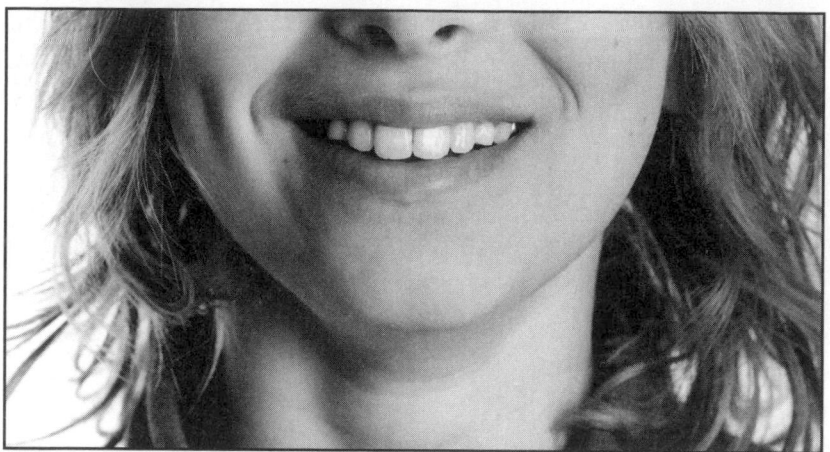

Fig. 25: A squared chin reveals an extra touch of practicality.

The Best Environments for the Water Nature

Water children will appreciate privacy, so if their rooms feel like secret hiding places, that will suit them well. As teenagers, they may even want to move down to a basement hideaway. But before that age, they may feel too frightened and cut off from you if their room is distant from yours.

These children will thrive with mood lighting in the house, or at least in the bedroom. You may want to hang sheer curtains over their windows to reduce the sunlight or thick drapes to give them the option to make it totally dark. They'll need spaces to be creative, and music will probably be an important part of their lives. And, of course, give them ways to be horizontal! They may work better on a laptop in the recliner rather than upright at a desktop computer.

Black and dark blues are the colors for children of this Element, so including these hues in their environment will be nourishing. Also add anything that has to do with water—such as a fountain or aquarium, art with images of water, or a map of the world—since Water is about exploration and adventure. They'll also need a bathtub and not just a shower!

A Few Thoughts for Teachers

These children do well with creative activities, but they aren't usually comfortable in a highly structured classroom. Their non-linear minds will be happy when they have as much freedom and flow as possible. Aside from loving art and music, they'll enjoy any opportunities to be innovative or to do things in unusual ways.

Please be aware that they may be inferring things from what you say that aren't true, or making up stories in their minds about what you're really thinking or feeling. Take more care when you're speaking to them and check in regularly to ensure that they understand what you've explained. Giving these little ones extra time to open up, ask questions, or tell you how they feel will suit their need for a supportive learning environment.

If a Water child ever closes his eyes when you're talking to him, this is a clue that he's overwhelmed and needs a break. If you give him some alone time and then try again, this can lead to success. Tears can flow in the classroom no matter how old these kids are, and you can empower them by showing that you honor their feelings rather than criticizing them for not being a "big" girl or boy.

Helping Your Water Child Flourish

Sometimes these youngsters will seem like old souls, and other times you'll wonder if this is their first visit to this planet; they carry the energy of both an ancient being and a newborn baby. There's an underlying wisdom but also a primal fear about survival existing deep within the Water nature that has the potential to emerge and affect their thoughts and behaviors. You can help these children by providing lots of reassurance and letting them know you'll always be there—not so much with words, but with your actions, your warmth, and your understanding presence.

Recognize that the best way for these children to communicate isn't with rapid-fire talking or lots of details. Flow with them, don't rush them, and don't expect them to work by the clock. You may think you have to try to change them to fit into a structured society, but I'd suggest that perhaps the world needs to shift rather than they do. Use their childhood to help them invent ways to continue developing who they are and still be wildly successful on their terms. The Water nature is about the journey, not the destination, and this is something everybody can learn from. Encourage creativity, innovation, and dreams in these youngsters; and try to see the world through their eyes rather than attempting to reshape their perceptions or behaviors. Make up stories together, play music, find patterns in the raindrops, and sing and dance . . . then allow them glorious silence and solitude!

You know your Water child and can feel just how deep his emotions run. There's a vast dark tide of feelings within, and this is his power and beauty. Assist him in learning how to ride the waves instead of being swept away by them. Create an environment where he can talk about his emotions in the best way for *him,* which probably means allowing him more time to open up than you might anticipate. Help him work on his tendency to misread people so he doesn't fabricate stories about others' thoughts or hidden motivations that may not be true, and examine if you might be contributing to his belief that people don't say what they really mean.

As teens, these kids can be drawn to the unorthodox: piercings or tattoos, Goth styles, the occult, fantasy games, or horror movies, for example. Don't be alarmed; this is just how these young people explore. A lot of weird Watery teens end up as financial planners or brilliant doctors. However, this Element can tend to float without direction, so it can be vital to supply them with guidance when you feel it's needed. Help them strategize a logical plan of action so they can move forward with their dreams.

Acknowledge and encourage their intuitive abilities and help them develop them. You can even make it into a game: before you open a newspaper or click on the home page of a news Website, ask them what they think the front-page picture will be today, and see how close they come. They may guess the main color, an object in the photo, or the subject matter. Look for other fun and no-pressure ways to practice this skill. Record their dreams; and have them tell you impressions they get about certain people, houses, or animals. You'll be deepening a talent that will serve your children well the rest of their lives.

⊙ ⊙ ⊙

<blockquote>
"We must be willing to get rid of the life we've planned, so as to have the life that is waiting for us."

— JOSEPH CAMPBELL
</blockquote>

THE WOOD CHILD: WARRIOR, PIONEER, ENTREPRENEUR

Chapter 7

Jacob

"He's got two speeds: stop and nonstop," Jacob's mother says. This five-year-old can't sit still. He jumps up on her lap, climbs on the back of the couch, leaps off, and runs around the room until he bumps the table and the coffee sloshes around in our mugs. He settles down for a few seconds to put a toy racetrack together, but then throws a ball to destroy what he's built. The dog starts barking outside, so he immediately races off to see what's happening then rushes back in to announce the latest news. This young boy is a human whirlwind.

Jacob's hairline goes across his forehead in a straight line and then juts in on the sides, virtually identical to actor Brad Pitt's. His temples are indented and he has thick eyebrows, especially for someone so young. This little body is so alert and at attention (even more than most kids), and every muscle seems to hold a dynamic tension. As he grows older, his muscles will look more sinewy and defined than most people's. It's likely that as Jacob reaches puberty, a strong and well-defined jaw will develop, only enhancing his lively traits. But right now, it's this energy that's stressing out his mother to the max. Just keeping up with his constant activity is exhausting, but she also worries that he's unable to sit down and concentrate on anything for more than a few breaths. "Jacob gets distracted by a fly on the screen," she says with a sigh. "And if there's nothing to distract him, he distracts himself." This is a child who can't sit through a meal—he hops out of his chair every few minutes, and his mother has to force him back to the table. When he is seated, he taps his feet and swings his legs, and soon his whole body is wriggling till he just *has* to get up!

Jacob is easily frustrated and has an explosive temper. He hits anyone who tries to restrain him at home or in day care, and he hates to lose in games so much that he'll throw anything within reach at the other children or even hit or bite them. All kids go through stages of learning to manage their feelings, but this is more than a phase. Jacob is wired to be reactive, and his energy will always shoot forward first—his brain only kicking in afterward. He's not a bad guy; in fact, he's a delightful, radiant little boy, and obviously very bright. There's a love of learning in his nature, and he has great confidence that he'll succeed in whatever he tries. He also doesn't hang back around new kids. "He really wants to be the alpha male in any group," his mother says. When playing alone, he loves to tinker and build racetrack configurations for his toy cars, although the last step in the building process is usually hurling things at what he's created until it's in pieces again.

Disciplining Jacob is very difficult for his mother, who's raising him alone. She ends up giving him lots of time-outs, but he tends to argue furiously with her and tries to blame someone else for his behavior. She's learned that it's better to use these times as opportunities for a cooldown rather than a punishment, which seems to just put an even bigger chip on his shoulder.

In school, his thoughtful teacher accommodates his learning style by giving him easy step-by-step instructions, and rather than demonstrating some new skill, she lets him attempt things on his own with her subtle guidance. She understands that he has to be in motion more than the typical five-year-old, so he's often chosen as the "volunteer" to get up and help her hand things out. This reduces the chances of him being overly disruptive to the group. She assures Jacob's mother that it's too early for ADD to be diagnosed and cautions her about readily accepting this label in the future.

Jacob's mother has already found that the more opportunities she can find to praise him rather than yell at him, the better he acts. She has set up a system of rewards that are immediately granted for good behavior and has even taken to videotaping the times when he's doing something unacceptable. Being able to actually see where he went wrong gives Jacob a real tool to learn from, rather than being yelled at for something that happened in the past.

Olivia

At age nine, Olivia is already an entrepreneur. With her mothers' help, she builds wooden birdhouses and sells them at a local shop, whose owner she approached on her own when she was eight. She donates half of her profits to a homeless shelter and is saving the rest of the money to buy the latest version of her favorite computer game. Her newest idea is to create a "fun run" for the kids in her school and give all the proceeds to charity, and she has visions of doing this nationally to really make a difference in the world. With her assertive personality, there's no doubt that she can.

With her tall, lanky body and full eyebrows, Olivia resembles a young Brooke Shields. She already tends to frown when she thinks, which is a typical Wood trait, and this will probably result in two vertical lines developing between her eyebrows at a fairly early age.

The verb that matches the Wood personality is *do!* Olivia is highly athletic; she plays soccer and softball, and loves to hike in the woods on the weekends. She's pushing one of her mothers to build her a tree house in the backyard; in fact, one of the most nourishing places for her is outside among the trees, as their energy resonates beautifully with her own. If this little girl stays indoors for too long, she can become a bit hyperfocused on her video games and won't be able to pull herself away.

At school, logic appeals to her linear mind, and she loves to do problem-solving exercises and prepare charts and graphs for homework. Once in high school, there's a good chance she'll join the debate club because it will satisfy her desire to argue *and* compete! Olivia tends to have frequent disagreements with both her teachers and parents, sometimes creating unnecessary conflicts, which seem to energize her. She can also be quite blunt with people, saying the first thing that pops into her mind; and she's made a few classmates cry with her teasing. Her parents are trying to help her understand that what she says can hurt others' feelings.

With her competitive nature and strong drive, Olivia needs many outlets for her energy, both physically and mentally. While Water children thrive with free time to just float and dream, this Wood child's mothers have done well by filling her life with lots of opportunities to exercise her body *and* her creative mind, including family brainstorming sessions about new inventions that will change the world.

Olivia hates to feel full and sometimes pushes away from the table too early, in her parents' opinion. As her pediatrician says, "She eats to live, not lives to eat," which makes it even more important that what she does eat is healthy. Since she is so athletic, a good tactic is to help her be aware of how different foods affect her body so she'll be motivated to make smart dietary choices. As Olivia moves into adolescence, her parents will need to be observant and keep lines of communication open, as Wood youngsters tend to become sexually active earlier than other children their age. In addition, because they may engage in risk-taking behavior, they can be more likely to experiment with drugs, reckless driving, or other dangerous activities. Despite these cautions, Olivia's mothers will also have the pleasure of watching their daughter mature and take on the world with gusto!

Fig. 26: This girl's Wood Element is shown in her eyebrows and strong jaw.

Fig. 27: This boy's eyebrows and jaw represent Wood Element as his primary energy.

The Wood Child's Nature

In this chapter, you'll learn about the inner nature and outer appearance of Wood children, and the following one will offer more detailed information about the physical features associated with this Element. To begin with, the following list shows what to look for in your child's face. Please note that not *all* of these characteristics have to be present for Wood to play a strong role— seeing any of them means it's a factor in your child's personality. The more aspects you notice, the more Wood there is in his or her nature! Look for:

- A straight hairline
- Thick or long eyebrows
- A protruding brow bone

- Indented temples
- A prominent or well-defined jaw
- A rectangular face shape
- A body type that is either tall and lanky or short and compact
- A complexion with greenish or brownish undertones

Well-known adults with many of these features include Barack Obama, Hilary Swank, Katie Couric, Bruce Lee, Mary Lou Retton, Anthony Robbins, Brooke Shields, and Simon Cowell.

As Your Child Grows

It's important to note that two Wood features, the brow bone and jaw, are at first underdeveloped, so they will form as children grow. Testosterone plays a big part in the emergence of the brow bone, so boys will normally end up with prominent ones. Additionally, the size of their jaws, the shape of their faces, and their body types will form over time. The meanings of these characteristics are covered later in this chapter; and as these features change as your child matures, you can then use this book to read the newer aspects of his or her personality.

Qualities of Wood Element

- *Facial features:* brow bone, eyebrows, temples, jaw

- *Other parts of the body associated with Wood:* liver, gallbladder, ligaments, tendons, neck, nails

- *Strengths:* vision, direction, change

- *Challenging emotion:* anger

- *Archetype:* warrior, pioneer, entrepreneur

- *What Wood feels like:* morning, spring, childhood, moving upward

I still carry a vivid memory of my little son charging up a grassy hill and shouting, every cell in his body alert and alive with enthusiasm. This is the essence of Wood—the dynamic energy of the "watch out world, here I come!" nature—and these children will have a good supply of this lively and lusty warrior approach to life (it's definitely their default setting). How many times have you heard someone say, "I wish I had their energy," as they watched little ones at play? Wood is the "full speed ahead and damn the torpedoes" attitude toward life!

This Element represents the stage of the cycle where, like plants in spring, life force shoots out with tremendous focus. Power is no longer hidden as it was in the Water stage; it's born into the world with great vitality, and there's no turning back now. Wood is about beginning the process of defining the self, creating structure, putting ideas into action, and making them real. This is the energy of "doing," and woe to anyone who stands in its way!

All Wood qualities can be seen in the children who carry them, although they can manifest in many different ways. To best understand the true spirit of this Element, and thus your little ones, learn the essence of Wood. The following sections describe its basic aspects and include a few examples of how it can reveal itself in your child's behaviors, emotions, needs, and perceptions.

The Spirit of Wood

The image of a tree can help you understand the true nature of this Element. A tiny seed breaks up the earth in its drive to be alive, and the green sprout shoots straight up with enormous force. This little being is following a plan, a predetermined strategy for the most efficient way to achieve its goal. There's no hesitation as it confidently heads up on its vertical path into the world. Wood children possess this enthusiastic zeal for life, and you may marvel at, or be exhausted by, their tremendous vitality and energetic personality. From the moment they open their eyes in the morning till they close them at night, their ambitious outlook never wanes.

Plants have a set intention, and there's logic in how they grow to achieve it. Likewise, people with this Element carry great potential for logic, linear thinking, and practicality. Wood children will value what makes sense and may enjoy problem solving and figuring out how to get from point A to point B in a straight line. Kids with this nature often love to build things or tinker, taking household appliances apart and then trying to put them back together. As they mature, they'll excel at organizing their thoughts to come to the most sensible decisions, but may become frustrated by those who don't share their abilities for this kind of clarity and vision. There's a directness to this disposition and a firm view of the world.

These youngsters may be frank in how they communicate, possibly too much so at times, blurting out whatever pops into their minds without realizing that their words may be blunt and hurtful. In addition, their firm confidence in their own viewpoints often causes them to be judgmental and leap to conclusions. These two qualities don't always bode well for smooth relationships, and at the very least, you may have to help them learn to think more carefully before they speak or accept that they may have to apologize at times. Unfortunately, "I'm sorry" doesn't flow easily off of Wood children's tongues.

In order to follow its growth plan, the seedling needs to break through the earth to reach the fresh air and sunlight that will further its progress. The tendency of Wood to break things up can manifest in children's lives in different ways: for example, they might set up their car racetrack and then bomb it with blocks to destroy it, or they may tease their siblings or constantly interrupt others at meals. This same energy is seen in the image of thunder in Taoist philosophy. Thunder's sudden, loud clap can show up in Wood children's natures as they play the drums, pound things with tools, or slam doors when they're upset; and it may even be heard in their voices. In Chinese medicine, the sound of this

Element is described as a shout, so these youngsters may be naturally inclined to literally shout; or they may speak with a clipped tone, unlike the melodious flow of some Water people's speech, for instance. President Barack Obama's communication style is a good example of a Wood voice.

Wood is about a focused push forward in life, but this quality needs to be balanced with flexibility and an ability to adjust to changing conditions. The design of a tree once again helps us understand the perfection of nature's plan. It's held firmly in place by roots growing deep into the ground with its trunk straight and firm, yet it possesses the ability to grow around obstacles, and its branches sway constantly in the changing breeze. Balanced Wood children have strong convictions, but they can adapt to the fluctuations life brings them. At their best, they're able to roll with the punches, get along with everyone, and be wonderful influences on those around them.

Morning

Imagine waking up refreshed with hope and a sense of optimism, ready to take on the day. Morning also brings the new vision that developed as you slept that gives you options and possible directions that you hadn't considered before. This is also when you see things realistically in the light of day without being immersed in the emotions that were washing over you the previous night.

Wood children overflow with energy and enthusiasm for all the possibilities that lie before them, and they're full of confidence to tackle whatever they decide to go after. As they grow up, they'll value being realistic about things rather than get lost in their emotions, but they may have trouble understanding why some people have to talk about feelings all the time and just can't move on.

Just as most people are more energetic in the morning, Wood children always personify this energy. They are always on the go, and if they ever rest, it's not for long. This irresistible impulse to move can be a problem if it's too strong. They may be unable to sit at the table for an entire meal, constantly badger you for new things to do, or cause you to always be on alert for the latest mischief they're getting into. It's essential for parents to provide lots of opportunities for activities, especially those with physical movement, so these little ones have an outlet for all this energy. If you need to talk to your Wood child about something important, don't expect him to be able to sit down for a chat—you'll find more success going for a walk or building with Legos together while you discuss the matter at hand.

Spring

This is the season of change, when life pushes forth to become visible at last. Baby animals are born and tender green plants burst through the soil. It's a time when things manifest in the world, and this is a significant impulse for Wood kids, as they possess a desire to create something from an idea and actually make it work. This isn't the nature of the Watery dreamers who dwell in their imaginations; these children often want to make something they can hold, see, or play with. Your little ones will thrive with toys they can build or assemble, and as they get older, they'll be looking for opportunities to do something that makes a difference in the world.

Just as plants break up the earth in spring, Wood youngsters feel an urgency to break up the old to make way for the new. For instance, they may want to get involved in community projects to improve the lives of others. Brad Pitt is a good example of this Wood benevolence, with all the aid work he's done to help rebuild New Orleans after the devastation of Hurricane Katrina. (It's said that he built more homes in that city than the U.S. government did in the years directly after this tragedy.) Or these children may fight for causes as a way to influence positive change, wanting to join protest groups or work to reform the existing system. However, these youngsters can take the rebelliousness and rule breaking too far, so it's your job to ensure that they understand the difference between changing things for the better and going against the grain just for the heck of it.

Another problem may be that these children have heads so full of ideas that they can't get them out fast enough. Wood minds are active, and it's vital for them to *do* something with this energy. Their entrepreneurial spirit may have them starting a business at an early age, and they may love to invent things or learn diverse skills. They'll be lifelong students, always on the lookout for ways to advance and improve themselves.

But don't expect them to be able to stick with projects over a long period of time. The energy of spring is about new growth, so these kids tend to look for what's next rather than go in-depth into what's here now. They'll start something but become impatient if it requires too many details, and then quickly move on to the next thing. You may need to help them develop what's actually a hidden strength of theirs: the tremendous potential for discipline that will enable them to achieve their goals.

Childhood

Every Element is associated with a particular time in the cycle of life, and Wood specifically represents the archetypal energy of childhood. Little kids at play are bursting with vitality and a fascination with exploring everything around them. It's their nature to approach life full throttle, so inherent in this personality is a tendency to dive right in and have a great time. There's wonderful optimism and confidence running through Wood children's bright spirits, and they don't have to be pushed or persuaded to try something new. But they can get so caught up in moving forward that they tend to rev up too fast and forget some important steps in a plan or project, become disorganized, or get into trouble by acting before they think. These youngsters are also predisposed to pushing the envelope, procrastinating right up until the deadline, and then enjoying the adrenaline rush as they put their foot on the gas and race toward the finish line at the last minute. They do well, though, if they have a step-by-step learning process, a preset timeline for projects, or other ways to help them stick to a plan.

Wood Element kids tend to be concrete thinkers—in other words, they'll take your words at face value rather than understand abstractions. One mother told her Wood son that they were going to the airport to pick up his aunt, who'd lost so much weight that they wouldn't be able to recognize her. Hearing this, he protested, "Well, how will we know we have the right person then?" All kids are said to move through a stage of literal thinking (approximately from the ages of 7 to 11), but Wood types can maintain this tendency throughout their lives. In accordance with this straightforward nature, they'll consider it foolish for others to beat around the bush in conversation rather than just say what they mean!

These children love to do things themselves, rather than be helped, to gain the sense that they're the masters of their own domains. Showing them how to do something may be less effective than letting them learn in a hands-on fashion with your close guidance. Remember that these are little ones who love to *do,* so don't assume that they'll watch or wait for very long.

And this brings us to why we can't expect Wood people to be overly patient: it's due to their challenging emotion, anger, which we'll discuss next.

Wood Challenge: Anger

Every Element has one emotion that consistently arises under stress and sends someone's system spiraling out of balance. The challenging emotion for Wood children is anger, and it can manifest itself throughout their lives. Psychologists have found that one of the few ways to make babies angry is to hold their arms so they can't reach for what they want. In other words, being blocked from a goal irritates anyone; but because Wood is all about moving toward goals, there are more opportunities for anger to manifest. This is the "push"—the strong drive inherent in this Element's nature—and it can also reveal itself in milder emotions such as frustration, impatience, or impulse-control problems.

You may watch them have a meltdown if they're told no; or if a project becomes too hard for them, they'll explode in exasperation. There's also a good chance that they'll talk back or argue, and up to this point, you may have been puzzled as to why they always seem to want to challenge, or disagree, with others. Creating conflict is another version of the plant breaking up the soil. This is a natural impulse, but it can certainly make parenting Wood children interesting! As for their anger, it's like thunder: a big initial bang, but then it's over and they feel much better . . . even if you're still trying to calm your jangled nerves.

Wood Strength: Vision, Direction, and Change

The salvation for Wood children's struggle with anger comes from their need to *do*. When they start to become frustrated or upset, help them choose a direction for their energy, a healthy way to blow off steam. For younger children, let them get physical; but instead of throwing things, encourage them to pound pillows or work out with a punching bag until the surge is out of their systems and they're feeling balanced. Interestingly, psychological studies have shown that people make better, more logical decisions immediately *after* they've felt angry, almost as if experiencing that emotion clears their minds.

An older child can be guided to use her Wood talents to look logically at a situation and create a strategy to solve the problem. Help her organize her thoughts by breaking things down into manageable parts to form a workable plan. Don't be the "bad cop" by yelling at her, because you'll only increase her reactivity. Instead, be a calming influence in response to her exasperation.

The more opportunities for Wood children to be physically active, the less of a chance that frustration and anger will be a problem, because moving their bodies provides an outlet for their enormous supply of bottled energy. But please know that they also need plenty of downtime to keep their drive well nourished. Help them find balance with soothing activities like playing with their toys or reading, and avoid anything with a screen (such as a computer) during these times.

"You will not be punished for your anger,
you will be punished by your anger."

— Buddha

READING THE WOOD FEATURES

Chapter 8

Certain features on our faces have to do with Wood, and the more prominent or noticeable they are, the more we possess this Element as a major part of our original nature.

However, it's important to keep in mind that we all have Wood Element in our faces and personalities, just in differing amounts. The Wood characteristics can be examined to determine the unique ways in which they show up in your child's design, whether or not they're predominant.

Straight Hairline

Although the hairline is a Water feature, I want to mention one specific type that goes in a straight line across the forehead and sometimes juts in at the temples. (This was also discussed in the section on "Hairline" in Chapter 6.) A sign of Wood, this is an indication that some rebelliousness exists in a child's temperament.

A straight line on any feature, no matter what Element it belongs to, is a sign of Wood. For instance, a squared chin at the bottom (rather than curved or pointed) is one way it shows up. It doesn't matter if there are no other aspects of Wood on a child's face; this feature will add at least a small influence.

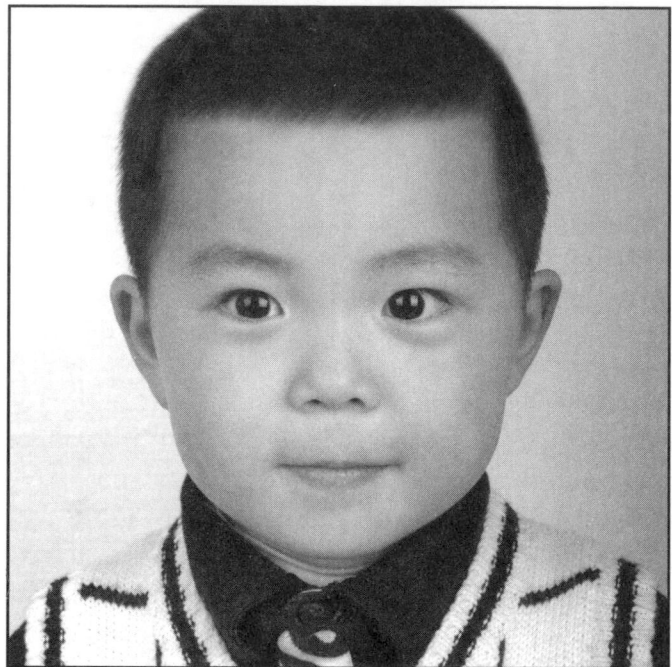

Fig. 28: A straight hairline indicates a rule breaker.

Eyebrows

The major indicator of Wood is the eyebrows. If they are full or long, this reveals a strong supply of confidence, drive, and assertiveness. Children with these eyebrows know what they want and will go in a straight line toward that goal. This feature also indicates the potential to develop an especially logical mind. For example, they'll be able to organize their thoughts, make decisions, develop a plan of action, and then go for it. Because of this talent for linear thinking, they'll thrive in structured learning environments.

Fig. 29: Full eyebrows signify confidence, drive, and assertiveness.

But you may not have observed all of these wonderful qualities in your Wood child yet! If not, watch them emerge over time. Right now, you may be seeing the other side of what these eyebrows add to his personality, such as the classic Wood tendency to be easily frustrated or angered, which we discussed in the last chapter. (There are other features that can modify this effect, however.) These little ones can be impatient, impulsive, and reactive; and if they're stressed, even a small obstacle will cause these emotions to arise. In Chinese medicine, the eyebrows correspond to the liver—the organ that processes toxins in the body and is also considered to filter "toxic" emotions. So a child with this feature can handle strong feelings better than others.

Please note that anger isn't always a bad thing. It's a force that rises when change needs to happen, to right wrongs and break up the old to make way for the new. The energy of anger is that push forward—just like plants in the spring—and it's this same force that creates the athlete, the entrepreneur, and the humanitarian who's out to change the world. If your child is exhibiting these behaviors, understand that he has to stay active, particularly when he's stressed, and you might have to help him learn to channel that strong drive toward positive actions.

Kids with very bushy eyebrows may also be aggressive or even carry a desire to be the "top dog" in any situation. They could get upset if they lose in a game and may try to dominate any group

Fig. 30: Weak eyebrows may indicate a lack of self-confidence.

they're in. Youngsters with a strong "unibrow" (eyebrows with little or no space between them) may especially struggle with hostile tendencies or have issues with authority.

Weak eyebrows can indicate less self-confidence or a difficulty being assertive. Sparse ones mean that Wood is probably *not* a major influence—in other words, their strengths will be discerned by other facial features. Remember that if your little one has naturally weak eyebrows, this is just one part of her design; it doesn't mean that something's wrong! But you may need to help boost her confidence.

What sometimes happens is that Wood girls, in an attempt to fit the latest trends, pluck or wax their eyebrows. If they reduce their naturally heavy brows to thin lines, they're going against their inherent energy, which can send their systems out of balance. This can result in problems with anger that weren't there before, or at least cause them to lose their natural confidence.

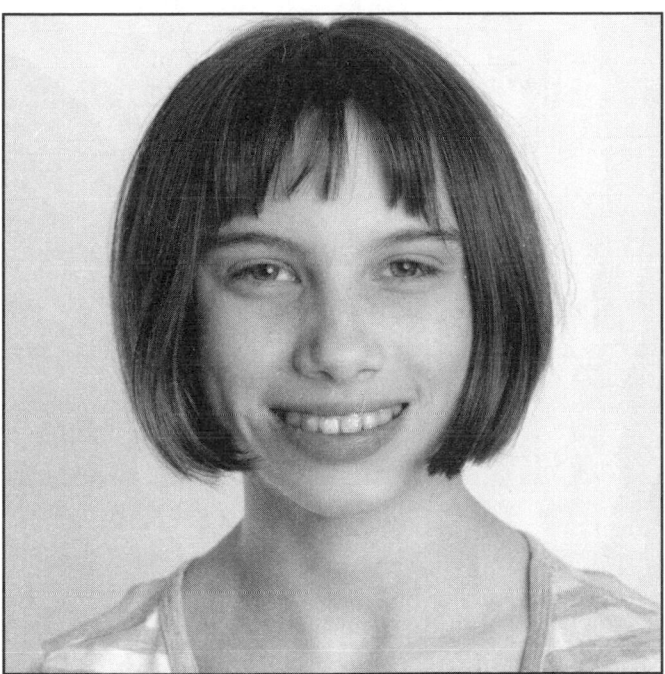

Fig. 31: Long eyebrows indicate the ability to have many friendships.

I always advise girls (and women) not to diminish their eyebrows too much!

Even the length of eyebrows has meaning. Long ones are said to be a sign of people who can maintain many friendships. Remembering that the liver processes toxins, it follows that children with this feature are capable of dealing with the toxic emotions of other people. In other words, they can handle all their friends' upsets and help them with their problems without getting overly stressed. Youngsters with short eyebrows are less likely to cope well with demanding peers, or else they may only be able to do so with smaller groups of friends.

Fig. 32: Eyebrows with a round shape are the sign of a pleasing nature.

Eyebrows come in different shapes as well. Those that are rounded indicate someone who wants to give others a positive experience, although if the brows are extremely rounded, this can be a sign that she tries too hard to please.

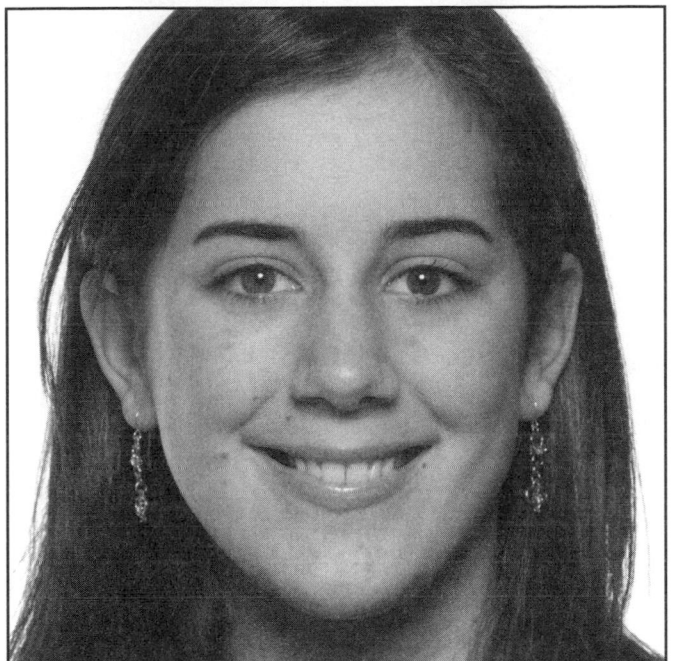

Fig. 33: Eyebrows that grow in a straight line reveal a logical mind.

Brows that grow in a straight line reveal an especially logical mind, someone who will carefully evaluate a problem and thoroughly weigh his options before making a decision. Then once these people have decided something, they're ready to go for it! Peaked eyebrows, ones that look like upside-down V's above the eyes, are the sign of those who react to situations much more quickly. These youngsters are spontaneous, but it can contribute to their tendency to leap before they look, act without thinking, or react without stopping to realize how their words or behavior will affect others.

Fig. 34: V-shaped eyebrows show a quick, reactive mind.

Fig. 35: Eyebrows that are set close to each other indicate the need to work independently from others.

Occasionally, you'll see eyebrows that dart up from the eyes in diagonal lines! These signify people who have the potential to react emotionally or jump into things too quickly. If this is representative of your child, it will be important to help her learn to pause and think before being swept away by her feelings or making any sudden decisions.

Some eyebrows grow very close together while others are wide set. The amount of space between the eyebrows is an indicator of how well someone gets along with others. If there's a very narrow space between them, this suggests a child who may be less flexible in dealing with various personalities. Unless there are other aspects of his face that lessen this tendency, he may fare better with a smaller group of like-minded kids. At school, these youngsters dislike being heavily supervised or having someone breathing down their necks when they're trying to work. These children may prefer to do things on their own,

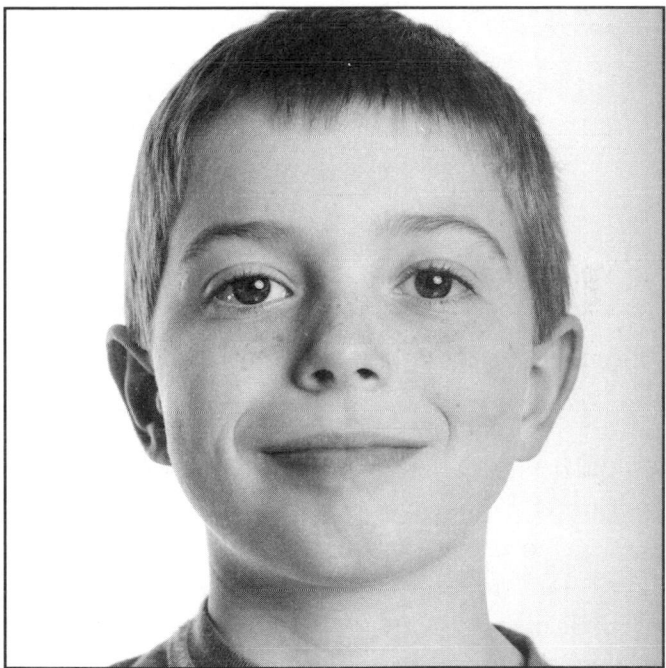

Fig. 36: Wide-set eyebrows reflect a more easygoing style of relating to others.

only sharing their projects once they're done. For instance, they might interpret a teacher's attempts to guide them as criticism.

Children with wide-set eyebrows, on the other hand, will be more easygoing about how they interact with different personality styles. They're not so bothered by authority figures monitoring their work and may relate well to various types of people. Youngsters with eyebrows that are narrow set grow up to be adults who enjoy jobs that allow them independence and privacy, while those with wide-set ones will better equipped to cope if they have to work in teams or a large corporate environment, for example.

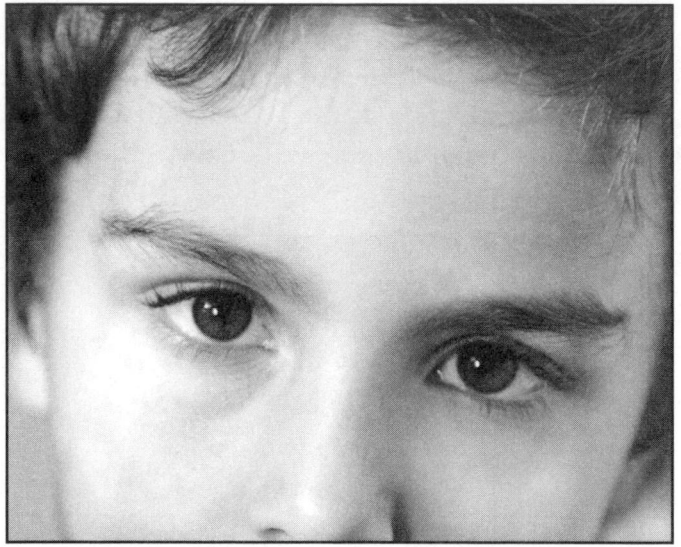

Fig. 37: The inner ends of the eyebrows set close to the eye show a tendency toward self-criticism.

Even the details of how closely the ends of the eyebrows reach down toward the eyes give us information. If the inner tips of children's eyebrows come down very close to the corners of their eyes, they'll tend to be self-critical and hard on themselves for making small mistakes, or they may hold the bar quite high for what they want to accomplish. Little ones whose eyebrows come down closely at the *outer* ends will find fault in others more often than themselves.

Brow Bone

The brow bone is the bone that lies beneath the eyebrows. In children, it's underdeveloped and only grows as the male hormone testosterone starts to flow through the body at puberty. Because its size correlates to the levels of testosterone in the system, boys will naturally develop one that protrudes more so than girls. Some women do end up with a relatively prominent brow bone, however, so it's necessary to pay attention to its size in both genders.

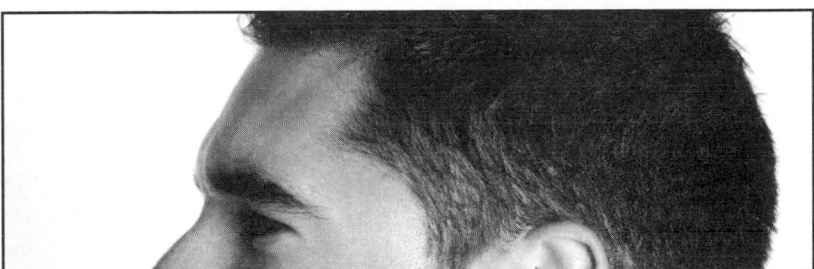

Fig. 38: A prominent brow bone reveals a need to be in charge.

Basically, this feature reveals the desire to dominate or be in power. The larger it is, the greater the urge. This characteristic produces an even stronger drive than heavy eyebrows do, and if a youngster has both, watch out! Anger may be a frequent visitor in his life, and he'll probably have an enormous need to stay physically active. People like this try to dominate any group they're a part of or be "on top" in relationships—to the point that if they feel they're capitulating in any way, they consider this "losing." These Wood personalities may have issues with authority, and they dislike being told what to do . . . and more than likely they'll perceive the rest of the world as ordering them around. For example, if you say, "Could you please mow the lawn today?" he'll hear, "I'm the boss of *you!*" Of course, this can create conflicts within families and in the outside world; however, one positive quality this feature provides is the potential to be a leader or achieve great success in business or athletics. And both of these activities are wonderful channels for all this drive.

The brow bone has to do with a kind of yang power that we all have an abundant supply of whether we're male or female. One particular part of this feature relates to the power people have that comes from their childhood relationship with their father or whoever was the authority figure in their young lives. This area is the very center of the brow bone between the eyebrows, and it's called "Father's Blessing." One of the father's most important gifts to pass down is this yang power, which is a sense of personal mastery in life. If you can envision a father telling his child, "You are the most talented, beautiful, and amazing person to ever walk the face of the earth. Go forth and prosper!" this is the feeling of the Father's Blessing.

Now, in real life, there's a range of how well fathers give this gift: some accomplish it with incredible success, but others have power issues of their own, and so they don't do a very good job of passing it on to their children. For instance, if a father has trouble with anger, this will interfere with his son's or daughter's ability to safely express theirs. If a father is emotionally or physically distant—or if he's left and no one has taken his place—this will have a negative impact on how blessed his children will feel with their own potential, and this can be read on their faces.

Ideally, the Father's Blessing area is broad, smooth, and slightly rounded; and the skin is a healthy color. This indicates a successful transfer of that yang potency. If a father wasn't able to pass along this energy effectively, there will be a sign of that here. It could show up as an indentation in the brow bone or a long-term discoloration in the complexion, but the most common indication is seen in maturity: a single, vertical wrinkle appearing right

Fig. 39: This boy has a beautiful "Father's Blessing" area on the brow bone right between the eyebrows.

between the eyebrows. This is called a "Hanging Needle" if it's a faint line or a "Hanging Blade" if it's deeper, and it reveals the extent to which someone feels cut off from her yang side and not fully connected to her inner power and the ability to express it in the outer world. The deeper the wrinkle, the bigger the problem this is in her life.

Like a needle or a blade, this issue hangs in front of her and will drop at some point to impede her progress if it hasn't been dealt with. The point isn't to project blame on the father for what he couldn't do. It's more a case of needing to take on the task of integrating her yang side and blessing her own power as part of a life contract, since her father was unable to. The Father's Blessing area is also where the third-eye chakra is said to be, and it's interesting that Wood energy is associated with activating this inner vision. I've found that many adults who have this mark on their faces have a spiritual focus, as if on some level they're aware of a need to access this unused power.

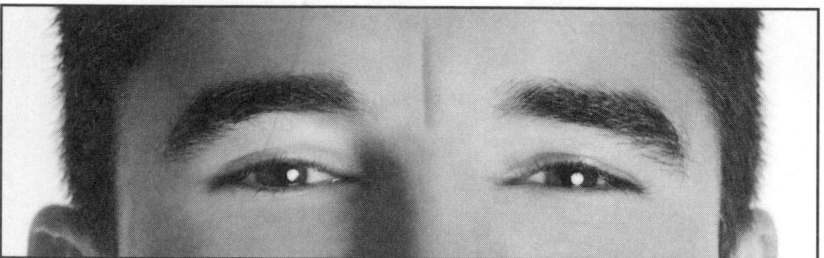

Fig. 40: A "Hanging Blade" is one deep line between the eyebrows.

Most young children don't have any wrinkles, but in case you do notice this single line developing in the center of your teenager's brow bones, it can be helpful to examine how he might not be expressing his yang power and consider what you can do to assist him in accomplishing this. If he's being overly dominated by a parent or authority figure, for instance, consider counseling for the family, or at least provide it for him. If you see some minor markings here, such as an indentation or discoloration, these aren't as significant, but pay attention to any evidence of this issue showing up later on in life.

A more common set of wrinkles that can appear fairly early in life is two small vertical lines right between the eyebrows. These are frequently found on Wood people, as they denote a tendency toward frustration and anger. After all, what kind of face do you make when you're experiencing these feelings? A frown! And the more you frown, the sooner you'll carve these creases into your brow. Many people develop these wrinkles eventually, as everyone occasionally feels these emotions, but seeing them at age 50 is very different from 17. If you notice these lines on your teen's face, this is a big clue that Wood is his or her home base!

However, don't be dismayed if you see them start to show up on your child's face. There's a more general meaning for this, and it has to do with the natural tension in this Element's physicality. There's an intensity in this kind of body—an aroused, alert tension held in every fiber—that's an aspect of this overall dynamic energy. These youngsters are able to focus with laserlike concentration; and whether they're studying, playing video games, or building a toy airplane, you'll probably notice their furrowed brow. This propensity to tense up is another way Wood people create these wrinkles between their eyebrows, and it's a sign of how intently they concentrate.

Temples

The temples are the sides of the forehead, and on most people they're unremarkable, but on some Wood faces, they'll be noticeably concave. Indented temples are another sign that this Element contributes to children's natures, specifically a tendency toward compulsive behavior. This is yet another indication of these children's inner drive of always wanting to "do." Most often this need to be in motion manifests as workaholism in adulthood, but even as youngsters they probably didn't have much desire to sit back and relax!

Concave temples can also reveal addictive tendencies, but not necessarily to the point of substance abuse. These kids can have obsessions with TV or computer games, for instance, almost developing a hyperfocus that puts them in a zone. There can be trouble with impulse control in Wood children, and this feature enhances that quality. Even though they know you said, "Don't do that!" they just can't stop themselves. Another term for indented temples is "Desire for Altered States," and compulsive behavior can indeed put someone into a different state of consciousness. In the big picture, this feature may also reveal a lifelong interest in spirituality, which is another way to achieve an altered state.

Fig. 41: Indented temples can signify compulsive tendencies.

Jaw

The jaw is the second most important indicator of the amount of Wood your child possesses. However, in infancy, this feature isn't completely formed and will develop later in childhood, so it's one you'll have to read over time. In Chinese face reading, it's called "The Roots of the Tree." A tree with strong roots can't be pushed over, so people with strong jaws won't be easily influenced or made to change their minds. A large or sharply defined jaw is a sign of a strong belief system and firm values, which is an excellent quality. This validates a study that I referenced earlier, which found that politicians with the strongest jaws tend to win elections, as the powerful jaw unconsciously makes us feel secure in the sense that these people will fight for what they believe in and won't be swayed. Additionally, this feature reveals a competitive nature and a natural draw to activities such as sports or politics—or any conflict where somebody comes out as the winner!

Fig. 42: A strong jaw is the sign of firm values and beliefs.

However, an exceptionally sharp or powerful jaw might indicate someone who is judgmental and jumps to conclusions about people based on his own rigid beliefs. This is a sign of an inflexible nature, such as the stereotypical military leader who has the attitude of "My country, right or wrong!" This trait is also a sign of competitiveness and the desire to be the winner at any cost. If your child develops this jaw, show him how to come to logical conclusions about others while still understanding their opinions and allowing for differences. He may also need assistance in learning how to be a gracious loser.

One wonderful benefit of these strong Wood personalities is that they want to make the world a better place, and this may be why people with strong jaws enter politics to begin with. If children with this feature can channel their forceful energy into helping others who are suffering, that will create positive results for themselves and everyone around them.

Fig. 43: A narrow jaw translates to a flexible nature.

A narrow jaw suggests someone who is more flexible and not so set in her ways. She'll listen to differing opinions, and even consider changing her own point of view if what she's hearing makes sense. Because of this more easygoing nature, she can sway others through the adaptability she radiates. A narrow jaw, however, can also indicate indecisiveness or being too easily influenced. Children with this characteristic may pay close attention to what their friends are saying and will want to go along with them, or they may be manipulated by others with firmer viewpoints.

Some youngsters have weak or soft jaws that seem to flow right into their necks with little definition. This merely reveals that they don't focus much attention on judging or competing, and I often see this detail in those who have many Water features.

Face Shape

In face reading, the overall shape of the face isn't very important; most people are a combination of shapes, and we get much more information from the details of the actual facial features. But in some cases, the shape further confirms an Element's major influence. The shape of a Wood face is long and rectangular; for example, TV news anchor Brian Williams has this look. Its meaning is similar to that of a narrow jaw, which, as I've said, indicates a flexible, more easygoing nature. People with these qualities are said to be classic diplomats, able to get along with anyone. Of course, the shape of your child's adult face won't be apparent early on and will develop over time. Also be aware that not all Wood faces take on this appearance. In fact, this shape usually appears with only one of two classic body types associated with this Element, and they're discussed next.

Body Type

A mature Wood body can be a tree or a shrub! In other words, these kids grow up to be either tall and lanky like basketball players or short and compact like gymnasts. The "tree" body often has the long rectangular face to go with it. This is a gentler yin version of Wood energy, and it's the more flexible of the two—much like bamboo swaying in the breeze.

The "shrub" body type is short in stature, but it's almost as if all that strong energy has been condensed into a small frame. These people have more yang and often have enormous drive. They're more like oak than bamboo, strong with less flexibility. Their face shape is less obvious, though it sometimes is a short rectangle or square.

The Best Environments for the Wood Nature

Green is the color associated with this Element, and incorporating shades of this hue in your decor will resonate with Wood children's energy. Actual living plants or images of nature are wonderful for these youngsters, especially any pictures of forests and trees or artwork that shows people climbing mountains or conquering challenges (which matches Wood's upward movement). Furniture made of wood is great, too, but please pad any sharp edges, as your little ones will probably be bouncing around the room quite a bit! A theme bed in the shape of a race car or rocket ship will be special for them, and so will a loft bed or bunk beds so they can climb *up* to go to sleep. Stripes in the wallpaper or sheets also carry that upward motion these children so enjoy.

Organized places for them to store books and toys work well because of their need for structure. When they're little, you'll be smart to put away breakables; it's not that these children can't be careful with things, but they're so active that the chances of things being damaged are higher.

It's also imperative that their rooms aren't filled with electronics, as these kids can spend far too much time watching TV or playing computer games. Too many of these activities really stress out their systems and can contribute to problems with impulse control or distractibility. Creating a calm oasis in their room as well as in other areas of the house will help them learn to balance their natural tension with relaxation.

Thoughts for Teachers

Because these children are so active, it's more difficult for them to stay seated for long periods of time than for other kids. Find every opportunity you can to let them get up and move around, whether that means handing out papers in class or running errands for you. In addition, they may have trouble concentrating if they're easily distracted. Experiment with either seating them close to your desk so you can help them stay focused or in a quieter part of the classroom where there's less to draw their attention. But don't make these little ones think that this move is a punishment. In fact, you may feel like you're always having to correct or discipline them; if this is the case, try to use more "do" than "don't" statements. Telling these children *how* you want them to behave will be more effective than yelling at them to stop whatever it is they're doing. The more *don'ts* they hear, the more criticized they'll feel, and this might lead to a vicious cycle of negative reactions.

Wood children do well in structured learning environments, with tasks broken down into manageable, concrete steps and a timeline or schedule to follow. These kids may forget to bring homework or schoolbooks from home each day, so some teachers allow for a second set of books to stay at home. You may also have to help parents realize that they must double-check to make sure homework is in their youngsters' backpacks before they leave the house each morning.

Helping the Wood Nature Flourish

These bright, active children are known for their enthusiasm, which originates from a word in the Greek language that, loosely translated, means "filled with God." There will be times when you feel your Wood child is just a little *too* full! It can seem impossible to keep up with him, since he's on the go all the time, and your life may seem like it only consists of chasing him around yelling, "Don't!" and "Stop!" for most of the day. Try to give positive commands and communicate what you want his behavior to change into rather than just demanding that he stop what he's doing.

These kids will respond well to positive reinforcement and frequent, immediate rewards for good behavior rather than punishment. If you do have to discipline them, don't use shame or blame. If you yell when they're immersed in anger, you'll only stress them out more and make it harder to regain balance. Remember that children of this Element have a strong reaction to feeling criticized or dominated. And, really, if someone was yelling and making you feel bad about yourself, would *you* want to hug them at bedtime?

Time-outs should not be punitive, as they'll just amp up these little ones' feelings of reactivity. Use these opportunities to teach them how to calm down and regain self-control. Don't make these children stand in an empty corner—instead, give them a project to quietly focus on, such as building with blocks or alphabetizing their books by author. Be a model for them by staying calm during their upsets (and your own!) so they can learn a new way of dealing with stress.

If your Wood child is older, you may be experiencing the result of years of frustration that have made family relationships degenerate into negativity, grudges, or sarcasm. Try to create opportunities to simply spend short periods of time with her where she gets to choose the activity and you just enjoy each other's company—with no criticism allowed. At this stage, you're rebuilding the supply of positive experiences to heal what's happened in the past. Play a sport together, or even better, get involved in something that appeals to this Element's strong benevolent nature. For example, volunteer for a nonprofit organization like Habitat for Humanity or anything that gives her the experience of making a real change in the world.

Look for ways to laugh and have fun together. Consider channeling their natural competitive drive into the types of sports where they can compete against themselves instead of others, such as swimming, track, or martial arts, which is also a brilliant way for Wood kids to develop their inherent powers of discipline. Teach them how to be gracious when others win a game, and create a daily gratitude exercise—perhaps to play at the dinner table each night—where everyone states something that happened that day that they're grateful for. All this will help you support these children to grow up to transform the world.

⊙ ⊙ ⊙

> *"People are like stained-glass windows. They sparkle and shine when the sun is out, but when the darkness sets in, their true beauty is revealed only if there is a light from within."*
>
> — ELISABETH KÜBLER-ROSS

Chapter
9

THE FIRE CHILD: LOVER, PERFORMER, FREE SPIRIT

Jayden

Jayden meets me at the front door, and the first thing I notice are his eyes sparkling with excitement. He asks me if I want to see his show and, not waiting for an answer, runs halfway up the stairs to start a dance of hops and kicks on each step back down to me. Holding an imaginary microphone, he starts singing at the top of his lungs. Losing interest in that, he launches into a monologue about his life story: "I'm seven! I live here! I didn't always live here. I used to live in another house and it was green. And I had a dog, but he ran away, but then he came back. And now we have a cat, too. Do you know a joke? I know lots of jokes." He then starts making funny faces. "This is my favorite shirt 'cuz it's red and I have red shoes—come see my new shoes! Come see my room!" Jayden shouts as he grabs my hand and we charge up the stairs.

Meanwhile, his mother has been trying to get a word in edgewise. Laughing, she follows us, saying, "Sorry, sorry. He's just got the biggest personality!" There's no need for her to apologize; the minute I saw his big dimples and peaked eyebrows, the jig was up. This boy is a natural performer and a talkative charmer who demands your attention but makes life more fun at the same time. Jayden loves the limelight and is always putting on shows for his family and anyone else who will stop to watch. He tries to copy the dance moves he sees on TV and often turns the playroom into a theater, complete with admission tickets and programs. The long-suffering family pets sometimes end up dressed in costumes as part of the entertainment, and he's always pestering his brothers and sisters to come see his latest show.

This is an extroverted little guy who loves his playdates with friends. "He can be gone all day and still not want to come home," his father says. At school, he's called the class clown but isn't a troublemaker; according to all reports, he seems to be the apple of his teacher's eye. He isn't disruptive, and in fact, probably keeps things lighthearted for everyone. Jayden is a highly affectionate boy who makes special drawings as gifts for everyone in his life, which he then demands his mother wrap up and mail or, better yet, that they jump into the car to hand deliver them. He also loves when relatives come over to the house, as this provides him with fresh audience members and playmates.

Jayden tends to get very excited when any big event draws near and becomes anxious and unable to sleep. His mother calls it "anticipation sickness." For instance, a few days before a big family trip recently, the normal bedtime rituals became useless. Nighttime for this little guy brought about agitated tossing and turning, and his system wouldn't relax. When he gets into this state, the only way he can sleep is if one of his parents crawls into bed with him or he can join them in theirs.

Daytime during these anxious periods isn't easy for him, either. Jayden seems almost manic, bouncing around the room and not focusing on anything for long. These episodes are hard for his parents, and at some point his father blows up at him, shouting, *"Put a lid on it!"* This results in hysterical sobbing on Jayden's part, and his mother ends up hugging him tightly and rocking him in her lap. Fortunately, "Fire-y" upsets can pass relatively quickly; however, he's become more shy around his father these days. As vibrant as this Element is, like a flame it has a vulnerable and delicate nature, and his father's strong reaction is like a shock to Jayden's system. This kind of flickering flame can be doused quite easily, and parents of these children do well to take it easy on them.

Sophia

Hot pink. Her entire bedroom is hot pink. The wallpaper, ceiling, rug, curtains, bedspread, and even the dolls' clothes all pulsate with this vibrant hue. And in the middle of the room, also dressed in the same electric color, stands Sophia. Her red hair, along with her pointed nose and freckles, makes it obvious that Fire is her home planet. She's just had a slumber party the night before (the room is still full of candy wrappers and crumpled pizza boxes), and she giggles at the mess. Waving her hands around as she talks, Sophia describes to me how they stayed up all night watching DVDs and playing with makeup. At 13, she's remarkably poised and naturally charming, and I flash back to what I was like at that age—certainly nowhere near as self-assured!

This fiery young girl tells me that she wants to be a movie and Broadway star. "By the time I'm 21, I'll be commuting between New York and L.A.," she confidently says. Despite these big dreams, she does well in school and especially loves creative writing. There are piles of notebooks filled with poetry written in purple, green, and red ink stacked on her nightstand; and although most of them are dreamy poems about various boys, she's got some talent with words. After school, Sophia juggles the demands of homework and drama club, and also earns a bit of money walking the neighbor's dog. This is a girl with energy to spare, and her only fear is being bored. *Highly doubtful!* Her phone vibrates and rings with texts and calls while her computer bings as e-mails fill her inbox. She has music playing in the background while her TV is on mute in the corner. It seems like there is never enough stimulation for her active mind, as half-done projects are scattered around her room and throughout the house.

Flames flicker and move, always looking for something new to burn; and Sophia's short attention span keeps her on the go, unable to concentrate on one thing for very long, which can be a real problem. Her parents have finally recognized that she's not a kid who will sit in one place for any extended period; and they let her spread out projects in the family room, on a desk in the basement, *and* in her bedroom. In this way, she can at least flit from place to place and they stand a chance of seeing something get finished. Often, though, Mom or Dad has to lay down the law and make her sit . . . and stay!

Sophia dances around the house, stopping to pet the cat and stroke the petals of the beautiful orchid her mother keeps in the foyer. Then she runs to the window when she spots a blue jay, gushing, "Oh! Isn't he the most gorgeous thing you've ever seen!" Her delight in just being alive is infectious. Fire nature spreads joy wherever it goes. Sophia glows when I compliment her on her sparkly shoes, and she immediately says she likes my necklace. Even if people of this Element can be somewhat self-absorbed, they're also very responsive to others . . . sometimes too much so.

"She's in love with being in love," her mother whispers as we meet in the kitchen. "It seems like every week she's infatuated with some new boy. Right now she's all talk and no action, but I'm worried about what's coming our way in another year or two!" Her mother's concerns may be justified. Fire people love to flirt and are thrilled when someone finds them special. They're so naturally affectionate and likely to respond to anyone who reciprocates. At any age, they can have trouble with discernment about others; for instance, they can get too deeply involved in romantic relationships before they've learned whether someone is worthy of their trust. Sophia's parents are trying to set a strong foundation now and keep the lines of communication open. This little girl knows they adore her, and she does want to please them.

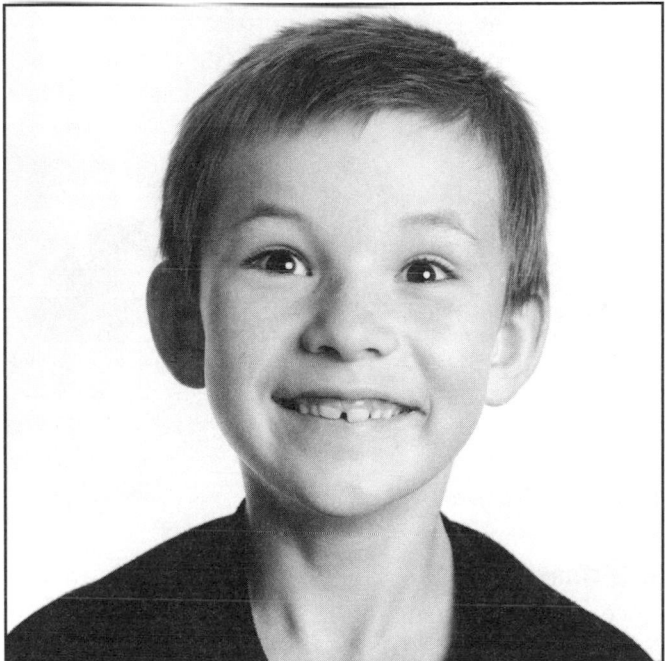

Fig. 44: This boy has the bright eyes, red hair, and pointed features of Fire Element.

Fig. 45: This girl's peaked eyebrows and wide-open eyes show her Fire nature.

The Fire Child's Nature

In this chapter, you'll learn about the inner nature and outer appearance of Fire children, and the next chapter will detail more information about each feature associated with this Element. To begin with, the following list shows what to look for. Please note that your child doesn't have to have *all* of these characteristics for Fire to play a strong role; seeing any of them means it's a factor in his or her personality. The more aspects you notice, the more Fire there is in your child's nature! Look for:

- Sparkling eyes
- Curly or red hair
- Dimples

- Pointed or cleft tips of features
- Freckles
- A pink flush or radiance to the complexion
- Skinny arms and torso

Well-known adults with many of these features include Billy Crystal, Shirley MacLaine, Ashley Judd, Jackie Chan, Jada Pinkett Smith, Lindsay Lohan, Jack Black, and Prince Harry.

As Your Child Grows

It's important to note that some Fire features are not immediately apparent from birth. Early in life, children's noses are more rounded at the tip than they may be later on. If your little one already has a pointed nose, then it definitely means she has some Fire in her nature! But if there's no sharpness there now, you may see more of a point form as she grows. Freckles also don't develop until later, usually after exposure to the sun, and whether the arms and upper bodies are destined to be thin will take time to be revealed as well. The meanings of all these traits are covered later in this chapter, and you can use this book to read the emerging aspects of your youngsters' personalities as their faces mature.

Qualities of Fire Element

- *Facial features:* light in the eyes, tips of features, vibrancy of complexion

- *Other parts of the body associated with Fire:* heart, small intestines, blood

- *Strengths:* passion, love, insight

- *Challenging emotion:* excitement

- *Archetype:* lover, performer, free spirit

- *What Fire feels like:* noon, summer, the prime of life, peaking energy, expanding outward

Fire is pure exuberance, the thrill of being alive, and the joy of giving and receiving love. It's the desire to dissolve like smoke and vapors, merge with life in divine passion, and dance in the world with wild abandon. The power of this Element is the heart, which the Chinese believe to be the center of consciousness in the body. The feeling of love makes our energy rise like a flame, connects us with our true spirit, and allows us to be intimate with others. This is only possible if the heart is open, but an open heart is a vulnerable heart, and it can be difficult to stay available emotionally and still be able to filter out what's harmful. Such vulnerability can result in injury to the emotional heart, and it may even end up shutting down as a result.

Fire energy is hummingbird-like: it vibrates in excitement or like a dancing flame, delicate and easy to put out. These youngsters' natural exuberance needs to shimmer throughout the day, filling their souls with joy and reaching out to exchange affection with those around them.

Every quality of this Element can be seen in those who carry it, although it can manifest in many different ways. To best understand its true spirit, and thus your little one, learn its essence. What follows are the basic aspects and a few examples of how Fire can reveal itself in your child's behaviors, emotions, needs, and perceptions.

The Spirit of Fire

People are drawn to fire by the light, warmth, and constant movement that entrances them to stay and watch the show. Fire children will have a bright inner warmth that reaches out to others, and they may even emulate a flickering flame by constantly waving their hands around as they talk. They move fast, think fast, and talk fast; and just as fire is constantly seeking something new to burn, they're always searching for something new to do. Change and variety are in their blood, and their worst fear is being bored—but that's virtually impossible. They're always finding things to be curious about or someone to talk to.

These are kids who are likely to get noticed or end up in the spotlight somehow, whether they want to or not. However, most do love attention, but not out of any egotistical desire; it's that they yearn for a connection with other people, because that's what lights them up. These little performers may love to put on shows for you, the whole family, the neighborhood, the crowd at the airport waiting for a flight, or even an invisible but adoring audience in their bedroom. These children like to feel special, and their preteen fantasies may be about the rock star who falls in love with them or the talent scout who makes them famous.

Fire also flares up; there's a sense of drama and amplification to it, which can manifest in the tendency to exaggerate or embellish a story. Please know that these children aren't intentionally lying or being dishonest. It's just that the truth sounds so lame compared to the actual experience! The school bus was an hour late, according to them, even though it was only more like 15 minutes. This is because a few minutes in no way conveys the intensity of what it felt like to be tardy. They'll run into the house screaming that the neighbor's dog attacked them, when it only barked at them through the fence. Understand that any exaggeration means an event was a big deal to them and they need your attention.

Just as fire is attracted to anything it can burn, these kids love physical contact. They'll want to touch whomever they're playing with, pet any animals they see, stroke interesting leaves on plants, and roll around on your nubby bedspread—life is one big sensual delight to them. The sense organ in the body that relates to Fire is the tongue, so they might also love to try exotic new foods as part of their adventure.

But just as flames are delicate in nature, these youngsters aren't always extroverted—they can actually be quite shy. It's very important to Fire people that they're liked, and this can translate into an overall anxiousness about being rejected. If they have a bad experience, they may pull back into themselves. But long-term isolation for personalities of this Element is unhealthy, and you may have to find ways to help them rejoin the world. They can become sad and morose if they're alone for too long; even if they're shy, they're nourished by being around others.

Fire kids can drive you crazy if they're a constant blur of activity or squealing and overly exuberant when you come home after a hard day. But it's so vital to understand that yelling or harsh treatment can easily douse their little spirits. Take great care not to come down hard on them. I've had countless adult Fire clients who had their lights extinguished early on by a heavy-handed parent, and it affected them for the rest of their lives. One woman in her early 30s was never able to develop close friendships because every time she started opening up to someone, she'd become so excited that her voice would get loud. At that point, she said she'd hear her father's voice in her head, snarling through gritted teeth, *"Keep it down!"* Immediately she'd pull back, terrified that everyone was thinking about how obnoxious she was being, and the new friendship would falter as a result.

Noon

At the height of the day, activity is at its peak. When you arrived at work in the morning, you got out your to-do list, organized your tasks, and then launched in. By midday, you're fully engaged, up to your elbows in half-finished projects, and things are scattered all over your desk; lots of balls are in the air. It's a natural process of getting something accomplished, but there's a lot going on at once. This is the energy of the Fire nature.

Talkative and full of vitality, these children will go nonstop throughout the day, their minds brimming with ideas. As they get older, they'll be able to multitask like nobody's business, juggling a million things at the same time. But right now, their rooms may be a mess with stuff in various stages of completion, and their lives can seem a bit out of control. Their hands may already be full, but suddenly they see something shiny out of the corner of their eye and say, "Oh! That looks like fun, too!" and they try to take that on as well.

At some point, the towering pile of projects can topple and create chaos. Inevitably, these kids may struggle with the classic Fire problem of having trouble completing things. After all, flames are always moving! Expecting them to sit in one place and finish a project from beginning to end is unrealistic. They do their best work if they can flit between tasks—15 minutes on one thing and 10 minutes on another—like a hummingbird flies among flowers. They'll stand a good chance of actually accomplishing their work efficiently if they're allowed to function according to their natural disposition, but perhaps with firm reminders from you not to forget to go back and finish!

Summer

When the sun is high, the days are long and hot, and all of nature is in full bloom, it's time to have fun! Summer is when people are spontaneous and carefree like at no other time during the year; it's all about party time, whether that means backyard barbecues with friends or playing at the beach. *Fun* is the operative word for Fire personalities—if something's not fun, it's not worth doing! You may judge your kids as irresponsible if they whine at the idea of having to do boring chores or homework, or if they joke around while doing these things. If they can, they'll try to turn anything into a chance to play or laugh to liven things up somehow. It might seem that these kids are being frivolous or aren't taking things seriously, but they're really just trying to adjust the experience to suit their needs. It feels right for them to have that exuberant energy soar in their bodies.

Summer is the season of stimulation, with bright colors in the garden and good weather allowing for a variety of outdoor activities. There's an expansive and inspired feeling during this time of year, and sadness or depression rarely lasts. Fire children will be as naturally cheerful as the season, and if they do run off in tears, they'll usually recover quickly. Don't be surprised, however, if there's big drama on a regular basis! Remember that it's expected of this Element to flare up, so a little upset may easily amplify into complete histrionics . . . for five minutes. Nothing lasts for long with Fire youngsters! In fact, change is a major theme with these little ones; they're adaptable and love variety in their lives. While other kids might be resistant to any deviation from the norm, if anything, it's a *lack* of variation that will drag these children down.

Prime of Life

Fire Element is the archetype of young adults; with hormones coursing through their bodies, they're passionate about life and thrilled at the possibilities of the outside world. No matter what age your child is, you'll be able to sense this passion, delight in being alive, and ambition to get out there and have experiences! He may dream of traveling the world, being onstage, or writing romance novels; whatever it is, he'll just want to go for it!

There's a warm charisma to this personality that radiates a natural expressiveness, responsiveness, and desire to give and receive affection. These little ones love to be touched: hugs galore are always welcome, they'll appreciate an arm around their shoulders when you're standing next to them, and they'll like the dog lying against them on the couch. They have a natural flirtatious quality, but this has nothing to do with sexuality. Fire reaches out to everyone, so they'll flirt with the cat, the neighbor's toddler, butterflies, or whoever comes to the door. This trait is apparent from an early age and is part of their wonderful talent for making others feel loved. As adults, they'll excel at any job dealing with people due to their genuine charm. Everyone feels better when a Fire person walks into the room.

But like the stereotypical young adult, they can be a bit self-centered. They'll dissolve into tears if you tell them they can't go out with their friends or buy yet another pair of shoes. They want your attention in every moment and will manage to turn the conversation around to *them* no matter how it began. "It's *all* about her," said one father, as he rolled his eyes while hugging his daughter with a big smile.

Fire Challenge: Excitement

Every Element has one emotion that consistently arises under stress and can send the system spiraling out of balance. This challenging emotion for Fire is *excitement,* and it can manifest in numerous ways. However, excitement may not sound like it poses the same kind of difficulties as Water's fear or Wood's anger! Traditionally, in Chinese medicine the challenging emotion for Fire is described as "excess joy," but this is a poor translation for the Western mind. After all, how can someone have *too much* joy in life? Fire's problem area is actually about *over*excitement. Their hummingbird energy can escalate into too high of a vibration, and they'll get excited to the point of emotional flare-ups, become hyperactive and highly anxious, or, at the extreme, even struggle with panic attacks.

Fire children's need to be liked can cause them to try too hard to please, or they may be devastated by someone rejecting them. As teens, they're more apt to throw themselves at any opportunity for love without stopping to think. But even at an early age, they may need guidance in how to choose healthy friendships. Betrayal is an issue that commonly shows up as a pattern of experience or perception in Fire people's lives, even for children, and can be the cause of great emotional distress.

Your little ones will also be so energetically open that they're highly empathic and able to pick up on what you're thinking with alarming talent. Because their spirit reaches out to others and lets them in so easily, they're sometimes too affected by the thoughts and feelings of others, which contributes to things like shyness, distractibility, and anxiety.

Fire Strength: Love and Insight

The part of the body associated with Fire is the heart, the seat of love that allows for the easy expression of affection. When these children become overexcited, your loving touch will calm them and bring the hummingbird to rest on a branch. Grounding them by being a relaxed presence and taking a thoughtful approach to problem solving can also help them shift their energy and learn to regulate their system and manage things better. Remember that yelling or harsh words are *very* damaging and can put out their flame at an early age.

Because these little ones will always crave close relationships, they'll need to develop two strengths: discernment and healthy boundaries. Instead of getting involved in something too soon, teach them how to discern which projects or activities are good choices and how to let friendships grow appropriately over time. You can even create exercises to practice judging what's beneficial and what's not by having them help you go through clutter and decide what to throw away or which of your e-mails can be deleted.

Help Fire children with the delicate balance between being energetically open and maintaining healthy limits. Because they've had permeable boundaries all their lives, they'll be used to letting everything in, but unaware of the effect this is having on them. Their empathic nature may even cause them to absorb the thoughts and feelings of other people that they'll think are their own. Realizing that not all the thoughts in their minds are theirs can be an incredibly eye-opening lesson. You can even turn this into a game; for instance, talking to them about what came into their heads when they were next to the woman on the elevator or what the dog is dreaming about can train them to recognize when this happens. Assist them in learning to manage their energetic boundaries, and you'll transform their sensitivities from a detriment to a skill.

◎ ◎ ◎

"To a true artist only that face is beautiful which, quite apart from its exterior, shines with the Truth within the soul."

— M. K. GANDHI

READING THE FIRE FEATURES

Chapter 10

Certain features on the face have to do with Fire, and the more prominent or noticeable they are, the more we possess this Element as a major part of our original nature.

However, it's important to keep in mind that we all have some Fire Element in our faces and personalities, just in differing amounts. The Fire characteristics can be examined to determine the unique ways in which they show up in your child's design, whether or not they're predominant.

Eyes

The eyes, in terms of vision, have to do with Wood Element, but their light is all about Fire. People with this nature will have a sparkle in their eyes, a radiance that shows their inner joy and exuberance. This light is called *shen* in Chinese medicine, and we all should have this luminous quality since it's a sign that our life force is healthy, our spirit is alive, and our heart is open. As I mentioned in the last chapter, the heart is considered to be the home of consciousness in the body and not, as Western tradition believes, in the brain. So if the eyes are bright, the consciousness is clear and the heart is available to give and receive love. It's a sad truth that as many people move through life, their hearts get hurt, their lights dim, and they close down. If someone's natural glow has been diminished, this can be seen in the eyes as a lack of light, or sometimes even a sense of deadness. How many of these faces do you see throughout the day? Far too many, I'm sure. Because shen is a part of all humans' inner nature, there should be light in everyone's eyes. But those who have Fire Element as their core nature will exude a special twinkle here.

Early in life, our shen is most likely still undimmed; therefore, *all* children's eyes should be bright. While this trait is a good indication of whether or not an adult is Fire, it isn't as meaningful of a place to start for kids. Instead, it's more effective to look for other prominent Fire features. However, if your little ones' eyes aren't bright, please give some thought to what might be extinguishing their spirits.

There are things you can observe about your youngster's eyes that give you information about some signs of Fire in her nature. For instance, her eyes reveal how she communicates—that is, how open she is to what others say and what's going on inside her. To find this out, notice how deep or shallow (more on the surface of the face) this feature is. There's an easy way to determine this: Simply lay your finger vertically over one eye, putting the tip of your finger on her eyebrow and the lower part against her cheekbone, as if you were making the "shhh" motion to silence someone. If you can feel her eyeball against your finger, she has shallow-set eyes. If you can't, she has deep-set eyes.

Fig. 46: Deep-set eyes reveal a private nature.

Children with deep-set eyes are more reserved in their communications. They'll tend to play their cards close to the vest in terms of what they're thinking, and they may have trouble expressing their more difficult feelings. This trait also shows a tendency to be skeptical and reluctant to accept what they're told without proof. As a result, these children are less gullible than other youngsters, though it may take them longer to really trust people. But once this confidence is earned, it's there for good.

Even if your children don't have deep-set eyes, narrowed ones (not open very wide) will have virtually the same significance: a private, withholding personality that doesn't openly share what's going on inside. If your little ones have either of these characteristics, you might need to give them extra time to communicate what's bothering them or to express their opinions. If you're carrying on with a long speech about your point of view, be aware that their silence may not he mean that they're in agreement. Instead, they could just be letting you chatter away while keeping their own thoughts to themselves. Suddenly, you realize that you've just delivered a lengthy monologue without much of a response from them! Try to create opportunities within a conversation for them to contribute their thoughts in a nonthreatening way. Part of the reason they're not open can be that they don't trust they're being listened to.

Fig. 47: Shallow-set eyes signify those who will openly communicate.

If your children have shallow-set eyes, or if they hold them in a wide-open fashion (the opposite of narrowed), they'll be more of an open book. These little ones will walk in the door gabbing, and you may have a hard time getting a word in edgewise. They tend to think out loud when trying to make decisions and often need to talk out their feelings instead of keeping them inside. These kids are natural communicators and have trouble understanding why others wouldn't want to share what's going on in their minds.

Communication is a two-way street, and if their eyes are held open quite widely, they're likely to welcome what others have to share. However, there's an alternative meaning for eyes like this: that they're too open to the energy of other people. This tendency to take in information from those around them is one sign of an empath's permeable boundaries, which can lead to being overwhelmed. Kids with such eyes may be so vulnerable to others' energies that they become quiet and shy. At the extreme, they can be too sensitive to influences or even manipulation, and helping them set healthy limits is extremely important.

Eye Shape

Eyes come in many different shapes, but three common ones you'll see are rounded, oval, and rectangular. Rounded eyes are more circular, while oval-shaped ones are almond shaped. Those that are rectangular are more stretched-out versions of the oval; they appear long and narrow.

Round eyes reveal the same approachable nature seen in children with shallow-set or wide-open eyes and show an additional supply of kindness. People with almond-shaped eyes still carry the tact inherent in those with round eyes; they're known for their diplomatic skills, but they're a little less open emotionally. Rectangular eyes convey a more logical nature, those who won't be emotionally reactive or vulnerable.

Lower Eyelids

The lower eyelids are actually governed by Wood Element, but they're included here because I'm discussing eyes in general. The shape of the lower eyelids will show you one aspect of how children deal with others. If they're rounded, this indicates that they genuinely care about others' experiences with them. They'll want to create a sense of win-win in any situation, and there's an extra emphasis on kindness in the way they interact with the world. If the lower lids are very rounded, however, they may not be concerned enough with their own needs.

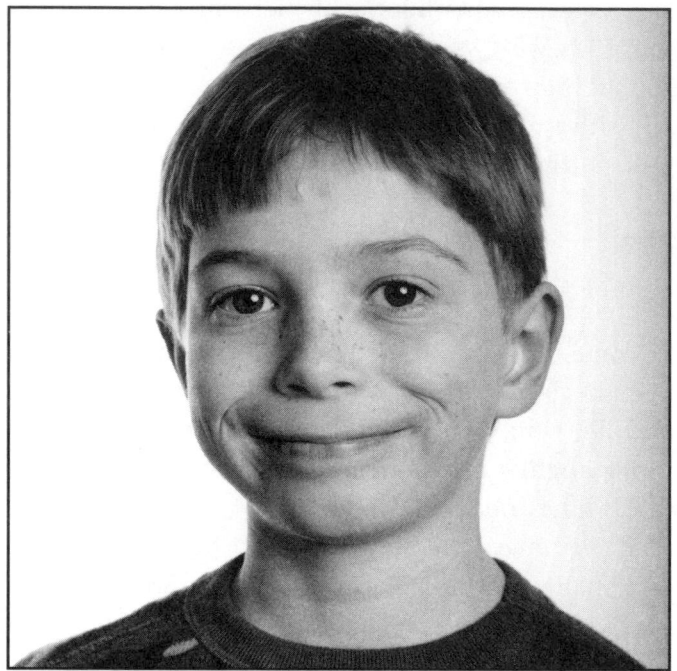

Fig. 48: Rounded lower eyelids reveal kindness in communications.

If children have lower eyelids that are more of a straight line, they'll place an emphasis on logic and have less concern for others' feelings. They may be the types who play to win or look for opportunities to get ahead. It's not that they're uncaring, but their own goals take priority, especially in negotiations. This could mean that they're less willing to compromise with their playmates about whose turn it is, or they'll be tough bargainers when it comes to how much allowance they want.

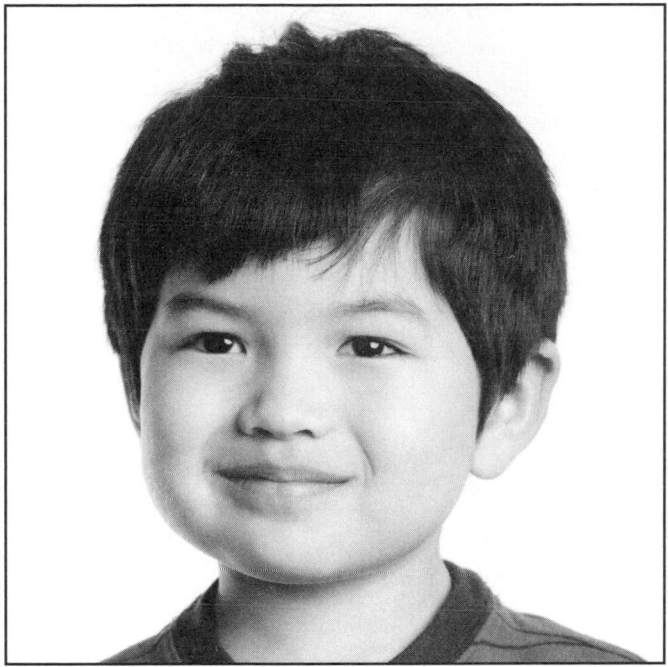

Fig. 49: Straight lower eyelids show a more logical approach to communications.

The lower eyelids tense up only when people begin to feel angry, so if you spot this in your child, be forewarned about what's arising in his system. For this reason, it's not a great idea for girls to use a lot of eyeliner on this specific part of the eye. Their desire to do so can be a clue that they're dealing with issues of frustration or anger. Know that amplifying this part of the face with makeup will actually stimulate more of these emotions in the system.

Eye Slant

Most people's eyes are set in a fairly horizontal line. However, occasionally you'll see eyes that appear to slant up or down; in other words, if you drew a line from the inner corner of the eye to the outer one, you'd get a slight diagonal rather than a straight line. Eyes that are angled upward reveal a more positive, optimistic nature—children who are always looking on the bright side of things. These are kids who may be opportunistic and ambitious, as their clever minds will see all kinds of possibilities in any situation.

Fig. 50: Eyes that slant up indicate an optimistic, ambitious outlook.

Eyes that appear to slant downward show a more kindhearted, tolerant nature. These kids' first thoughts in any circumstance are definitely *not* how they can take advantage; they're caring, but maybe a bit too passive. They'll tend toward a more pessimistic mind-set and may even give up too easily, assuming the worst or feeling that they don't have the power to change things for the better.

Fig. 51: Eyes that slant down reveal tolerance and kindness, but with some pessimistic tendencies.

White-Sided Eyes

When you look at most people's eyes, it's normal to see the whites on either side of their irises. Occasionally, you'll be able to spot the white in the lower eye (under the iris) or in the upper eye (above the iris). This isn't a sign of Fire, but rather of an imbalance that's usually the result of an overstimulated nervous system. Stress such as exhaustion, illness, or extreme emotional upset can cause what's called "three white-sided eyes," meaning that the lower or upper whites are visible in addition to the whites on both sides of the iris.

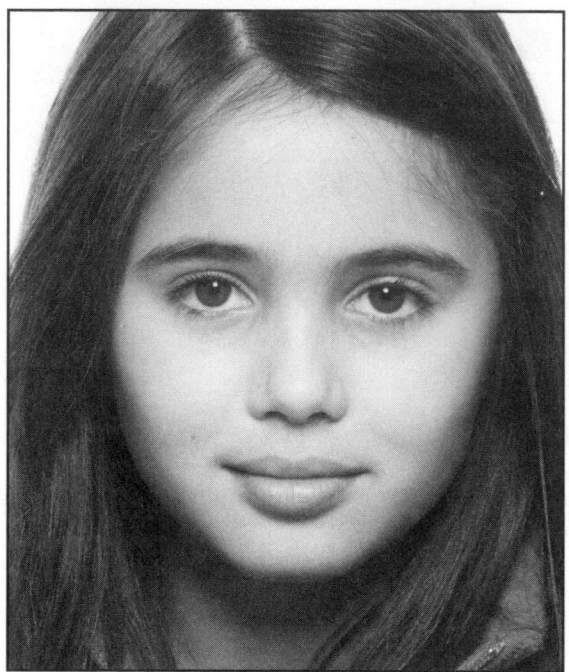

Fig. 52: Visible lower whites are a sign of temporary stress.

In order to accurately discern whether your children have white-sided eyes, be sure you're examining them straight on at eye level. (If they're looking up or down at you, of course the whites are likely to be visible.) If you can see the whites at the bottom of your children's eyes, this is a sign of short-term stress. Maybe they had three slumber parties in a row and are now very sleep deprived. They could also be coming down with the flu; be feeling devastated after breaking up with their first love; or be experiencing the impact of an overactive nervous system, which is a Fire trait that can cause high anxiety and even lead to panic attacks.

This type of eye is also called "danger from without" in Chinese face reading, which means that the danger comes from the outside world. For instance, kids may be so out of balance physically or emotionally that they become careless and, thus, accident-prone.

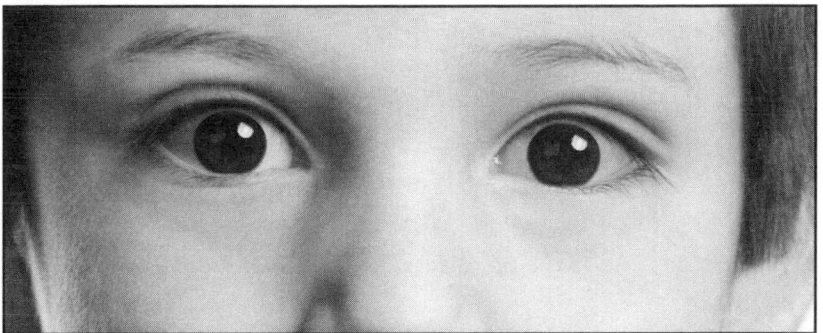

Fig. 53: Visible upper whites reflect more chronic stress in an individual.

Visible whites above a child's irises are called "danger from within." This reveals more chronic, long-term stress and is usually due to an emotional imbalance. One explanation is that the nervous system has been overextended for so long that it's now an ongoing disturbance preventing the person from living an emotionally healthy life. If allowed to continue, this can evolve into a more serious disorder.

Please note that some children will get extremely excited when they're talking and open their eyes very wide, which causes the upper whites to be visible. This just means that they're excited and want you to be, too; but it doesn't have the same significance as when you can *always* see the whites above their eyes.

There's also a feature called "four white-sided eyes," and this is when white completely encircles the eyes. If your child's emotions are out of control, you'll notice this as he speaks. This trait demonstrates extreme excitement on a temporary basis, and would only be a cause for concern if it remained even when the behavior subsided. I've never seen this in a child, and it's said to be an indication of a madman or a genius.

Red or Curly Hair

The color associated with Fire is red. So if your children's hair is this shade, or even brown with warm highlights, it means that they have some of this Element in their personalities. If it's dyed red, this has the same effect and adds more Fire to their nature. Hair that's very curly (not just wavy) is also indicative of this excitable nature. And yes, if your child curls her hair, this adds Fire as well! Additionally, any spiky or extreme haircuts add aspects of this Element, and these are often the kinds of styles these youngsters go for.

Tips of Features

Flames sear the tips of things as they move, so on the face, the tips of features reveal signs of the Fire nature. If any of these are pointed or cleft (an indentation through the center), this means your children have this Element in their personalities.

The most common is a cleft chin, which is called the "mark of a performer" in Chinese face reading and shows the classic Fire need to be noticed and appreciated. Your child may want to be the center of attention all the time as the extroverted class clown at school or a little performer at home who will put on a show at a moment's notice. These kids can also have the tendency to be pleasers, always trying to do things to make people like them. On a more subtle level, this trait can manifest as an underlying need to feel special.

It's remarkable how many actors, politicians, and people in the public eye have cleft chins. Since Fire is about naturally ending up in the spotlight, this makes sense. When my son was small, we used to play a game while watching TV where we'd try to spot

Fig. 54: A cleft chin is called the "mark of a performer."

everyone who had this feature . . . but sometimes we couldn't count fast enough to catch them all! Even when "the man on the street" is interviewed about the tornado that just blew through town, he's often a guy with a cleft chin!

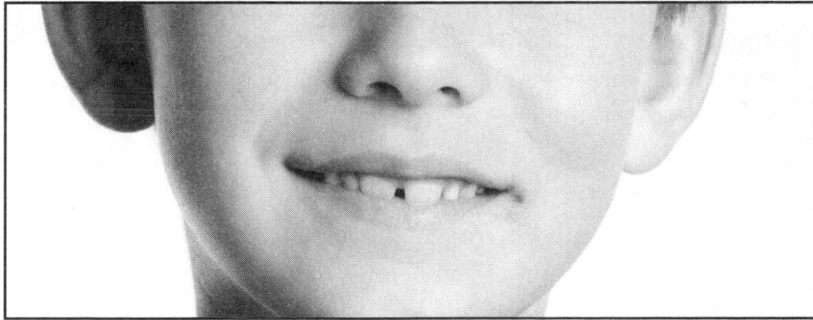

Fig. 55: A mouth with pointed corners is a sign of Fire.

Another common mark of this Element is seen in the tips of the mouth and lips. For instance, if the corners of your children's mouths come to a point, this indicates some extra Fire in their dispositions that's usually apparent in their naturally positive outlook. A highly defined and pointed upper lip is another place that reveals Fire. In this case, it's more an indication of a reactive personality. This little one's emotions will spike much more easily than other kids, sort of like an itchy emotional trigger finger. One last minor characteristic of this Element in the mouth is a cleft lower lip, which is the most obvious clue of a great sense of humor.

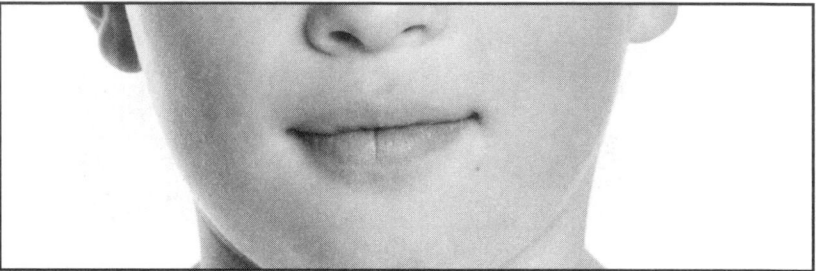

Fig. 56: A vertical line through the lower lip is a sign of a good sense of humor.

The inner canthus (corner) of the eye relates to Fire as well. The eyes directly correlate to communication style, and these inner tips reveal how people speak to others. Pointed inner corners here indicate that your child can be very precise when imparting information, whether it's spoken or written. But when she's upset, she might get so excited that she'll say hurtful things or be unable to censor her words. A rounded inner canthus is a sign that she'll be more tactful in how she expresses herself.

If the inner canthus of the eye is pointed and hooks down like a bird's claw, the tendency toward sharp words is more common. If youngsters with this trait are terribly upset, they have the potential to lash out to intentionally hurt others. Fights with friends or siblings, therefore, can be quite a show. They may

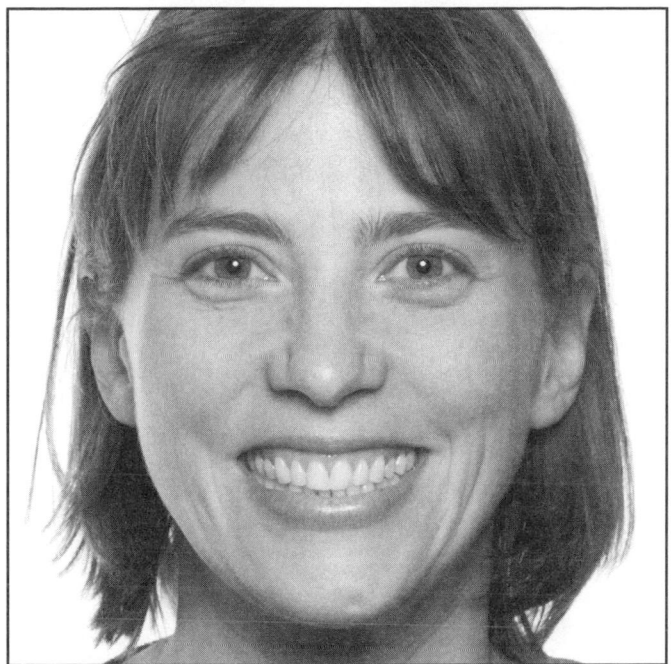

Fig. 57: If the inner canthus of the eye is pointed, communications are precise but can be sharp.

Fig. 58: A rounded inner canthus signifies tact in communications.

need to develop mindfulness about the impact of their words when they're emotional.

Fig. 59: A hooked inner canthus shows the potential for using hurtful words when upset.

Examining the tip of the nose is another way to detect Fire. If it's pointed, this is the sign of a curious nature and the need to find out how things work or all the latest news—it's no wonder these kids are sometimes described as nosey! But the tip of the nose is also where you observe the vulnerability of your child's emotional heart. In Chinese medicine, there is an organ called the "heart protector," which is associated with the pericardium (the membrane that surrounds the heart). The heart protector's job is to guard the "gate of intimacy" (the emotionally open heart) and act like a discerning energy field around it that screens harmful experiences and allows in beneficial ones.

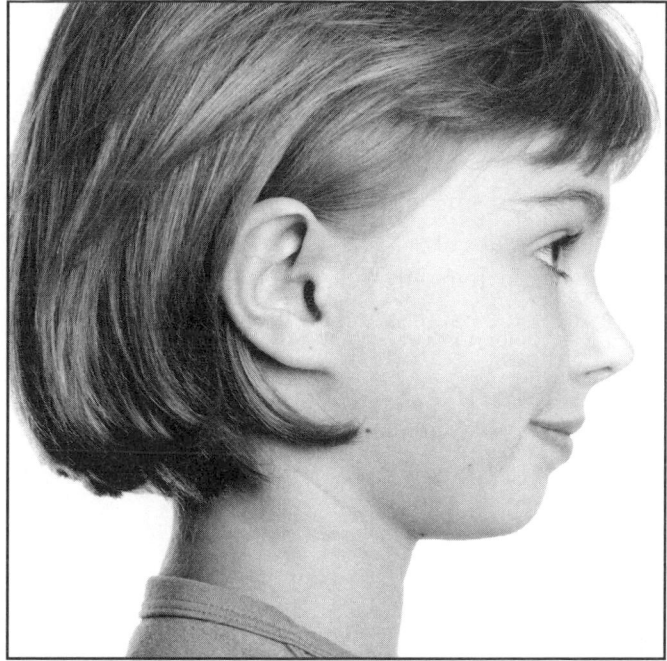

Fig. 60: A pointed nose reveals a curious nature.

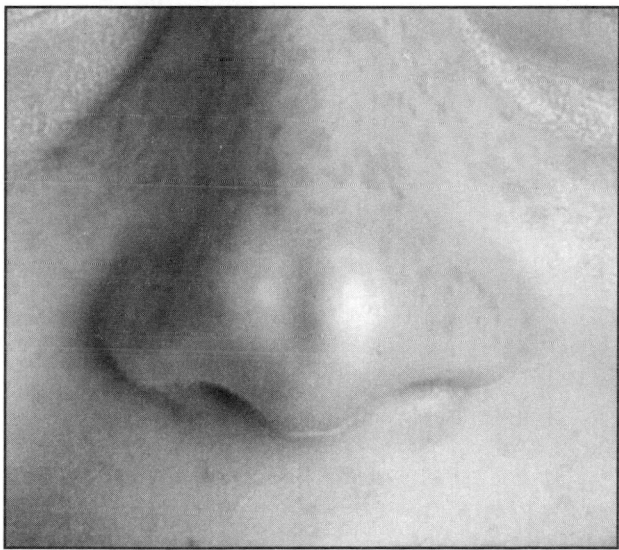

Fig. 61: A line through the tip of the nose shows a vulnerable heart.

If there's a cleft on the very tip of your little one's nose, this indicates that his heart protector may be leaving him too open emotionally with the potential of being hurt as a result.

This can also be another reflection of his highly empathic nature, letting other people's energy in without the ability to block what stresses his system. Seeing this on your child's face isn't cause for alarm, but it can help you understand the importance of teaching him how to create healthy boundaries.

The tips of the ears are the last major area that indicate Fire's influence. Points at the tops aren't seen very often, but if your children do have these ears, it's a sign of Fire excitability acting on Water emotions. The result of this characteristic is a more volatile nature and will likely show up when kids are very stressed.

Dimples

Dimples in your youngsters' cheeks mean they have adorable, "Fire-y" charm and may be able to wrap you around their little fingers . . . but you probably already knew that!

Freckles

A face full of freckles, a feature that's very common on red-haired children, is indicative of an overall Fire nature. Just a few freckles, however, will not convey the same meaning as many. Freckles develop after exposure to the sun, so they're never seen on newborns' faces. As time passes, you'll see just how freckly of a child you've brought into the world. (Markings on the face will be covered in Chapter 16.)

Fig. 62: Dimples are a sign of natural charm.

The Best Environments for the Fire Nature

You might think that you should give these children calm bedrooms to counteract their excitable nature, but this is a case of fighting fire with fire! Providing a stimulating decor will actually help them relax (as much as they ever can). Bright, warm colors are good; and so are lots of eclectic decorations, art on the walls, or anything eccentric and fun. One Fire child I met had a cuckoo clock wrapped in feather boas! These kids love change and variety, so you might put their furniture on wheels so it can moved. Expect the walls of their personal space to be an ever-evolving art exhibit, as the same things won't stay up for very long.

These children will probably want electronics in their room—and this is usually unavoidable these days—but even for the Fire personality, it's best to refrain from having too many things that plug in. Bedrooms are meant to be sanctuaries for true relaxation and rejuvenation, and large electronic devices will keep even these fiery systems too jazzed. It's also extremely important that they don't leave the TV on as they go to sleep. The Chinese say that the heart goes out into the world by day but it must return to settle back into the body at night. The flickering and noise of the TV will prevent your children from finding that necessary calm; even if they can drift off, their sleep will be disturbed and unrefreshing.

Thoughts for Teachers

Fire kids are often a delight—fun, cheerful, and eager to please—but they have the potential to be little manipulators who may use charm to get their way. And even though you know it's happening, you still can't help but go along with it! Occasionally, they can be disruptive in class, making jokes or clowning around, but their motivation is not to interfere. Focusing for long periods isn't their forte, and the completion of tasks is a major issue for them. Therefore, if you can find ways to let them shift between projects frequently, they'll actually be more likely to finish. A short spurt at one work space and then on to something different suits their energy very well.

Some Fire children are quite shy and will need your urging to participate in class. Remember that their timidity may actually be a result of their sensitive and empathic nature or a need for others to like them. These kids can get terribly upset if they're rejected or laughed at. If you have delicate Fire children, pushing them to stand up in front of the class without giving extra support might not be a good idea. Compliment these little ones when others are around, because they love to feel special. If they get too exuberant and loud, don't forget the vulnerability of their hearts. Use gentle guidance to ground them rather than stern discipline. If there are no school restrictions on touching students, a calm hand on the shoulder or an affectionate hug will do wonders.

Helping the Fire Nature Flourish

These children are bundles of joy because they're so naturally exuberant, always looking for ways to please you because the thrill of exchanging love is their reason for living. Give them opportunities to shine, heap affection upon them, show them they're special, and give them compliments; praise won't make them vain or egotistical. Teach them how to share the spotlight with others, however, and make them aware when they're talking too much. Physical closeness is important to them as well, so take advantage of every chance to cuddle.

Don't judge their mile-a-minute style as wrong, and don't rain on their parade by forcing them to focus on one thing for a long period of time. These children thrive by keeping a number of balls in the air with lots of change and variety. Your job is to allow them to multitask, but at the same time show them how to fully complete something. They may do well if they can develop their ideas and reach conclusions by thinking out loud, so be a good sounding board in that way. Guide them in creating an organized plan for any project and then meeting a firm deadline.

It's so important to not react negatively to their exuberance, and this will sometimes be a challenge, as Fire kids can get loud and shrill. Remember the vulnerability of their open hearts, and be gentle if you need to calm them down. Don't yell or criticize your children for this natural tendency; if you can respond to their flare-ups with warm and quiet words, they may be able to naturally ground themselves.

Little ones of this Element can struggle with anxiety due to their high-speed systems, so simple calming techniques—such as taking full, deep breaths down into their bellies—are good for them to learn. But also teach them ways to let the tension out. Literally jumping up and down to release their excitement can be beneficial in this regard, so encourage them to give that a try. Or let them use their flare for the dramatic to act out what they're feeling by creating a show or using puppets, for example. They might even be able to come up with their own solutions.

These are passionate children who move through the world seeking ways to touch hearts with others. Your job is to keep them lit up about life but teach them to develop healthy boundaries. Give these Fire personalities a container for their flames by helping them discern which friends they should be spending time with and which activities they should be focusing on. Practice ways to calm their nerves, allow them to exuberantly express their joy, and, most of all, keep your heart wide open to theirs.

◉ ◉ ◉

*"There are only two lasting bequests
we can hope to give our children. One
of these is roots; the other, wings."*

— HODDING CARTER

Chapter
11

THE EARTH
CHILD:
DIPLOMAT,
MOTHER,
GATHERER

Conor

Conor is a stocky 17-year-old with a beautiful full mouth, a wide bridge to his nose, plump cheeks, and a peaches-and-cream complexion. Dressed in an old T-shirt and sweatpants, he's trying to overcome his self-consciousness because he genuinely wants to assist me with my research. He and his mother bring in iced tea and cookies, and when I see him squirm uncomfortably on the dining-room chair, I know he'd be much more at home on the big leather couch I spotted in the family room!

Conor has an iPhone filled with photos of all his friends, and he also shows me a big box full of pictures from family vacations and parties. He tells me he's the photographer for the school newspaper, along with being involved with student government and the yearbook.

"I just want to help," he explains, worried I'll think he's sounding self-important. *That* would almost be impossible! This is a kid who exudes kindness, and as we're talking, I notice him trying to decide if he should move the cookie plate closer to me now or wait until I've actually eaten what I already have. At school, teachers have tended to seat him next to any challenged children in the class because they know he'll help, and not tease, them.

When I ask him how he'd describe himself, he replies, "Well, my mother would tell you I don't keep my room clean, my father would say I'm too much of a pushover, and my sister calls me a slug who never gets off the couch." This is a typical Earth response—seeing himself through the eyes of others!

His mother adds: "Conor is the most giving person you'll ever hope to meet. He'll be anyone's friend, and he really cares about others. What he didn't tell you is that he volunteers to serve food at the homeless shelter. When he was little, it was his idea to make cookies and hand them out to poor people on the street at Christmas. Just before you came, he was next door helping the neighbors load their moving truck. He's just a good kid."

Conor blushes and says, "My dad tells me I should stop giving away my time so much and start charging people for helping them." But it's obvious that's a bit of a foreign concept to this boy's mind. Naturally other-directed, his first thought is to find out what someone else might need and how he can make that happen, without any regard for what's in it for him. He admits that he has a hard time saying no, and the last time he had to turn someone down, he confesses, "My stomach just churned."

He also worries about disappointing his father and tries to make him proud by getting good grades. Dad says he just wishes his son would be more assertive. "I don't know how he's going to get anywhere in this world if he doesn't set better boundaries and stand up for what he wants. A leader needs to lead," he explains.

But the Earth personality is often more of a follower and supporter than a leader whose main focus is the harmony of the group—if it has to be defined in such black-and-white terms.

With big decisions, Conor will always consider the needs of the people in his life first and how they'll be affected before he can move forward. This is already being demonstrated in his process of determining where to go to college. He's been accepted at a school a thousand miles away from home and one in a city just an hour away. He's leaning toward the one nearby and living with his folks, as it's difficult for him to imagine moving so far from family and friends. What would happen if he fell out of touch with what's going on with everyone, and what if his family needed him in some way? Change isn't attractive for Earth people, and their first impulse is to maintain the status quo.

Grace

The playroom at Grace's house has a full toy kitchen, washer and dryer, and a miniature ironing board. There's a little white table with tea service all set up, and in the corner of the room is her old crib filled with baby dolls. For her birthday, she wants a dollhouse, too. "It's pretty embarrassing," her mother says with a laugh. "From the beginning, I gave her blocks and toy trucks to play with and tried to screen out gender-biased toys as much as possible." But as she grew, Grace gravitated to only the most traditionally feminine things. "At friends' houses, she'd run for the girly stuff like she was finding water in the desert!" her mother recalls.

At five, Grace is already feeling the full force of this Element's Mother archetype coming through her little spirit. Although this can manifest differently in people's lives, it's not uncommon for Earthy little girls to start assuming that role at an early age. Grace loves to play house, and her kindergarten teacher calls her "my assistant" because she's such a good helper at school. A cuddly little girl, Grace has a large mouth framed by chubby lower cheeks and big round eyes. Most children have extra plumpness in their cheeks early on, but this feature will stay as Grace matures.

Even at such a young age, this girl knows how to contain herself. She can be content playing with her dolls for long periods, although she's even happier if someone will play *with* her. She already loves books and often climbs into their big easy chair and pretends to read. She sits calmly at the dinner table, doesn't fidget in the car seat, and is a cooperative little girl in general. "When Grace was a baby, I finally had to face her out in the baby carrier because she was so quiet I worried she wasn't getting enough stimulation," her mother says. "But that just seems to be her temperament."

In new situations, she does hang back, staying by her mother's side until she feels comfortable enough to join the group and make new friends. When it's time to go home, there are no tantrums; she obediently rejoins her mother. However, she follows Mom around the house, even waiting for her outside the bathroom door, and still struggles with separation anxiety whenever she's left with a babysitter.

Grace notices when other kids are distressed and always tries to comfort them. She'll call the teacher over, hug them, or give them the toy she's been playing with. At her recent birthday party, her favorite part of the day was stuffing the goody bags she handed to her friends as they arrived, and she insisted that each girl immediately empty her bag to see all the candy and little trinkets inside. When her mother had a migraine last week, Grace brought her candy as medicine to try to make her feel better. Care and thoughtfulness run through the veins of Earth personalities.

Her bed is hard to find under all of the stuffed animals and pillows piled on top. Although she usually doesn't sleep there— much preferring the family bed with her parents—each cushy animal has a name and gets daily attention, as she doesn't want any of them to be left out. Grace's favorite place in the room is actually her window seat, also full of pillows. There she has a cozy, enclosed space where she surrounds herself with all this padding and watches the neighbor kids play with their dog. Lately, she's been begging her parents for a pet of her own to take care of.

An easy way to keep Grace amused is to have her help create decorations for an upcoming holiday. She loves the idea of decorating the house, and until her mother came up with this idea, Grace kept hauling out the Christmas ornaments to play with. Now they always have some craft project going, making some doodads to hang around the house for St. Patrick's Day, Arbor Day, or whatever obscure holiday they can find! Grace also enjoys the concept of family traditions that are repeated each year, and it's even more exciting if they involve everyone gathering for meals, such as Thanksgiving or Passover.

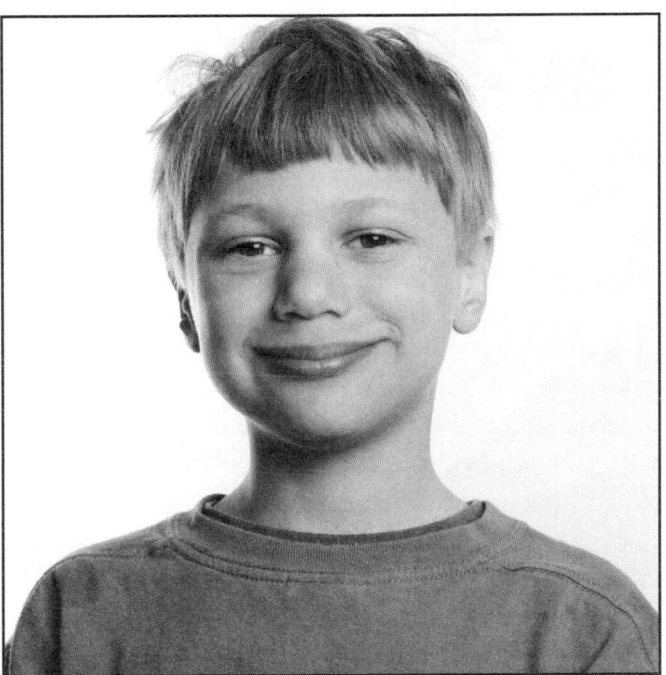

Fig. 63: This boy's large mouth and full lips are classic features of the Earth Element.

Fig. 64: This girl has the full mouth, fleshy nose, and plump lower cheeks of the Earth Element.

The Earth Child's Nature

In this chapter, you'll learn about the inner nature and outer appearance of Earth children, and the next chapter will detail more information about each feature associated with this Element. To begin with, the following list shows what to look for. Please note that your child doesn't have to have *all* of these characteristics for Earth to play a strong role; seeing any of them means it's a factor in his or her personality. The more aspects you notice, the more Earth there is in your child's nature! Look for:

- A large mouth and/or full lips
- A wide bridge of the nose
- Plump lower cheeks

- A fleshy nose
- A round shape to the face
- Puffy upper eyelids
- A peaches-and-cream complexion or one with yellow undertones
- A round stomach or stocky body
- Thick calves

Well-known adults with many of these features include Renée Zellweger, John Krasinski, Sonia Sotomayor, Rachael Ray, Oprah Winfrey, Tim Russert, Rosie O'Donnell, and Al Roker.

As Your Child Grows

It's important to note that in infancy, most children have a lot of Earthy aspects to their faces. Babies naturally have a thick layer of fat under the skin and, therefore, tend to have very round faces with chubby cheeks. An infant's mouth can be quite small early on, and the nose, and its bridge, doesn't begin to take its mature shape until later in childhood. As your child grows and these changes begin to occur, use this book to read the emerging aspects of his or her personality.

Qualities of Earth Element

- *Facial features:* Mouth, bridge of nose, upper eyelids, lower cheeks near the mouth, area above the upper lip

- *Other parts of the body associated with Earth:* stomach, spleen, pancreas, muscles, flesh

- *Strengths:* intellect, devotion, compassion

- *Challenging emotion:* worry

- *Archetype:* diplomat, mother, gatherer

- *What Earth feels like:* afternoon, early fall, middle age, moving downward, settling

Harvesttime brings feasts and family gatherings. The crops are coming in, the fruit is hanging ripe on the trees, and everyone is well nourished and satisfied by the results of their hard work. This energy is similar to how you feel in the afternoon as you sit at your desk: a bit heavy from lunch, with your mind and body more relaxed than when you first arrived in the morning. Earth is also associated with middle age, when you've had some accomplishments in your life and don't feel so driven; you can now take it a little easier and enjoy the success your labors have brought you. This period is about that pause in the seasons, the day, or life to absorb and digest the benefits of your previous activities.

This Element is the archetype of the Mother: the nurturer and the one who provides a "home" for us all. She gives us the lap to crawl into and the comforting arms that are always there to embrace us and make things better—that safe place we can count on. Earth people truly care about others, and their first thought is: *How can I help?*

Every quality of this Element can be seen in those who carry it, although it can manifest in many different ways. To best understand its true spirit, and thus your little one, learn its essence. What follows are the basic aspects and a few examples of how Earth can reveal itself in your child's behaviors, emotions, needs, and perceptions.

The Spirit of Earth

This is our planet, our home in the universe, and it's filled with wonderful pleasures to enjoy. Great food, loving families and friends, beautiful surroundings . . . who could ask for anything else? The Earth person, more than any other, likes being here. Some kids of other Elements can feel as if this is a foreign world, but not these children. They're comfortable on this planet and their energy is in sync with it. They savor their food, enjoy being at home, and revel in spending time with their loved ones. And like the actual ground beneath their feet, they'll be solid—sometimes in both personality and physicality. These children aren't high-strung, but instead are steady and easygoing; and their body types tend to be rounder or thicker than others. Boys may grow stocky, muscular bodies or develop bellies as adults, while girls can also be plumper around the middle and sometimes also heavyset in their upper bodies, with large breasts at maturity. Not all Earth kids look like this, but if you do see this body type, it's a definite tip-off that this Element is part of their nature.

But the most important thing to understand about these children is that they carry the archetypal nature of the Mother. The more you learn about this inherent energy, the deeper you'll comprehend how it defines them. Mother is the nurturer, and she truly wants to be of service to her family. Your little ones will be natural helpers—for you, their teachers, their friends, and everyone in their lives. Earth children might share their allowance with kids who don't have as much or try to take all their friends along with them to the theme park. Such sweetness brings them much appreciation and love, but it also opens up opportunities to be taken advantage of.

And like the caregivers watching out for their family's welfare, these youngsters will tend to feel overly responsible for others. If Earth children see someone in distress, their first impulse will be to assist, even if it's not a problem they should be taking on. They're other-directed and can have trouble maintaining good boundaries in that regard. Just as Mother spends her day thinking about her family's best interests, and often has trouble saying no, your little ones are predisposed to feel obligated to others, devoted to making sure everyone's needs are fulfilled.

The typical maternal image isn't of the dominating parent; instead, it's the modest and kind figure who doesn't take all the credit. This can translate into children who lack self-confidence or give away their power too easily. They may be overly dependent on others, insecure, or uncomfortable with their own decisions. These kids can seem to be needy and clingy, or the type of people who don't want to bother others with their problems and feel guilty about sharing what's troubling them.

However, there's another kind of Mother archetype: the one who does so much for her family and carries such a huge load that she feels underappreciated or taken advantage of. The result can be a victim attitude, and resentfulness can grow from this. It's as if she's done so much and gone so far out of her way for everyone, yet she has never received a thank-you or gets to do what *she* wants. Instead, the demands keep piling on; and that perception causes her to become negative, bitter, and even angry.

This can show up in children's personalities as being too easily stuck in their own opinions or approaching every chore with hostility. They may even refuse to do what you ask if they feel they've done too much already. Youngsters with this attitude may choose to ignore your rules out of anger or spite and because they think, on some level, that they know better than you do! In their hearts, these children still want to be a loving part of the family, and one way to bring them back into balance is to heap hugs and appreciation on them for all they do to help out.

In general, all Earth kids are friendly, thoughtful people for whom friends and community will be very important. They love family gatherings and doing things in groups much more than working on their own. They'll enjoy taking care of pets and giving little gifts to people, and will always be looking for opportunities to make others feel nurtured.

Afternoon

At this time of day, most people just want to sit. They've just had lunch, and after working hard all morning, the last thing they want to do is exert themselves. You'll notice that your Earth child's favorite position in life is sitting—sometimes for hours—as if he's been glued to the couch or easy chair! Once he gets into a relaxed position, it can be really hard to get him up and going again . . . it's just so comfortable there!

Exercise isn't an Earth priority, so if you want to encourage these children to stay in shape, give them opportunities to exercise with other people. Since the energy of this Element is all about gathering, any activity done in isolation feels unnatural to them. If they can take walks with the family or participate in a group fitness session, this will suit their needs. And if they think they're helping someone else by going, they'll definitely be motivated!

Autumn

Early fall is a harmonious time, almost like a pause *between* the seasons rather than an actual season. People are a bit worn out from all the frenzied fun of summer, and it's not quite time to prepare for the scarcity of winter. This is a period of relaxation with loved ones and to just take it easy for a while. There's a calm, grounded energy to this season, and this extends to your child's temperament. These kids will be the patient diplomats who don't like to ruffle feathers, but they *will* be more easily upset by conflicts or arguments. In some situations, this can mean that they have the potential to become the family peacemakers, feeling responsible for preventing any discord in the home. This is a heavy weight for kids to carry, and it isn't appropriate for their position in the family. Parents going through stressful times may need to be careful not to share too much about their personal problems with their Earth children or allow them to take on a parental role.

This phase of the year, when the crops are piled high, is also connected to issues of clutter. The Earth energy of gathering often shows up as a predisposition for your children to love their stuff. They may be collectors and have everything on display in their rooms, keeping each gift everyone has ever given them—as well as mementos from family outings and all the photos, too. This is the sentimental nature of this Element's personality. The idea of giving—or *throwing*—away anything someone else has given them is a painful one, since they feel pleasure at the sight of their wonderful belongings around them. These aren't kids who enjoy living in a minimalist environment! They'll need to be allowed to have more around them than most because it's a form of nourishment. Forcing them to get rid of too many of their possessions would be no small task. You may have to monitor the situation, teach them that there has to be space between things, and probably provide a lot of storage for all their beloved treasures.

Middle Age

Most people have had some accomplishments in their lives by this age—a job, a house, and a family—and they aren't as driven to achieve as when they were younger. Their energy is starting to settle at this point, and they to want to rest on their laurels and look with satisfaction at what life has brought them. (Or they're distinctly *dissatisfied* with how few hopes and expectations have come to fruition.) The theme of this stage is the desire for satisfaction. You may notice this in your children by how important eating is to them. In the body, this Element relates to the stomach and digestion, so food may be a bit of a hobby for these kids! Cooking, gardening, sharing meals with friends, and, most of all, feeling full are vital for Earth youngsters, and this can result in their being a bit plumper than other children.

Not *all* Earth children have a rounder body type, but it's important for you to understand this information so that you don't criticize your little one for something that's a part of his or her nature. I'd ask any parent to remember how limited this culture's current parameters for beauty are. Unless your family is eating an unhealthy diet, or your son or daughter has an emotional problem that is contributing to overeating and a true weight problem,

I hope you'll enjoy your child's strong appetite and reinforce the idea that his or her body is absolutely beautiful.

Middle age is also a time when we've matured, learned from our experiences, and developed thoughtfulness and integrity that are in line with our years. Earth kids make excellent tutors, as they can effortlessly put themselves in someone else's shoes and understand how to be of assistance. They can be so trustworthy and protective of others that they might even want to start babysitting at an early age. Like adults who have years of life lessons under their belts, these children are diplomatic, have patience, and can easily cooperate in nearly any situation.

Finally, because this era is when people focus on ease and contentment, comfort is an important issue to Earth children—and this includes what they like to wear. Of course, most kids aren't fashion plates and, until a certain age, they'll want clothes that they can easily play in. But Earth youngsters will thrive in sweats and T-shirts or prefer to lounge in their pajamas all day . . . and regardless of the situation, they'll choose furniture where they can sink in and relax! This can also help you understand why they tend to take their time and don't rush to do anything: comfort is requirement number one.

Earth Challenge: Worry

Every Element has one emotion that consistently arises under stress and can send the system spiraling out of balance. This challenging emotion for Earth is *worry,* and it can manifest in numerous ways in your child's life. This goes back to the archetype of Mother, who is the Olympic champion of worrying. Imagine the typical mother crawling into bed at midnight, having just finished three loads of laundry, a couple of hours of paperwork, cooking dinner and washing the dishes, moving the kids through their usual bedtime rituals, and making the family's lunches for the next day. But now she's wondering whether her daughter really finished her homework, trying to remember if she gave everyone their vitamins, and contemplating getting up to put a note on the mirror to remind herself of the parent-teacher conference tomorrow afternoon!

The concept of digestion actually applies here, too. Just as this Element relates to the stomach and food, it also involves the process of thinking: Earth people don't always digest their thoughts well. As if they're chewing the same bite for too long, thoughts can go around and around, cluttering their brains and making it nearly impossible for them to think clearly. Because of this constant worrying, their minds can become cloudy, and they can have difficulty with indecisiveness or confusion. Just as poor digestion creates stagnation in the body, overworrying slows the brain and drains energy from the system, causing lethargy or someone who's too set in her ways and resistant to change.

In children, this can show up as difficulty getting to sleep at night due to all of the worries going through their heads. If there's a major life change, such as moving to a new city, they'll struggle with it more than kids of the other Elements. Or they can show a tendency to stew about what might be going wrong on a daily basis, making you wonder why they have such a pessimistic attitude. Keep in mind that it's not negativity; it's just that they can't stop thinking.

Earth Strength: Intellect, Compassion, and Devotion

The salvation for these children is to bring in the *strength* of this Element. Like the Mother, they have such a beautiful devotion to others and are so good at being compassionate, while rarely expecting it for themselves. To ease Earth children's minds, show your own caring devotion by frequently giving them a sympathetic ear and taking the time to listen to their worries while cuddling together. Talking things out with you can lead them to create a strategy to ease their fretting. A thoughtful touch, like a loving note tucked into a lunch box or preparing a favorite treat after school, will reassure these little ones that they're well taken care of and have no reason to worry.

The word *intellect* is associated with this Element but has nothing to do with intelligence—rather, it refers to the process of thinking. This is one of Earth's strengths—the ability to sit and reason out all of the details in order to bring something to fruition. However, imbalance occurs when they overthink. You can be your child's guide in learning how to keep the thoughts moving and not getting stuck.

Since the proverbial Mother gives so much to others but never gets a thank-you, she can begin to feel starved for appreciation. Noticing and acknowledging the things your Earth child does, such as helping around the house or performing well in school, will ground him and make him feel more empowered in his world. Also, providing Earthy children with opportunities to nurture by giving them a pet can do wonders.

When they're upset in the moment, they'll feel so much better if you wrap your arms around them or give them a pillow or their favorite stuffed animal to hug, even if they're past the age that you'd expect this to help.

⊙ ⊙ ⊙

"If a child is to keep alive his inborn sense of wonder . . . he needs the companionship of at least one adult who can share it, rediscovering with him the joy, excitement and mystery of the world we live in."

— RACHEL CARSON

READING THE EARTH FEATURES

Certain features on the face have to do with Earth, and the more prominent or noticeable they are, the more we possess Earth as a major part of our original nature.

However, it's important to keep in mind that we all have aspects of all the Elements in our faces and personalities, just in differing amounts. The Earth features can be examined to determine the unique ways this Element shows up in your child's design, whether or not it's predominant.

Mouth

The mouth is the most significant part of the face when it comes to understanding how much Earth there is in your child's makeup. Of course, infants' mouths don't look as they will at maturity, but you can monitor how this feature develops as they grow, which will give you valuable information about all the aspects of this Element in their lives. To determine the size, compare it to the other features. A small mouth on one person might look quite generous on another, so you'll want to know the status of the mouth on this particular face. One way to check is to draw an imaginary line down your child's face from the centers of the irises in his eyes. If these lines intersect with the corners of his mouth, it's an average size. If it extends past the lines, it's a large one; and if it doesn't touch them at all, it's a small mouth.

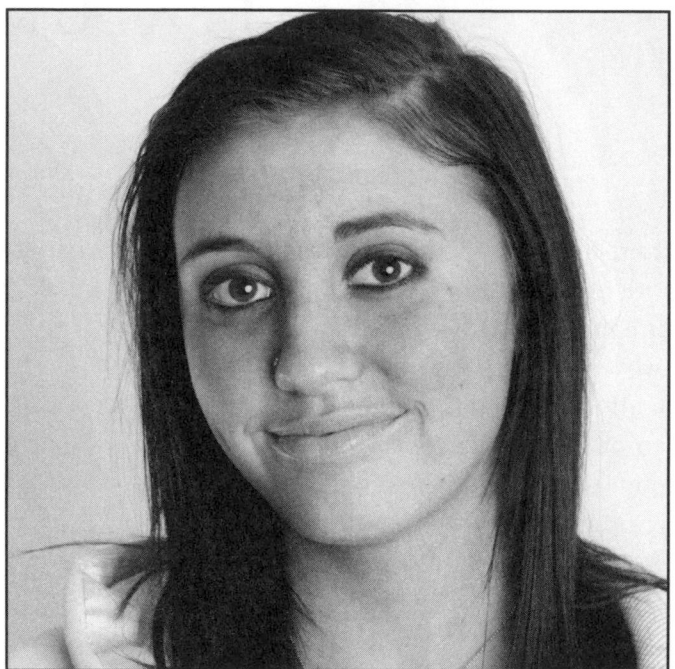

Fig. 65: A sense of connection is important to someone with a large mouth.

Children with large mouths have Earth as a major part of their inherent nature. Relationships and community will be exceptionally important to them, and they have the capacity to work well with others because they place such an emphasis on a cooperative attitude. This kind of mouth denotes a giving nature and an emotionally expressive personality who makes a great friend. Kids with this trait feel best if they can talk out a problem or collaborate on a school project rather than work alone. Their idea of a good time is being with other people, *not* being by themselves. Earth is a gathering-together energy, and these children feel best if they're surrounded by loved ones.

In addition, the fuller your little ones' lips are, the more Earth qualities they possess. This feature enhances the generosity that's always a big part of this Element, as well as the need for close

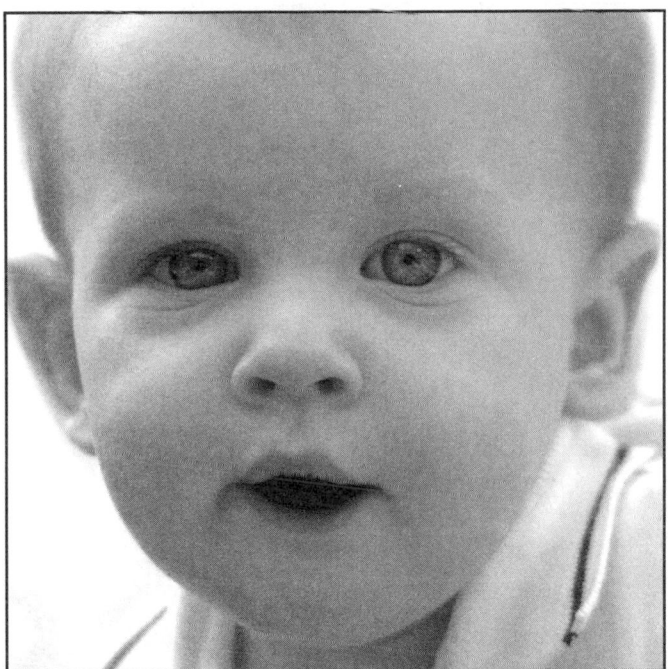

Fig. 66: If this infant retains her full upper lip, she'll desire intense experiences.

connections to others. From a very early age, friends and family will be important to these children, and thicker lips enhance the basic Earthy desire to enjoy the finer things in life: good friends, good food, a comfortable home, and overall contentedness. You may notice how exceptionally talented your little ones are at finding ways to savor their time on this planet! Kids with extremely full lips will have the potential to be a bit hedonistic, for example, seeking indulgences as a first priority or not wanting to work very hard at anything.

In some faces, you'll see a difference between the size of the upper and lower lips. A thicker upper lip indicates someone who enjoys intense emotional experiences, especially within relationships, and if there aren't enough to suit her, she may contribute some drama to them!

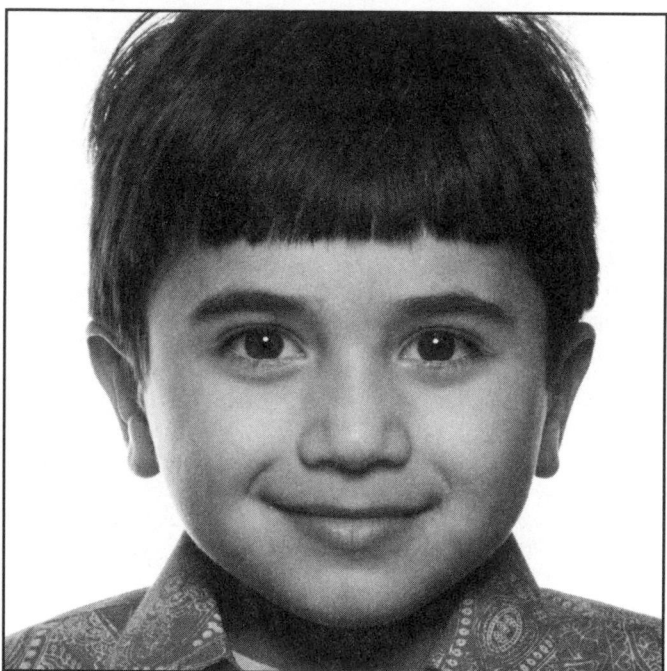

Fig. 67: A full lower lip shows a desire to be pampered.

Children with lower lips that are much fuller than their upper lips love to be pampered. For example, giving them little treats or preparing a special bubble bath will make them so very happy. However, they may have a tendency to go overboard with certain pleasures, such as eating too much of their favorite foods or lounging for hours and not getting their work done. Whether this feature is full or not, if you notice that your child's lower lip looks flaccid or loose, this can be a clue to a more significant problem with self-control or a lack of discipline. Or it may indicate a physical health issue instead, which could be a sign of digestive problems in the lower intestine such as constipation.

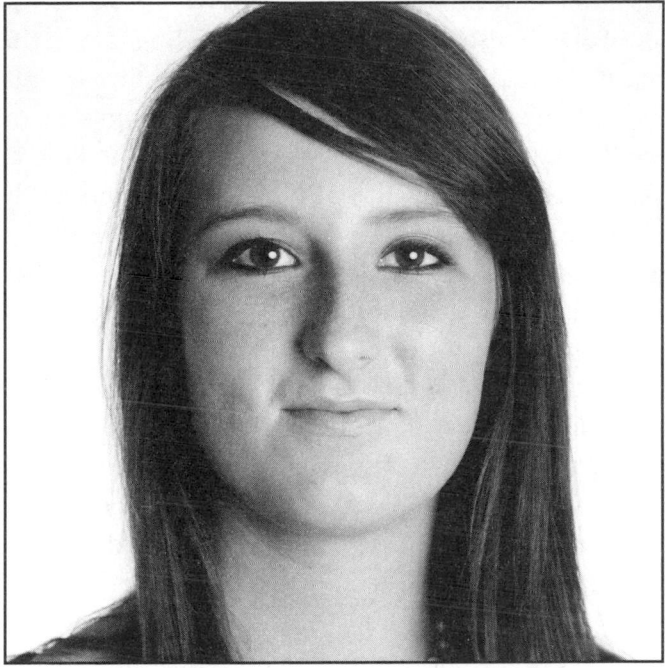

Fig. 68: Someone with a small mouth may put less emphasis on a sense of community.

Children with small mouths probably don't have Earth as their main Element. This is neither good nor bad; it's just an indication that you need to look elsewhere to discover how they perceive the world and what's important to them. But this characteristic can tip you off to certain patterns within their personalities, even if they primarily show another Element. A small mouth shows less of an emphasis on friendships and community overall and not much of an awareness of how to make others feel well nurtured. This certainly doesn't mean that they can't have good relationships, but it's probably not their main focus in life. They might be more introverted and only need a couple of close friends at one time. Knowing that this is normal for them will ease your worries if this is different from their siblings' behavior or your own needs.

Since Earth is also about "home" and feeling safe in the world, children with small mouths may feel less stability in their lives. Therefore, changes such as a new school or a big move can trigger anxiety. It will be important for you as a parent to be aware that these kids need a firmer sense of home than others or that they could be insecure about their place in the family or at school.

Finally, because this Element is also about the Mother archetype, children with *significantly* small mouths (not just slightly small) may have specific mother issues, such as difficult relationships with their own mothers and whoever acts as a nurturer in their lives; maternal figures who are emotionally distant; or a perception that life is conspiring to create a physical distance between mother and child, such as a loss of custody. This experience is even more likely if the mouth is small and the lips are extremely thin. These aren't the only scenarios that can manifest for children with this feature, but the issue may well have to do with mother, home, a sense of connection, or safety in some way.

Thin lips, like a naturally small mouth, merely tell you that this child probably isn't based in this Element. They also indicate someone for whom community or taking care of others isn't a main priority, as well as possible issues with feeling safe or protected. For instance, a youngster could have a pattern of belief that he's not well looked after, even if this isn't the reality of his situation. Because the mouth is also about receptivity, he may have a harder time accepting sympathy from you when he's upset. But knowing this tendency can help you find ways to counteract it by giving him lots of positive attention and affection. And as discussed previously, very thin lips combined with an extremely small mouth can mean difficulties in the relationship with mother or caregiver.

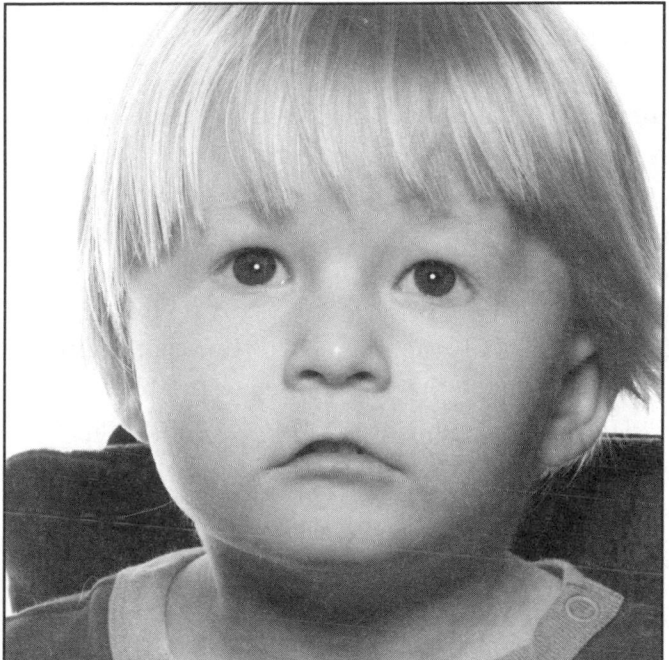

Fig. 69: Thin lips are a sign of those who are less focused on personal connections.

A woman who came to one of my workshops had a very Earthy appearance overall, with the exception of her mouth. She had a very round face, beautiful plump cheeks, a peaches-and-cream complexion, and a fleshy nose. She even radiated the sweet kindness of the Earth energy, but her mouth was exceptionally tiny with very thin lips. Once she shared the story of her childhood, it all made sense.

When she was just an infant, her mother's mental illness became so severe that she had to be institutionalized. As a little girl, the woman first lived with family in her hometown, but in grade school she was sent to stay with distant relatives in Germany. If it wasn't bad enough that she had to adjust to a new language, school, and culture, this family didn't have a bedroom or even a bed for her. She had to sleep on the living-room couch once everyone had gone to their rooms for the night. After a few years, she was sent to Holland to live with family friends and was again forced to adjust to a different country and start over. In this house, she didn't even have a couch and had to sleep on a pad on the floor in the corner of the dining room.

When this woman was 13, her mother was released from the institution, and they were reunited. Her mother didn't like to be touched, and wouldn't even hug her daughter to welcome her home. She *was* allowed to sleep on a bed in the den—finally, a bed of her own!—but her mother loved the beautiful mattress and box-spring set so much that she wanted to be able to see it during the day. Therefore, this girl wasn't allowed to put sheets and blankets on it until bedtime, and each morning she had to immediately take them off and store them so her mother could gaze at the fancy mattress. Although she was back "home," there really wasn't a soft place to land. This was pretty serious Earth deprivation that revealed itself through the message of her tiny mouth.

Upper Eyelids

Earth has to do with accumulation—of friends, food, possessions, money . . . you name it. In Chinese face reading, the upper eyelids and the area above them are called "Assets" because they show how well people gather resources. Fleshiness here reveals a talent for saving or investing, often with success in real estate; and as adults, those with Assets are also well represented in the fields of construction, property development, and even feng shui! However, accumulation is not always a good thing. Puffy upper eyelids reflect a tendency to collect clutter or have energy stagnate in the system, resulting in weight gain or general inflexibility in life.

Fig. 70: Fullness in the upper-eyelid area indicates the ability to accumulate wealth, especially in real estate.

Bridge of the Nose

This part of the face is a minor Earth feature that mostly relates to the concept of stamina. Remember, this Element relates to the archetypal Mother who must have enormous strength to work long hours to take care of the family. The bridge of the nose reveals how energy comes into the system. If it's wide, this is a broad channel, so they're likely to have a good supply. This is the second of three Reservoirs of Wealth on the face. In traditional Chinese face reading, the nose is called "the money box," and the bridge is said to show how money comes in. If you have a lot of stamina, you'll be able to work hard and, therefore, keep money coming in . . . so I guess this makes sense!

Fig. 71: A wide nose bridge shows plenty of energy flowing in.

If your child has a narrow nose bridge, this doesn't indicate that she's weak; she just doesn't have a six-lane highway for energy to rush in. So the advice is that she take care with her resources, conserving and using them wisely.

This part of the face can offer early warning signs about self-care issues. If someone develops faint wrinkles or a mark here, for example, she might be wearing out her vitality by working too hard or not taking good care of herself. Alternatively, marks here can indicate digestion difficulties. It's said that children might have food allergies if a horizontal blue line appears across the bridge of the nose.

Area above the Upper Lip

Aside from the mouth itself, the area around it also relates to Earth, including the space between the nose and mouth (but not the philtrum, which is associated with Water). This part of the face usually becomes important to look at much later in life to see if wrinkles develop, since it has to do with the status of giving and receiving and how satisfied people feel. In childhood, this area should be of normal complexion and clear. If there is a marking, discoloration, or scar here, you may notice that your child is struggling with an imbalance in the Earth actions of giving and receiving. It's pretty common for Earth people, even as youngsters, to overgive, be too "nice," or even get taken advantage of. Markings on this feature can be a clue for you to watch these tendencies in your children and help them learn to maintain a healthy balance.

Lower Cheeks

Babies often have marvelously fat lower cheeks that you just want to kiss! The true shape of this feature will begin to emerge as they mature, and then you'll be able to more accurately judge their level of this Earth characteristic. Plump lower cheeks denote kids who are naturally kind and caring. These children want everyone to be happy, and their first instinct will be to create harmony in any situation. This disposition makes them wonderful friends, but it could cause them to get especially upset by conflicts of any sort. It might also lead to them taking on the responsibility of being the peacemakers in the family, which isn't an appropriate role for young people.

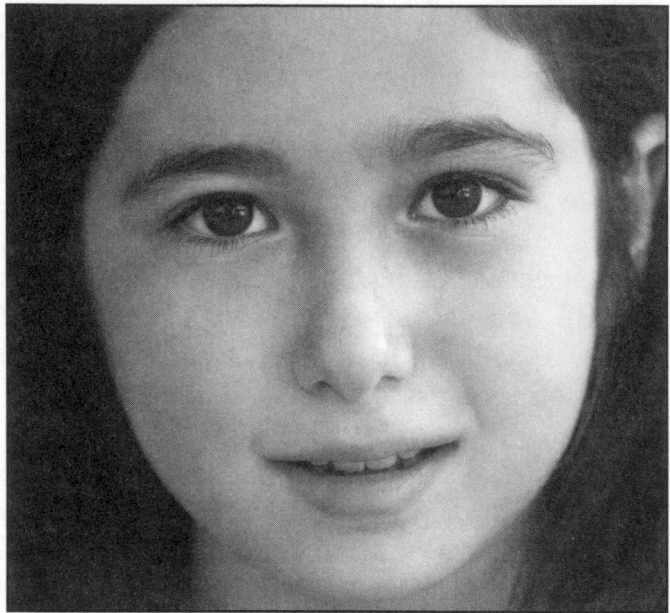

Fig. 72: Plump lower cheeks are a classic sign of the Earth nature.

If your little ones' lower cheeks are especially plump directly on either side of the mouth, then they have the mark called "moneybags" in traditional Chinese face reading that's considered very lucky! It's the third and most important Reservoir of Wealth on the face (the other two are large earlobes and a wide bridge of the nose), and if you had this trait in ancient China, you'd have been married off easily. Just as with the bridge of the nose, I find that if you exchange the word *energy* for *money,* you'll understand the concept better. Moneybags indicate children with reserves of energy and lots of stamina who will be able to work long and hard and, therefore, always be able to bring in money. Similar to plump lower cheeks in general, fullness in this part of the face indicates those with a kind, caring nature whose first concern is the welfare of others.

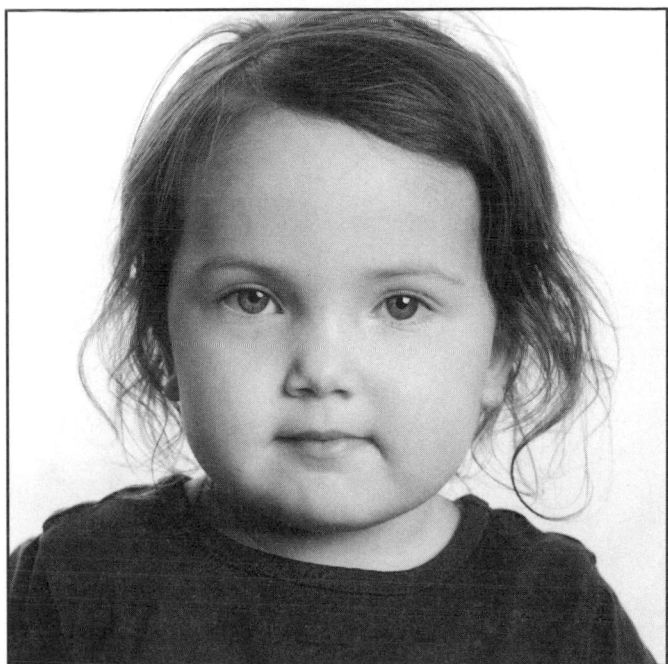

Fig. 73: Plump areas next to the mouth are called "moneybags" and reveal stamina and kindness.

Heavy Lower Face

In some people, the lower face goes beyond just plump cheeks and appears fuller and heavier throughout. Kids with heavy lower faces often have thick, sturdy upper bodies; less roundness; and more of a blockish look that translates into an energy that carries less of this Element's sweetness and more of its power. This isn't to say that these children aren't total sweetie pies, but this shape might indicate that they're forces to be reckoned with. The personality is consistent with the archetypal Mother energy as the one in the family who is in charge, and demands that things be *her* way. You may find that these children are less easygoing than other Earth people, more insistent on what they want, and less willing to do what they're told if they disagree with instructions.

However, this feature can also enhance their stability and stamina, and in no way does it diminish their underlying desire to assist others and have good relationships.

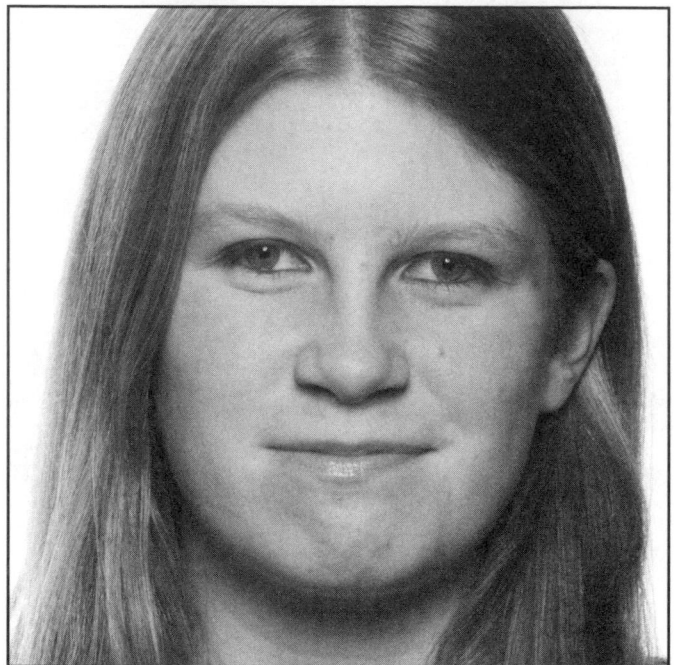

Fig. 74: A heavier lower face shows stamina and strong opinions.

One father told me that his nine-year-old daughter was like a steamroller; no matter what he and his wife said, their little girl just went ahead and did what *she* wanted to do. He explained, "We told her she couldn't go to a friend's house, so she sneaked out anyway. She stole half of her brother's Halloween candy, and when we caught her, instead of owning up and apologizing, she argued that she deserved it because she was the one who took him trick-or-treating. She just won't back down."

This trait has to do with that part of the Mother energy that feels taken advantage of for having to do more for her family than they do for her. Children with this feature can behave as if they're victims of your unfair rules, so they disobey just to even the score. Of course, people who predominantly exhibit any of the other Elements can be resentful in their behavior, but you'll see this as more of a consistent pattern in those with heavy lower faces. One way for you to deal with this tendency is to actively recognize all the wonderful things your little ones do and show your appreciation when they help out or follow your rules. Keep in mind that these issues are really just the essence of Mother craving acknowledgment for her hard work and sacrifices.

Fleshy Nose

Extra fleshiness anywhere on the face connotes an extra supply of Earth. The most common place to look for this is the nose, even though it's not a feature related to this Element. There are three general types of noses: average, bony, and fleshy. If your child's nose is the third type, this is an indication of some additional Earthiness in his or her nature—specifically, enjoying the pleasures of life and a talent for accumulation. A large percentage of successful businesspeople have fleshy noses, which is a reflection of their gift for gathering riches. People who like to collect things or enjoy fine food usually possess this trait as well. Remember that children aren't born with the size, shape, or fleshiness of the nose they'll have later in life; this feature doesn't begin to take on its mature appearance until about age five.

Fig. 75: Extra fleshiness of the nose shows an ease of accumulation and enjoyment of life.

Round Face Shape

Earth is another Element that has a distinct face shape associated with it, but not *all* of these kids have round faces. Seeing this shape just means there's some extra Earth in their nature; they tend to be exceptionally good with people, exuding that cooperative disposition that makes them so easy to relate to. Studies have found that we trust those with round faces more—especially if they're also wide—and adults with these characteristics are actually exonerated more often in court. Of course, this isn't to say you should encourage your Earth kids to lead a life of crime since they'll be good at getting away with things—and their responsible personality would cause them too much guilt to do anything wrong anyhow!

Environments for the Earth Nature

Cozy is the word for these children! Earth is about softness, receptivity, and a safe place to land; and this sense can be created with lots of pillows, stuffed animals, fabric wall hangings, fluffy comforters, and cushy furniture like beanbag chairs or plush couches. Let their rooms be full of pictures of family and friends; mementos from get-togethers; and if there's space, artwork such as pictures of landscapes, pastoral settings, or gatherings of people or animals. The color for Earth is primarily yellow; but earth tones like brown, beige, and warm pastels are good, too.

A special room in the house for arts and crafts is a dream come true for these kids. Consider having a second bed in their room to allow a friend to stay overnight, and don't be surprised if they want the family pet to sleep with them. For small children, having sturdy stools around the house so they can step up to help Mom or Dad at the counter or table will be nice, as they love to feel useful and part of everything. Because these children do tend to have a lot of stuff, good storage is mandatory; you might even build a window seat over that storage container to allow them to sit and read, which is a common Earth activity.

Thoughts for the Teacher

These children are likely to be your little helpers and easy to deal with overall. They're the ones you'll want to seat next to the more difficult kids and whom you can rely on to watch the class if you have to dash out for a moment. But know that self-confidence may be an issue, and they may be quite shy or tend to worry much more than you'd expect about disappointing you or their parents. They may also not want to bother you if they need assistance, so don't assume that because they're quietly working away you don't have to check in. Your help in boosting their confidence will do wonders. Challenging them to push the envelope a bit will keep them from getting stuck in a limited comfort zone; just be there so that they feel supported during the process.

Earth children will enjoy working in groups or helping others. It will be upsetting for them to encounter conflict or anger in the classroom, and it may be hard for these kids to watch you discipline troublemakers because they'll worry that you might treat *them* like that. Be aware that they may need reassurance or clarity about the situation.

Any change will be tough for Earth children to manage, and they'll be the ones who don't want the school year to end. They'll cope better if you let them document the experience with photos and mementos!

Helping the Earth Nature Flourish

These are sweet, kind, caring children whose first thought is to be of service. Their reason for living is the close connections they have with parents, family, and friends. They'll take advantage of as many opportunities as possible to do things with those they love, such as: family dinners, cuddling on the couch watching TV, or taking pictures at any gathering or group outing.

Although they may be outgoing by nature, these kids will almost always exhibit shyness, a lack of confidence, a need to feel safe, and difficulties with change. This all factors in to create distinct discomfort if they have to tackle a new situation by themselves, and they can become clingy and unsure as a result. Be mindful that it may not be wise to thrust them into something without you or a friend nearby, so sympathize with them rather than urge them to get with the program. The sense that someone else understands what they're going through is what all Earth people crave.

These kids tend to give to others, but often fail to look out for themselves. They need someone to talk to on a regular basis just to get their worries out of their minds and feel understood, not necessarily to find a solution. When they're upset, embrace them warmly and let them hug a stuffed animal or pillow.

You'll need to be aware that these children can try to please too much or feel responsible for keeping peace within the family. They'll also get very upset by arguments or discord in the house, so be sure to use these situations to show them how people can talk out their problems and come to an agreement. If a divorce occurs, they may seem to be coping well, but consider that this could be because they feel too guilty to bother you with their problems. Or they may feel the need to help you during your distress and end up being more of the parent in the relationship, which isn't healthy for either of you. Encourage them to speak up for their needs and not be so worried about everyone else.

These are children whose lifelong issues will include a tendency to give their power away. Cultivate their ability to build confidence, teach them the necessity of saying no, and provide them with the opportunity to learn how to be independent while still knowing you're always there as a safety net. They might also feel that they're not as smart or imaginative as their peers, but the truth is they have wonderful minds and their thought processes are often far more mature than those around them. They'll be more comfortable in the background, but if they can get some experience in a position of power, it will do wonders for their self-confidence.

Teach your Earth child that it's okay to take risks. One way he'll be willing to do so is if he's convinced that his actions will help others. With loving support, he'll grow up to be surrounded by loving relationships and help others in powerful ways.

◎ ◎ ◎

"He who knows others is wise. He who knows himself is enlightened."

— LAO-TZU

THE METAL CHILD: VISIONARY, FATHER, SENSOR

Chapter 13

Aiko

Finger paints always held a horror for Aiko—to dip your fingers in cold, wet paint; rub them on paper; and then end up with messy hands . . . *what* is fun about that? And even with an apron, you might still get paint on your clothes. Aiko can't stand having dirty or wet clothes, and she has to change them immediately if even a speck gets on them. Fortunately, now at age eight, she no longer has her mother offering her finger-painting sessions. But their recent trip to the beach ended early because Aiko wasn't comfortable with sand sticking to her feet. She'd run into the waves to wash it off, but as soon as she ran back onto the shore, they were coated again. Nothing her mother suggested helped, so they finally gave up and went home.

The first things you notice about Aiko are her remarkably full, prominent cheeks; eyebrows set high above her eyes; and a pale glow to her complexion. She also exhibits the predominant quality of the Metal personality: a highly sensitive nature. Soon after birth, she was deemed a "difficult" baby by her pediatrician because of how reactive she seemed and how hard to console she was when she cried. Aiko has certainly shown that little things can bother her—scratchy labels on her clothes, different foods touching on her plate, or certain smells that the rest of her family barely notices. When she was smaller and still taking afternoon naps, she'd refuse to lie down in her day clothes. She insisted on changing into pajamas, a bathrobe, and slippers before getting into bed, and then getting dressed once again when she woke up.

This is a child who notices all the little details of life, which is both a wonderful attribute and a tremendous challenge. She sees the waitress handle money in the restaurant and then doesn't want to eat the food the same woman delivers because her hands are sure to be full of germs. She spends an hour double-checking her homework each night, and is mortified if her teacher marks an error on one of her papers. However, this level of attentiveness allows her to create meticulously detailed jewelry with tiny beads and crystals, and draw page after page of her initials with intricate decorations reminiscent of the illuminated manuscripts of medieval monks. As she matures, Aiko will discover even more benefits of her high level of sensitivity, including her ability to read people's energy and make them feel understood and welcome in any situation.

Her family's nickname for her is "the Empress" because of how bossy she is. Aiko likes things just so, and if something isn't right in her opinion, she'll demand that it be changed. She still requires very complicated bedtime rituals, with her blue blanket pulled up exactly to her chin, her hair smoothed out on the pillow, her stuffed bunny in her left arm, and her teddy bear in her right. Her mother has to read her two stories and then close the closet and the curtains—in that order. After that, Mom must tuck the sheets in extra tight, pressing Aiko down into the bed so firmly that she can hardly move. In addition, she wants a heavy comforter and as many blankets as the season will allow because the weight allows her to relax. The bedroom door has to be wide open and three night-lights must be plugged in. If any of these steps are missed, the whole family will hear loud complaints until the situation is remedied!

Because of Aiko's vocal nature at home, her parents were shocked to hear at a parent-teacher conference how quiet and shy she is and that she should contribute more in class! For Metal children, home is often the only place that feels safe. The outer world can be overwhelming—a cacophony of sensations and energies emanating from the people and places around them—and they pull back into themselves just to survive it. At school, Aiko doesn't easily join in with other kids and is reluctant to try new experiences. She insists on bringing her own lunch instead of buying it in the cafeteria like the other students because she worries that the food might be unfamiliar or have flavors that are too strong.

Rules and manners are important to this girl. She does best when given clear guidelines on a project, and if instructions are at all ambiguous, she becomes anxious. Aiko notices when others are rude and is quite concerned about learning the right way to behave in different situations.

"She got hysterical last month when I parked in a handicapped spot for 30 seconds to run in and drop off a letter at the post office. She was afraid I'd get arrested, and won't let me forget it. Every time I pull into a parking space now, she asks me if it's for the handicapped!" her mother exclaimed.

Blake

We're all gathered outside Blake's bedroom door to talk and take a peek inside. This 11-year-old has a large bony nose and fine bone structure, with narrow wrists and ankles, both classic signs of Metal. "He knows when someone's been in his room, even if we haven't touched anything," his dad tells me. "He says he can just feel it." The room almost looks as if it might belong to an adult. On each wall is a single, framed scientific chart of fossils, rocks, or crystals. His desk is spare, with a laptop, an art tablet, and a series of fine-point pens laid in a straight line. Blake loves to create exquisitely detailed sketches, filling the entire page with tiny, exact lines; and his freehand work looks almost like someone designed it on a computer.

At one end of the room is a large white wardrobe, which his mother says holds his books and rock collection. "He said it made him nervous to constantly have to look at all that stuff, so we finally ditched his bookcases and brought in the wardrobe so he can close the doors and have no visual clutter," his mother explained. The last thing a Metal personality needs is more stimulation since they're already so hyperaware. Minimalist environments are more comfortable for them.

Blake's favorite activity is to go rock and fossil hunting, and the family recently returned from an expedition to eastern Oregon where he reveled in the big skies and wide-open spaces. Metal people can tend toward being claustrophobic, and Blake's worst memory is the day his class took a field trip to a submarine. "I just had to get outta there!" he says, turning a bit gray at the memory. In fact, his grandfather calls him "the Family Fire Marshal," because whenever they go to a store, the first thing Blake does is locate the exits in case of a fire!

This boy has mild OCD (obsessive-compulsive disorder), which is a common Metal challenge. In Blake, it shows up in minor ways, such as a need to line up his shoes before going to bed at night or repeatedly rereading parts of a book, worried that he's missed the last few words on the previous page. He also has difficulty with transitions; when he was little, his mother quickly learned that the worst thing she could do was rush him to get ready to go somewhere. She used to often run late in the morning and then suddenly realize that she only had five minutes to get him to day care. She'd run in the room where Blake was watching TV and shout for him to hurry up, put his shoes on, and grab his jacket. As a result, this little guy would just fall apart. She came to realize that as long as she gave him plenty of advance notice, things were fine. In fact, once he figured out how to tell time, Blake would be the one following her around, making sure she knew it was getting late. "Yeah, just call me the human alarm clock," he says, smirking, often managing his hypersensitivity with dry humor.

This is a bright boy who's learning how to function in the world with his high level of awareness. He knows he's a perfectionist and too self-critical, but says it helps him understand how people must feel when they make mistakes. I ask him if he can ever physically feel others' energy, which leads us into a discussion on the concept of being a sensor, a new idea to him. I explain that sometimes sensitive people act as sponges and soak in what others around them are experiencing. His mother adds that he gets worn out quickly in crowded stores and wonders if that has anything to do with it. Blake admits that some kids at school feel prickly to him, while others feel really heavy and damp. Sometimes when a classmate gets sick, he starts feeling ill, too.

This is a guy who requires a lot of time to be alone and recoup at the end of the day because of having dealt with all the energy around him. In order to stay balanced, even as an adult, he'll probably need to create daily opportunities for solitude.

Fig. 76: This girl's prominent nose is a strong indicator of the Metal Element.

Fig. 77: This young man has the bony nose and sculpted features of the Metal Element.

The Metal Child's Nature

In this chapter, you'll learn about the inner nature and outer appearance of Metal children, and the next chapter will include more information about each feature associated with this Element. To begin with, the following list shows what to look for. Please note that your child doesn't have to have *all* of the characteristics for Metal to play a strong role; seeing any of them means it's a factor in his or her personality. The more aspects you notice, the more Metal there is in your child's nature! Look for:

- A large nose
- Plump upper or prominent bony cheeks
- Concave or sunken lower cheeks
- Fine bone structure (most easily seen in small wrists and ankles)
- High eyebrows
- Wide spaces between features
- A pale complexion (relative to racial heritage)
- Hypermetabolism and the tendency to be slim

Well-known adults with many of these features include Adrian Brody, Meryl Streep, Lyle Lovett, Michelle Pfeiffer, Nancy Reagan, Nicolas Sarkozy, Barbra Streisand, and Ralph Nader.

As Your Child Grows

It's important to note that in young children, the nose and cheeks don't look as they will later on, and evidence of a small bone structure may not be visible under a baby's chubby wrists and ankles! As your child grows, use this book to read the emerging aspects of his or her personality.

Qualities of Metal Element

- *Facial features:* nose, cheeks, skin

- *Other parts of the body associated with Metal:* lungs, skin, large intestines, chest

- *Strengths:* sacred awareness, bodily sensation, inspiration

- *Challenging emotion:* grief

- *Archetype:* visionary, father, sensor

- *What Metal feels like:* evening, late fall, old age, moving inward

Since ancient times, the late fall was when people were concerned with making sure there was enough food preserved to keep them alive through the scarce times of the approaching winter. This period is about ensuring that everything is in order, nothing has been overlooked, plans have been carefully evaluated, and necessary refinements have been made so everyone will be safe. The evening is when work is finished or set aside for the next day, desks are cleared, and preparations are made to rest for the night. In old age, as we approach the end of our lives, we feel compelled to let go of what no longer has purpose and focus solely on what has meaning in the time we have left. Metal has to do with refining our ideas, paying attention to what's important, and not wasting energy on the frivolous.

This Element is the breath as the lungs draw in divine life source, and it's also about letting go—breathing out and the endless rhythm of life. It's the sky where the ethereal vision of the future floats, and it's also the archetype of the Father and visionary who sees the big picture and leads the family toward new horizons with power and clarity.

All Metal qualities can be seen in the children who carry them, although they can manifest in many different ways. To best understand this Element's true spirit, and thus your little one, learn its essence. What follows are the basic aspects and a few examples of how it can reveal itself in your child's behaviors, emotions, needs, and perceptions.

The Spirit of Metal

Hard and shiny, Metal is an energy that contracts and tightens—it's the least flexible of any Element. There's a strong aspect of control to Metal people, but it's important to understand why, as their behavior can often be misinterpreted as a desire to dominate others. This couldn't be further from the truth: the reason even children of this Element can seem controlling is actually due to their highly sensitive nature, which makes their experience of the world entirely different from those around them.

The shininess of Metal reflects everything around it. Those with these traits see, feel, and sense more of what's going on in their environment than most people. When these children walk into a room, for example, they're immediately aware of a thousand details: the picture on the far wall is crooked, there's a smudge on the mirror, the rug has a loose thread at one corner, there's still a hint of the neighbor's cigarette smoke wafting through the window, and someone has just squirmed slightly in a chair as if her back is bothering her. And a highly Metal child can even enter an empty house and be impacted by the residue of emotional energy left over from an argument that happened there two weeks ago!

In Chinese medicine, this Element also relates to the skin. People with this nature are considered to have thin skin, which results in their soaking in others' energy as actual physical sensations. At times, this can be unbearable. While Fire children are empathic in that the thoughts and emotions of others appear as flashes in their consciousness, these kids actually *feel* this subtle energy physically in their bodies. If you have a headache, your Metal child may start to get sick herself. If you and your partner had a fight while she was at school, she may sense it in her body when she walks through the door and be very uncomfortable without knowing why.

These youngsters are often judged to be fragile or even hypochondriacs, but what many parents don't realize is how much they absorb compared with other kids. Anyone would struggle with this, and the fact that there's no language in our culture to define this kind of hypersensitivity can leave them feeling like aliens.

Even for adults, this kind of experience is enormously challenging, but for children it can be overwhelming; as a result, the tightening, controlling aspect of this Element shows up. Because these kids are so aware of the little things around them in every moment, they're forced to try to make things as manageable as possible and control the situation so they don't become too stressed. The consequence is that they may become inflexible and need to have things "just so" in many areas of their lives. I've done many private consultations for parents who've struggled with the misperception that their children are attempting to be the heads of the household, when they're merely trying to cope with the extreme challenges this kind of sensitivity can bring them.

One mother brought her nine-year-old daughter to me for a face reading with the hope she could discover why the little girl no longer wanted to spend time with her. She informed me that it must have something to do with her refusing to put up with this power play the child had been attempting, and that she was trying to order her mother around every chance she got. When I asked for an example, she said that her daughter demanded an elaborate bedtime ritual, culminating with the bedroom door needing to be left open exactly halfway. But her mother felt this was an attack on her position of authority in the family and, with strong emotion in her voice, told me that she ignored her daughter's pleas and firmly closed the door each night with the great satisfaction that she was teaching her little girl respect, despite the child's nightly sobbing.

In reality, her daughter was desperately trying to create a comfort zone for herself so that she could relax and go to sleep. It had nothing to do with challenging her mother's authority, and everything to do with her attempts to manage all the incoming information from her environment. Fortunately, to this mother's credit, once her eyes were opened to what was really going on, she was able to soften her judgment and change her responses so effectively that a week later I got a happy phone call: mother and daughter were a team again and enjoying each other's company. This new awareness prevented the problem from deepening into what could have been the beginning of more serious issues.

However, there's an important aspect of this Element that can contribute to parents feeling that their children are being defiant. Just as Earth relates to the archetype of Mother, Metal is associated with the Father—the paternal figure at the head of the household whom no one questions! Some of these kids project a subtle expectation of power that can be misinterpreted as stepping over the line of appropriate behavior. This might actually be true, but more often it's an energy that colors their interactions; if you understand the source, you won't react so strongly to it. The essence of Metal children is what makes them grow up to become visionaries, since they're able to see the big picture and the fine details at the same time. Their sense of strength will allow them to be in positions of power as adults, with the potential to be great leaders in their fields.

But right now, you're raising the child version of this future authority, and it's the sensitivity of your little one that will most likely be the source of any problems. These kids will often complain about the feel of the fabrics in their clothes or be picky about their food. And because the nose is the sense organ associated with this Element, they can be more aware of, and bothered by, subtle odors. Understand that these children aren't complaining because they're always looking for something to whine about; they just notice so many more details than everyone else that they're more likely to discover that something's off. For example, these are the little ones who will point out that the candles on the birthday cake aren't evenly spaced.

They'll be concerned about doing things right, and if something is *slightly* wrong, they won't relax until it's corrected. As you've probably already noticed, these kids tend to be perfectionists and self-critical, but this can also extend outward to other people in their lives. Metal children will recognize when someone else has made an error, and it will be virtually impossible for them to restrain themselves from calling attention to it. Therefore, they can easily be perceived as critical and nitpicky, which can instigate a spiral of negative reactions and misunderstandings where each person takes the other's behavior too personally.

This incredibly detail-oriented nature, however, also gives these children wonderful skills and abilities. They can maintain an intricate focus on their work and produce beautiful results due to their ability to make sure every aspect is exactly right. Metal kids are very conscientious overall with strong ideals and principles, giving them a level of integrity beyond their young years. Since they can literally feel people's energy, they're superb at sensing what those around them need in order to feel comfortable, and they can be quite talented at relating to others in a way that makes them feel welcome. People with this nature can be gracious and charming and are often excellent communicators, knowing how to express something in a way the other person can hear and accept. After all, the standard term for a Metal person is the Perfect Host!

Evening

As the day winds to a close, we also start to end our activities and prepare for the transition to rest at night. We clear off our desks, put away our tools, or clean up whatever we've been working on. Metal children carry this energy, and will feel best if they can have the least amount of clutter around them. While Fire kids thrive in as busy of an environment as possible, the last thing these little ones need is more stimulation, thank you very much!

This can mean that rather than having all their toys and books on display, they'll appreciate having closets and cabinets so that things can be kept out of sight until they want them. And they may not like their walls filled with posters or photos the way Earth kids do.

Interestingly, it's usually visual clutter that's most disturbing. If things are kept inside drawers or behind closed doors, to them, it's as if they don't exist. One image for Metal in the Chinese tradition is the surface of the lake—that perfectly still, reflective sheen of water that creates a sense of calm. People of this Element are always trying to make things look good on the surface.

This desire can even extend to other aspects of life. Your child may be very concerned with how her clothes look or bothered by the house needing a minor repair, for fear of what others will think. She might even worry about her social status or develop elaborate fantasies about being a princess in exile. One boy used an English accent every time he went out with his family for an entire year, trying to make people believe that he wasn't part of this shabby group, but a regal visitor from afar!

Late Fall

After the harvest and the feast, winter fast approaches; and the focus turns to safely storing supplies so everyone has enough to eat during the scarce times to come. Issues about "enough" can be significant for Metal children. They may even show up as a general stinginess: these kids might be unwilling to share their toys, pinch every penny in their allowance, or want to buy the cheapest birthday present for their friend.

There can also be major concerns about being good enough. These kids might be reluctant to try something new for fear that they'll fail or even just make a mistake. One way to ease this anxiety for your Metal child is to provide clear explanations for what's going to happen and what to do each step of the way. The more guidelines and rules there are, the safer these kids feel, because it gives them control over their experiences and reduces the chances that they'll do something incorrectly. When Metal children approach any project, the more they know about every stage, the better—even to the point of rehearsing in advance. One mother told me that when her son was old enough to start making phone calls to friends, he'd write out an elaborate script to follow and rehearse it several times before dialing the number.

Old Age

There's a fragility to elderly people, a brittleness or delicacy. You deal with them gently, expecting them to be a bit rigid in their outlook on life; and you don't challenge them with big surprises or intense experiences. All this applies to the Metal nature as well. Don't get me wrong, these kids aren't fragile or weak. On the contrary, they can be like little soldiers who persevere in even the most difficult experiences. But these children do best if they're helped with transitions in life so they don't become overly anxious. Allow them enough time to get ready for school without feeling rushed, for example. Also make sure that they know what they'll need in order to prepare for a new adventure.

One family woke their Metal daughter up on the morning of her birthday with a surprise trip to Disneyland several hundred miles from their home. They rushed into her room with a suitcase already packed for her and the plane tickets in hand, ready to quickly get her dressed and head to the airport. But how could they have known what she'd want to pack? And she'd have no time to find out which rides would be too scary, so she might end up on one that was too violent and get sick. Rather than excitedly jumping out of bed, this little girl burst into tears! Predictability is soothing, just as it is for older people; so surprises, even good ones, are unnerving. Developing and maintaining a natural rhythm for life helps these youngsters feel that things are under control and reduces their level of anxiety.

One of the most important things to know about disciplining Metal children is that all they need is a look from you. If they're doing something wrong, you don't have to yell; simply raise an eyebrow, and they'll immediately know they've gotten out of line. These kids are already extremely self-critical, so harsh words coming from the outside are too much on top of that. This is especially true if they're from a parent, whom they desperately want to please. They'll be crushed to think they've done something so bad that it requires an angry tone. And really, these little ones are so sensitive that strong words will literally feel violent to their systems. Please be subtle!

Some mothers and fathers spot this sensitivity but go overboard in trying not to upset their children. They're so afraid of a negative reaction that when they notice their sons or daughters doing something wrong, they try to distract them instead of pointing out and correcting the behavior. Understand that it *is* important to set firm boundaries and help your children learn how to handle distress. But a soft message is all it takes to make them aware of the right way to do things, which is what Metal always wants.

Metal Challenge: Grief

In the evening, during the late fall, and upon reaching old age, it's all about letting go. We end our day, the trees release their leaves, and elders recognize the preciousness of each moment as their lives come to a close. This is a loss, and it can be a poignant and wrenching experience to feel something come to an end and know we'll never get it back.

Metal is related to the lungs in the physical body, breathing in and out, taking in and letting go. When these children grieve, they may not easily take in comfort or let go of suffering—and they can be very affected by loss of any kind. They'll most likely hold on to their grief for a long time, but may not appear overtly grief stricken, however. It's the nature of this Element to tighten, and sometimes kids can show this by toughing things out and not opening up about their upsets.

Metal Strength: Sacred Awareness, Bodily Sensation, Inspiration

Metal's power is in valuing the preciousness of the moment, that awareness and appreciation for the sacred and miraculous beauty of what's here right now. Help your child relax and notice something small and perfect like a tiny flower in the grass or the magic of the light at dusk (the Metal time of day). Bringing in some lightness of spirit with humor will melt this Element's rigidity.

Guide them to understand that it can feel right to let go. Talk to them about how great it feels to clear the way for new things to come into their lives. Give them this experience by cleaning out their closet to make way for new clothes, or have them participate in donating discarded outfits to charity so they see the value of the end result.

Letting your Metal children care for some plants of their own will instill appreciation for each step of the life cycle: the flowers blooming and dying, old leaves falling, and new growth appearing. Keep a family gratitude journal of the little things that each of you noticed and the special things that happened in your day.

◦ ◦ ◦

"Making the decision to have a child—it's momentous. It is to decide forever to have your heart go walking around outside your body."

— ELIZABETH STONE

READING THE METAL FEATURES

Chapter 14

Certain features on the face have to do with the Metal Element, and the more prominent or noticeable they are, the more we possess Metal as a major part of our original nature.

However, it's important to keep in mind that we all have Metal Element in our faces and personalities, just in differing amounts. The Metal features can be examined to determine the unique ways in which this Element shows up in your child's design, whether or not they're predominant.

Nose

A nose isn't its mature size at birth, and it won't really begin to take shape until later in childhood, so this is something to monitor over time. You can determine the size of your child's nose by comparing it to other features on his or her face. What looks like a large nose on one person might look small on someone else, so be sure to judge them relatively. Also keep in mind that face reading is always done within races; in other words, compare Caucasian faces to other Caucasians ones, African faces to other African ones, Asian faces to other Asian ones, and so on. (You can read mixed-race faces, too, of course; it just takes a little more practice.) On Caucasian faces, for instance, a large nose tends to protrude quite far off the face, but with some African and Asian faces, the nose may spread across the face instead of sticking out. In discerning this Element, this doesn't really matter very much; what's important is whether the nose looks large on the face.

Fig. 78: The larger the nose, the greater the potential for personal power.

The major indicator of how much Metal children have in their nature is the nose. The larger it is, the more impact this Element will have on their temperament. One of the main things to understand about Metal is that it represents the potential for personal power. But it's important to understand what's meant by *power*. This isn't the drive to dominate or be the winner, as some Wood types feel. Instead, it's an emphasis on meaningful accomplishment and pride of achievement—whatever these people do will be of the highest quality, something they can feel good about, and for others to respect. The larger the nose, the more significant this will be for them; and as a result, a tendency toward perfectionism will be likely as well. If your child has a prominent nose, this may explain why he exasperates you so frequently with his insistence that there's only one right way to do things—his way!

Metal equates to the archetype of Father, but it also has to do with being the regal leader. This doesn't just mean the father of the family, but also the king of the country. In ancient times in the Middle East, the noses of the princes were pulled and massaged because there was a cultural belief that they couldn't be powerful rulers without equally powerful noses! We look at the size of the nose to understand the potential for authority. In adult life, this can translate into her being the head of an organization, just like Father is the head of the family, or even an idealistic visionary who can guide everyone to a better life. The joke about adults of this Element is that they always think they're right—and they are!—and this may extend to Metal children as well.

The larger the nose, the more likely these kids will think they're the only ones who know how to do things correctly—keep in mind that Metal tends to notice the fine details that most people miss. The more pronounced this feature is, the more this quality is amplified, and it can result in that person frequently experiencing how those around him lack the same level of awareness. This might lead to a subtle, underlying anxiety, and a propensity to not trust that others will remember to do everything they're supposed to. One teenage girl asked me, "Why does everyone keep saying, 'Why don't you trust me?'" Those with big noses may not be able to restrain themselves from correcting people or spelling out in great detail how to accomplish a minor task, and this can hurt relationships—even those between parent and child!

If your little one's nose sticks out more than an inch from her face, it's a sign that she not only can be a leader, but also may be quite the trailblazer. Google cofounder Sergey Brin has this sort of nose. For kids with extremely prominent noses, this can be helpful information to share with them, since their potential would be diminished if they ever decide to reduce the size of this feature.

A smaller nose reveals someone who isn't so focused on his own personal achievements and more easygoing about working with others. It's interesting that people with big noses are the ones who are said to work too hard, probably as a result of their perfectionism and anxiety about getting things right. I often find that grown-ups with small noses tell me, "I believe in working smart, not hard," and their co-workers say that, indeed, they're great at getting things done efficiently and easily.

We learned in the Earth chapter that a fleshy nose reveals someone who's got an extra supply of that Element. Here, a bony nose, like the one on the young man pictured at the beginning of Chapter 13, means extra Metal. If this feature is both large and bony, it's a sign that this child could be an extremely sensitive perfectionist who actively tries to reduce the level of stimulation in his life to increase his comfort level. For instance, he may really need his alone time after having been out all day; or he may be especially bothered by crowded shopping malls, clutter at home, or strong smells emanating from the kitchen.

In older children, this nose reveals an idealistic nature—one that may have a disdain for materialism or even be attracted to deprivation rather than seeking pleasure (an Earth characteristic). One boy with a very bony nose told his mother that he wanted to redecorate his room. Imagining new drapes and paint, she gave her son some interior-design magazines to get ideas from. "No, Mom," he protested. "I want it to look like *this*," he said as he held out a picture of a medieval monk's cell in one of his history books!

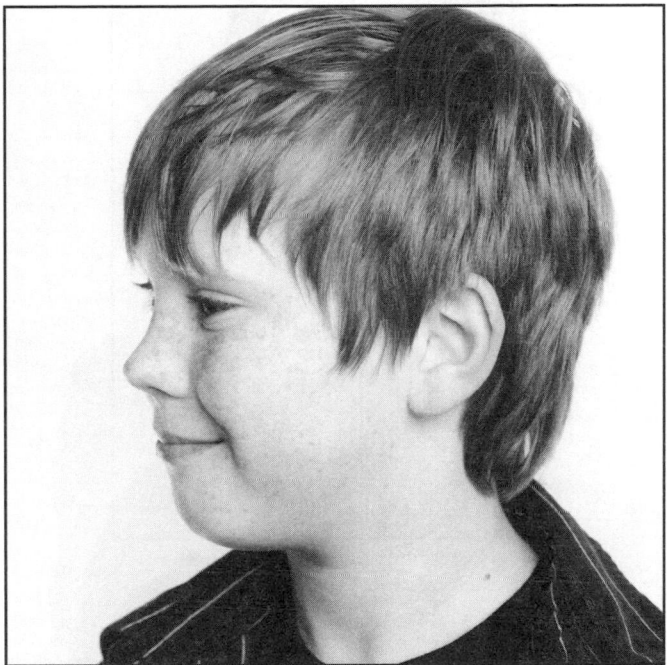

Fig. 79: An upturned nose signifies a sentimental nature.

An upturned nose has a different meaning—a sentimental nature reminiscent of Earth Element. These children will freely give to others and be able to receive as well.

Occasionally, you'll see someone with a nose that has a distinctly bony bump on it, usually about one-quarter to one-third of the way down from the top. It doesn't matter whether this appears naturally or is the result of an injury; regardless, it has the same meaning: the need to be in charge. Remembering that Metal Element is the essence of Father, you can envision the stereotypical paternal figure who is in charge of the family—and no one questions or talks back to him! A bump on the nose enhances this

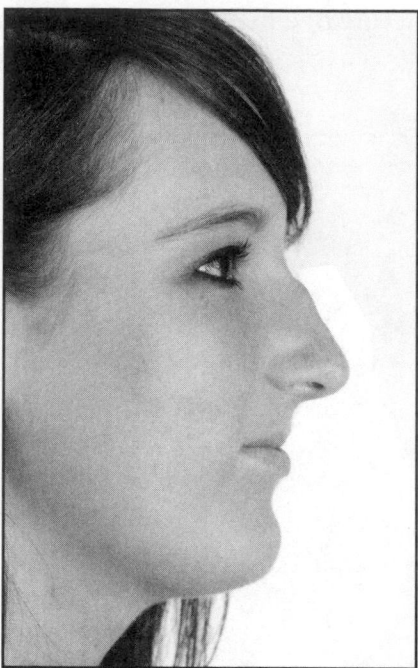

Fig. 80: A bony bump on the nose reveals the need to be in control.

need to tell others what to do and how to do it, what they've done wrong, or, more likely, all of the above. This can present problems for children with this kind of nose, because their place in the family is *not* at the head of the household. Knowing this may help you understand why your child may have trouble restraining her tendency to interfere or be critical, even though she knows you're just trying to help!

The last thing to consider regarding the nose is how straight it is from top to bottom. Most noses extend in a straight line down the face, but sometimes you'll see one that's curved. This can mean that there will be a change in career or life direction at some point in this child's adult life. But as you know, signs on the face relate to specific aspects of the physical body, too, and in this case it's with the spine. As strange as it may sound, the appearance of the nose is considered to be a direct reflection of the condition of the back. I've found that some people with scoliosis have noses that curve in the same pattern as their spines. When I read faces with noses that have bends or curves, it's not uncommon to discover that these people also have chronic back pain or had an injury in this area in the past. I've had several clients who had polio as children that resulted in weakness in their spines, and their noses all had deep markings on them.

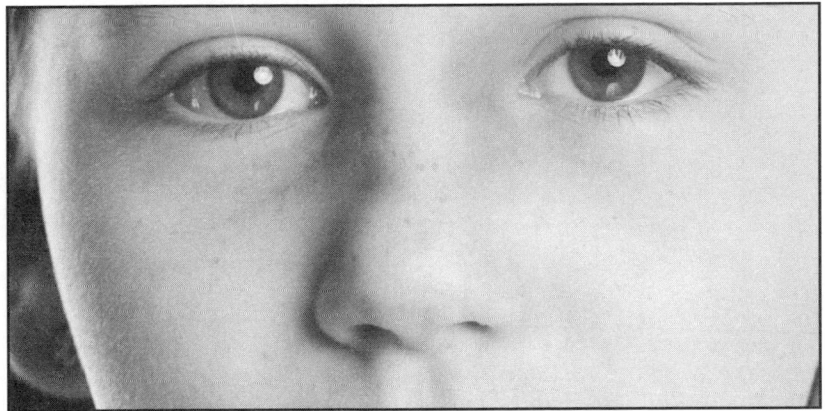

Fig. 81: A crooked nose can reflect the condition of the spine.

The bridge of the nose reflects the condition of the neck and upper back, the middle of the nose relates to the middle of the back, and the lower part of the nose shows the status of the lower back. Issues with the bone of the nose can mean problems in the spine, and anything irregular about the fleshy part pertains to the muscles in the back. Please note that if your child has an irregular nose, this does *not* guarantee that he'll have back problems. Any sign on the face can have to do with physical or emotional issues or even a certain time in life, as we'll discover in Chapter 16.

Even nostrils reveal information about your little ones' personalities! Just as the bridge of the nose shows us how energy and money come into someone's life, the nostrils show how they go out. Large ones indicate a person who will spend these things easily—for instance, devoting her time and efforts to friends without a second thought and possibly loaning them some cash as well. She'll also love to shop, since these nostrils show the ability to spend easily!

Fig. 82: Large nostrils indicate an easy outflow of money and energy.

Small nostrils signify the opposite—that is, kids who will be careful about how they spend and may be reluctant about giving away their resources. Long and narrow nostrils (rather than rounded) reflect a similar style but with the additional information that they're bargain hunters who want some return on their investment if they donate their time or funds.

Only one type of nostrils is really a cause for any concern. If you look at your child's face straight on at eye level and you can see directly into his nostrils, this is an indication that he may let energy flow out too freely. This reveals that money will immediately be spent, or he could be an easy target for any friend who wants a loan. These kids might not plan well before tackling a

Fig. 83: Small nostrils reveal more care with money and energy.

project, and could find that they're having to give far more than they anticipated. There's just too much potential for life force to leave their systems. However, I find that the impact of large nostrils is often modified by other aspects of the face. For instance, if the bridge of the nose is broad, this means that the supply of energy flowing in is strong and will balance what's going out. Or, if these children have large earlobes—which indicate excellent long-term planning—despite their nostrils, they'll always think ahead and have enough in reserve. So if you see these nostrils, don't leap to conclusions; wait to see what other information you discover in the rest of their features.

Upper Cheeks

The lower cheeks reflect the quantity and quality of your children's Earth characteristics, but the upper cheeks (the area of the cheek over the actual bones) have to do with Metal. Kids with prominent upper cheeks have a supply of Metal's ability to hold authority, the potential to speak up and give orders. If you're in power, you must be able to express your needs and tell others what you want them to do, and someone with strong upper cheeks is very capable of doing so.

If your child has this feature, you may find her readily bossing you around! These kids will have a hard time staying quiet about what they want or holding back from giving advice. As adults, this can serve them well, as they'll have what it takes to run a business or a household, taking charge and supervising as necessary. If there's some extra padding to those cheeks, it adds some Earth kindness, and others will be happy to follow their orders because they sense the caring energy behind them.

Fig. 84: Prominent upper cheeks reveal the ability to hold authority.

If your child has strong cheeks that are bony instead of padded, this still means the same power of authority, but with a lesser supply of tact. The Metal inclination to speak his mind, make demands, or criticize will be expressed in a manner that can at times be a bit too sharp for the recipient. But regardless of whether children's large cheeks are padded or bony, they still carry the sensitivity of the Metal nature. This will suggest that they're quite vocal at home where they feel safe, but more shy and quiet at school.

Flat cheeks have the opposite meaning: kids with this feature aren't interested in telling others what to do, and they don't like to be heavily supervised either. It's a weight on their shoulders if they're held responsible for a group's success, for instance, and they get uncomfortable if you hover over them as they do their homework.

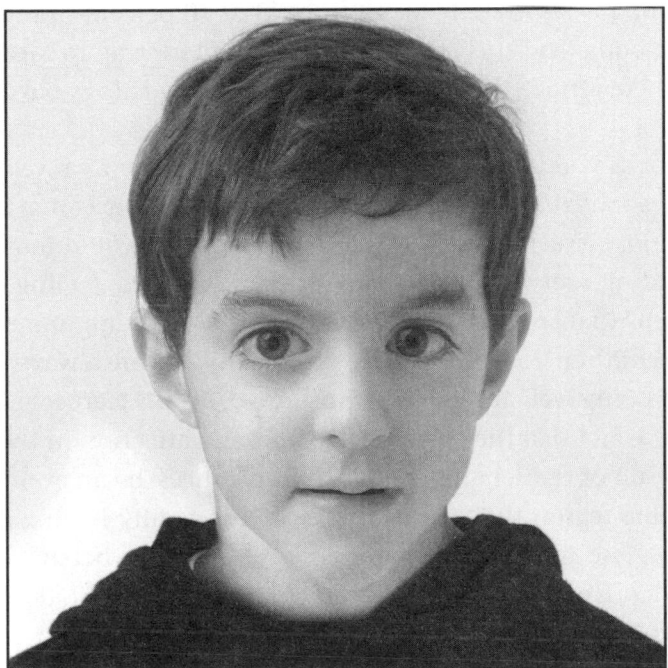

Fig. 85: Flat cheeks indicate a dislike of supervision or being responsible for others.

Rear Lower Cheeks

The cheek area directly on either side of the mouth has to do with Earth, but the part behind that area is associated with Metal. It's not common for this part of young people's faces to look sunken or concave, but if you see this, it might have to do with one particular aspect of this Element's nature: the tendency to breathe too shallowly. Because these sensitive spirits feel bombarded by all the energy around them, they can easily develop a constant underlying anxiety, which results in their not breathing deeply enough. It may be important to help your youngsters be aware of when this happens and how to correct it. Belly breathing is what most small children naturally do, so this will be familiar to them.

One fun exercise is to have them lie down while you put a lightweight toy on their stomach to assist them in breathing deeply in and out, making the toy go up and down. It's said that breathing is responsible for getting rid of 70 percent of the toxins in the body, and this may be especially interesting to Metal kids, as they're attracted to the concept of clearing things out and letting go.

But as you know, a sign on the face can not only reveal something about the function of the physical body; it can also show emotional issues. Rear cheeks that are indented could indicate an overriding sense of lack in some way, such as the feeling of "not enough" that Metal people often struggle with. It might mean that these children don't believe they're worthy and are always worried about doing well at school, for instance. Or this feature might reflect the fact that they feel a lack of enough affection in their lives as a result of challenging family circumstances. It can even be that for some reason they're uneasy about the family having enough money, and in this case, you might even observe behavior where they deprive themselves. For example, they may try to do without new things so that they'll be less of a financial burden or worry that the groceries you're buying are too expensive.

It's rare for these cheeks and issues to show up in childhood. If you do observe them, you could have a very Metal child on your hands, and it would be wise to pay attention to how he may exhibit patterns of lack in his life. Sunken rear cheeks are an extreme way for this tendency to reveal itself in the face, but a more common sign is the development of "lack lines," which are vertical wrinkles that develop in the rear lower cheeks. These lines can show up temporarily, signifying a stressed system. It would only be if lack lines start to carve themselves into your children's cheeks that you'd need to look for deeper issues to heal.

Fig. 86: Vertical lines in the lower cheeks can reveal an inherent sense of scarcity.

Fa Lin Lines

Most children don't have wrinkles, of course, but there are some that you may notice your little ones developing at a relatively early age: the nasolabial folds that extend from the sides of the nose down toward the corners of the mouth. In Chinese face reading, these are called Fa Lin lines, and they're literally translated into English as "orders of law." When these characteristics appear on a child's face, it means that he's on the right path: he's living according to his own inner laws and being true to himself. These wrinkles are also sometimes called "purpose lines," meaning that those who have them are at least on their way to fulfilling their purpose in the world.

Having Fa Lin lines doesn't mean a person has life all figured out or has no more to learn. But when they emerge on children's faces, it's a sign that they've already begun to discover their path.

Fig. 87: The nasolabial folds are called "purpose lines."

I've often seen these lines on kids who have special talents that they're already successful at, such as actors or musicians. If you notice them on your youngsters' faces, this isn't a sign of early aging, as some parents might assume. Instead, it's an indication that they've already discovered at least one of their special gifts.

Space Between Features

Metal has to do with spaciousness, and this can be reflected in the face by wide spaces between features. Aside from this suggesting that your child has Metal in her personality, specific meanings can be found in a few places as well. The two main areas I look at are above the eyes. If your little one's eyebrows are placed high above her eyes, she has what I call "Queen's Eyebrows." For one thing, this is a sign of someone with

Fig. 88: High eyebrows are called "Queen's Eyebrows."

strong principles and high expectations. Like the queen, she prefers things to be done just so, and she'll voice her concerns if her decrees aren't carried out as ordered!

These are also the mark of highly sensitive children who can be affected by other people's energy so much that they take a while to warm up to new acquaintances. Therefore, they may hold back at first from joining a new group of friends and probably won't like to be touched by those they don't know well. For instance, having to hug Aunt Deborah, whom they've never met before and smells funny, will be difficult. Kids like this can be judged as unfriendly or aloof and can have a harder time being accepted by their peers. High eyebrows actually cause other people to feel a bit intimidated by this royal energy and afraid they're going to offend those who have them.

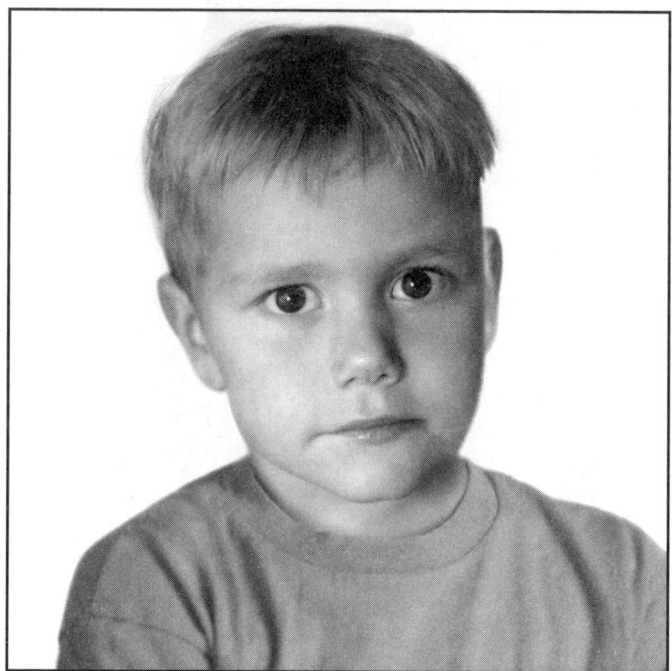

Fig. 89: Low eyebrows are the mark of an approachable nature.

The opposite kind of eyebrow placement is where they're very close to the eyes, hiding almost any view of the upper eyelid. Children with this feature will be very approachable and not at all flustered about having new people in their lives. These eyebrows also show those who won't hold back within a relationship. One term for this feature is "Coach's Eyebrows," indicative of the energy of sports coaches who get so caught up in how their teams do that they fall apart upon losing. Kids with this characteristic will keep their promises to friends and not give up if the going gets tough, but they may become overinvolved in others' lives.

The second area to pay attention to in terms of spaces between features is the upper eyelid. If you look at your child straight on, not standing above or below him, and you can see a large amount of his upper eyelid, this is a sign of Metal in his nature. This aspect is sometimes called "hooded eyes," and kids with it will be more likely to struggle with grief and suffering if they experience a loss.

Fig. 90: Hooded upper eyelids show difficulty with the grieving process and letting go.

For example, if the family pet dies, these youngsters may mourn more deeply or be unable to accept a new one. Under emotional distress, they'll have a tendency to lose sleep, not want to eat, or contract into themselves, instead of reaching out for comfort.

Environments for the Metal Nature

The less visual clutter in a Metal person's space, the better, so providing closed storage for your Metal children's things is a good idea. While elegant minimalism is an important concept, what is most essential is that these children are given control over their environments. Let them have a voice in every detail of their surroundings, if at all possible. They'll be the only ones who know how something *feels,* so you won't be able to decide what will work best for them. They'll be most affected by the placement of the furniture—believe them when they say that the bed has to be moved two inches to the left! The colors and textures for Metal are white; gray; pale pastels; actual metallics, such as gold and silver; anything that has a sheen to it, as in pearlescent paints; and silks or satin fabrics.

These kids love to be up high and see far into the distance, so a bedroom on an upper floor is great. The larger the windows, the better; and the more expansive the view, the happier they'll be. And a ceiling painted with a scene of clouds and blue sky will give them a wonderful sense of spaciousness.

Metal children are the most prone to developing allergies or environmental sensitivities. If they're having these problems, watch for fumes from things like paint, varnish, or carpets, even if they're not new. Be especially careful about anything that touch- es their skin—for example, soap, shampoo, and the fabrics they wear—and research natural bedding products for them. Remem- ber that these kids are also very sensitive to subtle energies, so be mindful of that aspect of their surroundings. One girl I met had trouble sleeping until her parents removed all their financial re- cords from under her bed!

Thoughts for the Teacher

These children are often very self-conscious. They can be such perfectionists that any mistake can be devastating for them, especially if it's pointed out publicly. Give them as much praise as you possibly can, but it's got to be genuine and not just for the sake of it, because they'll see through that in an instant. Metal kids love to be acknowledged by an authority figure, so your words will have a deep effect.

Any opportunity you can find to get them to lighten up and be silly will melt their anxiety and help them not take things too seriously, but don't try to force them out of their comfort zones. The more control they feel they have, the more relaxed they'll be. These kids need to feel safe, and it will be upsetting if you push them into a new situation prematurely. One way to circumvent this is to rehearse anything new that they're going to attempt so they'll know what to expect every step of the way and won't feel as anxious.

Metal children need clear procedures and guidelines at school. For instance, any ambiguity about homework deadlines or boundaries of behavior in class will be disconcerting. A consistent rhythm in the daily routine is important; if there's a sudden change to the structure, this can be unnerving unless there is plenty of explanation about details. Finally, the thin skin of this Element means these little ones can soak in the upsets of other children, even to the point of their taking on the symptoms of those who are ill. They can be judged as hypersensitive, or even hypochondriacs, but unlike some kids who respond to stress emotionally, they take it on physically.

Helping Your Metal Child Flourish

Metal children are highly aware little spirits who experience life on a different level of consciousness than most. They'll sense more of the energy of any environment or person and can be quite impacted by the sensations this produces in their bodies. Part of their lifelong challenge may well be to learn to manage all that they sense, to feel it and still stay in balance. Not knowing how to deal with this can cause them to become hypervigilant and create an ongoing undercurrent of anxiety. Your job as you raise them is to acknowledge, allow, and even trust their sensitivity. It's not what's wrong with them; in fact, it's their greatest strength. But at first they may often experience the downside of taking in so much from their surroundings, and their task in life is to learn how to handle feeling so much. First of all, it will be so empowering for them if you validate their awareness rather than treat them as if there's something wrong with them. Just the fact that you listen and believe will do wonders.

Creating a game that involves verbalizing all the impressions they're receiving will help their talents bloom and develop their ability to manage the cacophony of information coming from the world around them. This can be as simple as focusing on their five senses. For example, tell them to close their eyes while you put a piece of dried fruit in their mouths and let them describe all the sensations of that experience, or have them stroke the textures of different fabrics and talk about how each feels on their skin. You can even expand this game into playing with the idea of merging their senses—for instance, pretend colors have sounds or tastes by having them sing what kind of sound blue would make or decide what flavor red is.

The next level of this game would be to become aware of how they feel when they're standing next to different people, or what the energy of their brother's bedroom feels like compared to that of the den. These exercises will really empower their systems to take charge of their sensitivity rather than be so overwhelmed. Don't underestimate the transformative power of helping them realize that not everything they feel is *theirs*.

Many parents of Metal children are judged as being over-protective. Try to resist letting this misunderstanding affect you. You know your children and that they may need more help in preparing to do something for the first time or being protected from too much intensity. Understand that this isn't because they're fragile and that you're not being overbearing by responding to their unique needs. Of course, this is hard to explain to others, and you may feel embarrassed by their judgments. But don't pressure your little ones to do things too far outside of their comfort zone without your support. That can mean rehearsing for a new experience or having a secret code word they can use to alert you of their need to leave *now*. Discuss solutions to the worst-case scenario for any situation so they'll feel equipped and capable as they go out for that new adventure. Respect their need to know the plan if something were to happen, and provide a predictable rhythm in their lives in every way you can.

Make sure to praise them on a regular basis—find something they've done to applaud as a high-quality job . . . but your words must be genuine and specific. Don't just give it generally, for if there's any forced enthusiasm, they'll notice. Continue to give them compliments even if they seem to be shrugging them off, because every comment you make will work its magic over time.

Last, know that one of the most valuable things you can do for Metal children is to teach them not to take everything too personally or seriously. The way to do so is with laughter and lightness of spirit. Bringing play, humor, and silliness into their lives will melt Metal's contracting nature and allow them to relax and feel comfortable being their authentic selves.

◦ ◦ ◦

"Faces are as legible as books, only they are read in much less time, and are much less likely to deceive us."

— JOHANN KASPAR LAVATER

TWO FACES, THREE FACES

Chapter 15

The Two Sides

There's even more information waiting for you on each *side* of your child's face. The right and left sides provide you with different insights into the messages your child shares with the outside world, as well as the deeper aspects of his or her inner terrain. The right side is called the "public" side and is said to reveal those parts of someone's personality he's allowing others to see. This area is controlled by the left brain, the half that deals with logic and linear thinking.

The left side is the "private" side and is governed by the right half of the brain, which is the home of the emotions. This part of the face is where the deepest feelings manifest, and where you'll see clues to the more intimate parts of a person's character. For instance, someone's left eye may be more open than the right, or her smile may be stronger on one side. All these details offer new information for you to use along with the rest of the facial features.

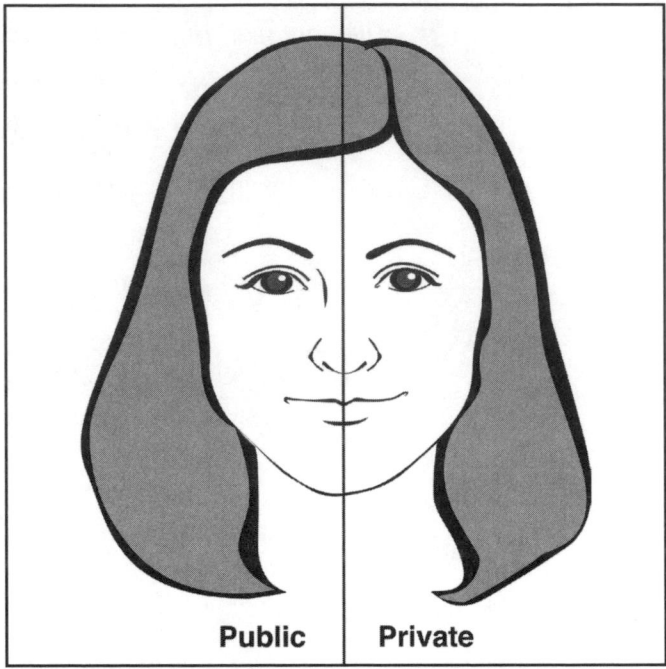

Public   **Private**

Fig. 91: The right side of a face is the "public" side and the left is the "private" side. This is true for both boys and girls.

A young mother in one of my workshops noticed a difference in her daughter's eyebrows. Her right eyebrow was rounded (suggesting a willingness to please others), but her left one was shaped more like an upside-down V (indicating a tendency to react quickly and emotionally). The woman realized this and confirmed what she'd observed about this girl: she interacted with others in an easygoing way and went along with jokes even when teased, but privately it was a different story. Once this little girl was alone with her mother, she showed her inner feelings and sobbed, so hurt by her friends' behavior. Her public eyebrow showed a desire to please, but her private one revealed her more strongly reactive emotions.

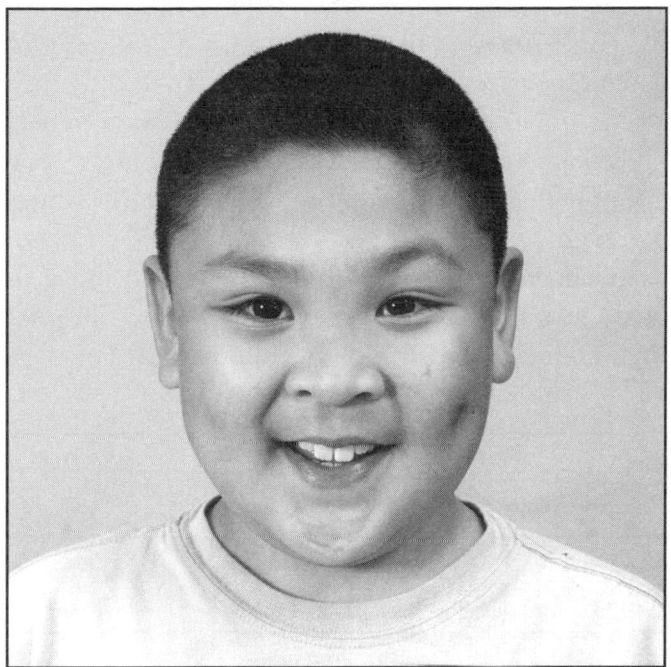

Fig. 92: The two sides of this child's face give us different information based on the size and shape of the features.

Even Western science has found that the left side of a person's face is more expressive than the right, since it's where more of his or her emotions are revealed. Studies have also confirmed that most of us tend to look at the right side of another person's face when we speak to them, which means we're viewing the public side and not seeing the private nature.

The Three Zones

Children's faces can also be viewed in three horizontal zones: the "Analytical Zone," the "Practical Zone," and the "Intuitive Zone." These zones reveal how they tend to think and how they make decisions, and what they need in order to feel comfortable in their thought processes. What you discern from reading this aspect can give you clues to their best learning styles, ways to help them in the classroom, and how their decision-making processes work.

Please note that in very young children, the face is much more wide than high, and the nose and jaw are not yet developed. Don't rely too much on these zones until kids start to move through elementary school and you begin to see what information is emerging in terms of which zones seem especially large or small.

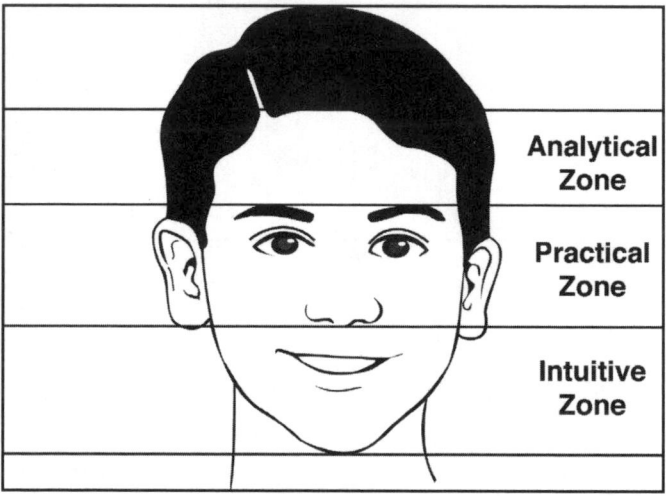

Fig. 93: The Three Horizontal Zones offer insights to a person's decision-making process and are read the same for both girls' and boys' faces.

The Analytical Zone begins at the hairline and extends down to the eyebrows, the Practical Zone goes from the eyebrows to the bottom of the nose, and the Intuitive Zone is found from right under the nose to the bottom of the chin. To understand what these areas are telling you, simply observe if one has a significant size difference compared with the others. Many children (and adults) have zones that are very similar proportionally without one in particular being remarkable. If this is the case, these individuals will have the ability to use all of the qualities each area reflects pretty equally. However, if one zone is considerably larger than the others, this represents a dominant way of thinking and making decisions. If one area is small, its method isn't an important part of how someone's mind works. Knowing this will help you understand where your children's strengths lie, and you'll be aware that you should support those attributes rather than trying to force your little ones to fit into a mold that doesn't match who they are.

If your child's Analytical Zone is the largest, he'll need time to think through decisions in order to feel certain about them. Unless there are other details on the face to modify the characteristics of this trait, these kids are less likely to be spontaneous or impulsive in their choices; instead, they'll want to evaluate things carefully and thoroughly. In their studies, they'll be more analytical and enjoy researching all the little details of any problem or homework project. You may find that they're excellent students because they'll tend to study hard and put a lot of time into their work. But it won't be comfortable for them if they're pressured to act without enough information. Kids with strong Analytical Zones rely on their minds so much that they may overdo it and get too wound up thinking about all possible options, details, and consequences; and not be able to move forward with a decision.

Children with dominant Practical Zones are often those who do well with a hands-on style of learning—by actually doing what they're trying to learn. If their foreheads are very short as well, this enhances the need for on-the-job training. Their decision-making process focuses on what's most practical and efficient and what makes the most sense. While kids with high foreheads will presumably possess the tendency to overthink, these youngsters consider it a waste of valuable time to analyze things to death. They may place too much emphasis on taking action, however, and, therefore, may not consider other people's feelings or the finer nuances of a situation.

If the Intuitive Zone is your child's strongest, she will make decisions based on gut instincts and not have as much faith in analysis or practicality. These kids may act before thinking things through completely, but their sixth sense is often correct, so their choices turn out to be right after all. Families or teachers may judge these children as being too impulsive without realizing that they're trusting that inner voice, which might give them the answer before someone has even finished the question! This method suggests that they won't be poring over books, but will still grasp the information all the same. On the other hand, kids with a dominant Intuitive Zone can let their emotions influence their decisions too often, preventing them from easily fitting into the usual classroom structure that values linear thinking. If parents see this happening, they may need to act as advocates for this more unusual style and help the teacher understand that their child may require a slightly different approach.

It can be interesting to watch how these zones show up as your little ones maneuver through their days! One couple who'd been to my workshops e-mailed me with a story about a trip to the mall. Once a month, Sunday afternoon was set up as a treat for their children, where they could choose how the family would spend the day. Sometimes it was a trip to the zoo or a hiking excursion, but this time the kids chose a large shopping mall that had a theme park. In preparation for the big event, the father told me, "Our Practical son found local coupons for free rides and two-for-one sodas; our Analytical daughter researched the mall on the Internet, printed out a map of all the stores, and made a list of which ones she wanted to visit and in what priority; and our Intuitive son made absolutely no preparations and just ran to the first play area he spotted. And everybody had a wonderful time!"

These happy parents saw their kids' distinctly different styles and honored them, rather than trying to make them function *their* way. If one of your child's zones is larger than the others, recognize that this is where her strengths lie and support that. If one area is weak, know that this just isn't so much a part of her world, and let that be okay.

• • •

Far more important than dividing the face vertically or horizontally is what can be read about a child's entire life journey. Next you'll see how you can help your son or daughter navigate through life by going with the flow rather than fighting the current.

⊙ ⊙ ⊙

Part III

THE JOURNEY

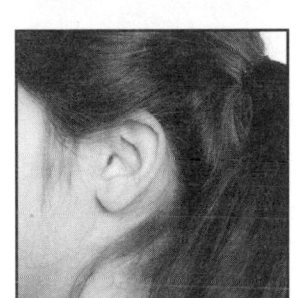

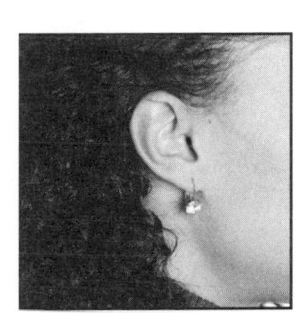
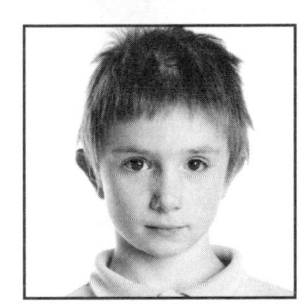
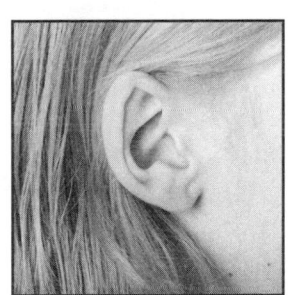

"The great thing about getting
older is that you don't lose all the
other ages you've been."

— MADELEINE L'ENGLE

Chapter
16

THE MAP OF
YOUR CHILD'S
JOURNEY

Every year of your child's life is represented by a point some-where on her face, just like a map of where she's been and where she's going. Each major feature represents approximately one decade, so you can even scan the general course that's being charted overall.

But here's where we need to have a heart-to-heart talk. I'm a mother. I know that your love for your child rings in every cell of your body, and just the thought of any difficulty for him or her is almost unbearable. We're wired by nature to protect our little ones, to turn into mother (and father) bears if we ever see anything we think might be threatening them. It's probably been hard at times to read this book and see that there are aspects of your child's nature that will likely cause challenges. We realize logically that every human life includes difficult times and painful experiences, and that because of these we grow and evolve. But in our bones we never want our children to endure any hardships. So the prospect of seeing a map of your little one's entire life may make you fearful . . . but that's obviously *not* the purpose of this chapter!

Some periods in any life will be positive and others will have difficulties, but we all deal with issues that cause us to struggle and grow, and that's natural. At other times, life feels golden, usually as a result of all the hard work we did during the arduous stages. The quality of each phase can be read on the face, but this does *not* guarantee that bad things will happen to your child during a challenging phase, nor that a powerful time will be completely joyous. As parents, one thing we must acknowledge is that our little ones will have to walk their own paths as adults, and our job while they're with us is to prepare them for whatever comes their way.

If your daughter's face indicates that her 20s will be especially demanding, for example, this might mean that she'll experience marriage and kids of her own along with a new job—all of which, although stressful and challenging, are normal parts of life. If her face also reveals that her 50s will be positive, this may suggest an era of transformation to happier times but still may include a lot of personal work to get her to this new level.

It's also essential to recognize that one of the universal principles of life is that everything changes, and that includes your child's life circumstances and self-development. Chinese face reading considers the face to be a reflection of who someone is inside at this moment in time. As he evolves, so does his face.

Of course, your children will mature as they grow physically, but aside from that, their features will develop as the inner selves do. So what you see now that's predicting a certain challenge may fade or even disappear based on what happens in their lives between now and that stage in the future.

All this may sound hard to believe, as a face is flesh, bone, and cartilage. Logically, it seems that it would only shift due to physical developments and aging, but *everything* is energy that responds to its environment. I've seen astonishing changes in people's faces, sometimes within very short periods of time as a result of important transformations in their inner or outer progress.

Children's faces don't reveal their destiny, so to speak, since that's constantly changing according to the choices they make, the experiences they have, and their responses to them. What's revealed is their potential at this point in time based on their journey up till now. There's a wonderful quote that's attributed to the Buddha that embodies this idea: "What you are now is what you have been. What you will be is what you do now." So who we are is everything we've experienced up to this point—a culmination of all the choices that we've made and the emotions we've felt; and in every moment there is the possibility of an entirely different future.

So with this understanding in mind, let's take a look at your child's map, starting out with the big picture and then homing in on the details.

Rivers and Mountains

The Chinese believe that we go through yin and yang periods in our lives. A yin time is one of looking inward and dealing with emotional issues and personal growth. A yang time is more outward directed, and it's about being active in the external world and not undergoing as much inner development. The yin periods are called "Rivers" and the yang ones are "Mountains," and each is said to last about ten years.

These eras correspond to major features on the face. The Rivers are the soft areas that tend to have some moisture: the ears, hairline, eyes, and mouth. The Mountains are those bony, protruding features: the forehead, nose, chin, and jaw. Let's start by getting a general overview of your child's terrain—his or her personal Rivers and Mountains.

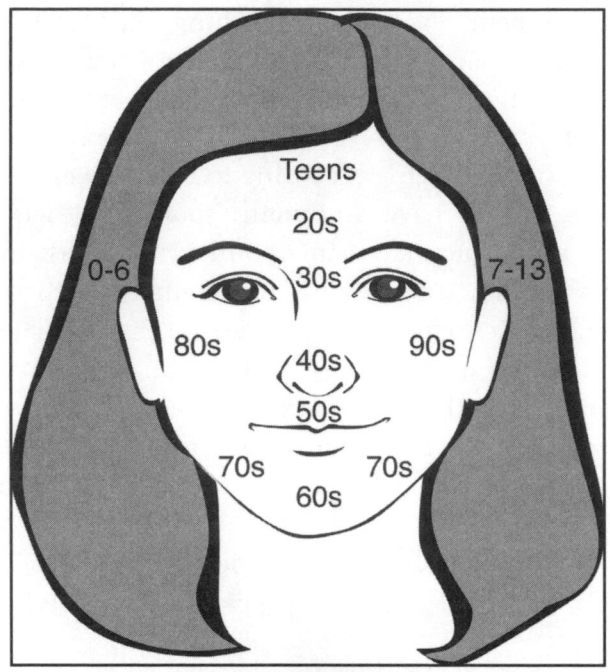

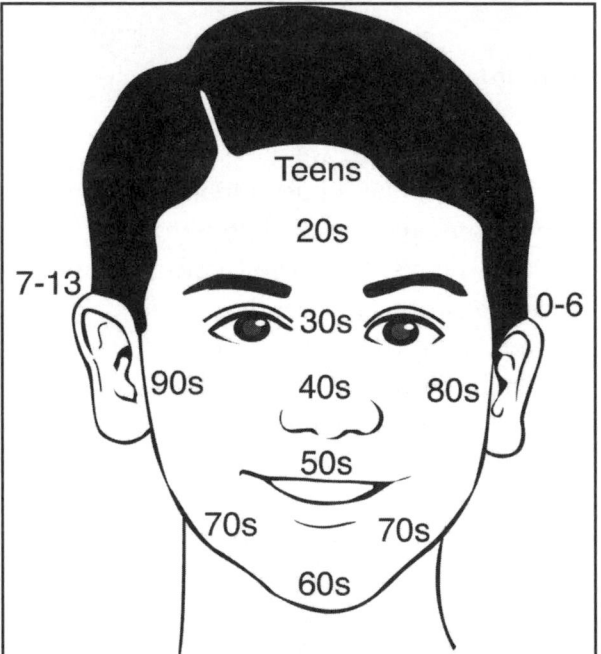

Figures 94 and 95: Each decade corresponds to one feature of the face.

Ears = Childhood

You begin to read people's life stories by looking at their ears, where conception, birth, and life experiences through age 13 are revealed. For a girl, begin with her right ear, which shows her history from the very beginning through age 6, and then turn to her left ear to see ages 7 through 13. For a boy, it's the opposite: look at his left ear first to discover events that happened from inception through age 6, and the right ear is associated with ages 7 through 13.

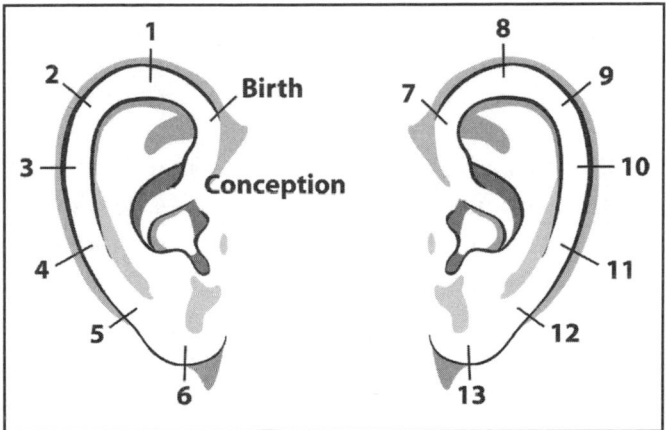

Fig. 96: For girls, the right ear maps life experiences from conception through age 6, and the left ear reveals anything that happens from ages 7 through 13.

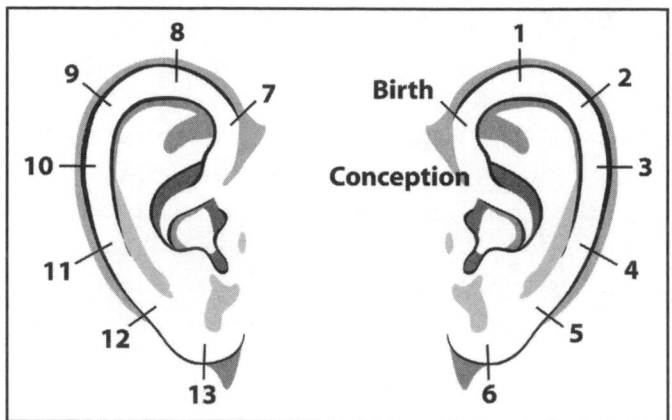

Fig. 97: For boys, begin with the left ear to identify life experiences from conception through age 6, then examine the right ear to read events that occurred from 7 to 13.

In reading this aspect of the ears, look mainly at the rim, or "helix," of the ear to note anything unusual. As we'll soon discuss in detail, any marking that's out of the ordinary, like a thin area on the rim, indicates a time when there may be some stress in your child's life. Of course, this will be the recent past, the present, or the near future, so you may be fearful about discovering anything that indicates a challenging time for your little one. Let me hasten to assure you that any sign on a child's ears suggesting stress can mean a very minor event—such as the birth of a sibling or starting school for the first time—and not some trauma or tragedy.

Childhood is when we've just landed on this planet and are beginning to figure out what's going on. We are innocent and vulnerable and don't have the emotional maturity to cope with what might not cause as much stress a few years later. What could look like a minor challenge may be genuinely difficult for a child, even though it can be a perfectly natural stage of life.

Most important, it's not so much what happens to you, it's how you *feel* about it. For one child, if the family dog runs away and they get a new one, that's okay. But another youngster will remember and mourn the loss of that dog for a long time to come.

In the latter case, it's possible that the rim of the ear would show a mark from that stressful situation. It's only if you see an area of the ear that's mangled or deformed that you'd understand it to be a time of more serious stress.

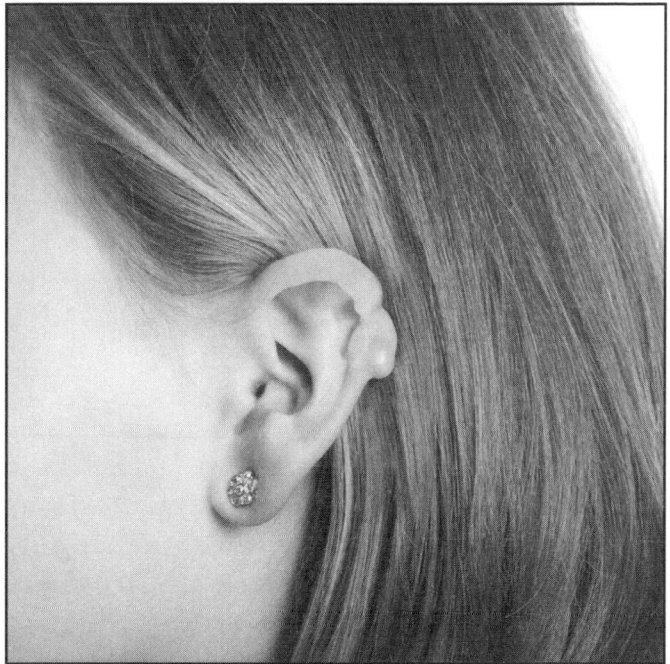

Fig. 98: This marking shows severe stress occurring around the age of ten.

As you begin to read your child's ears, first look at the right for a girl and the left for a boy, and begin at the top of the ear where it attaches to the side of the head. This relates to the time period of conception through birth. It's now known that the experiences in utero do matter; a mother's stress, whether emotional or physical, can be transmitted through the placenta into the bloodstream of the fetus.

To determine if there was an influence between the time in the womb until birth, feel the region right before your child's ear separates from the side of the head. Nothing may be visible, but when you touch this part, you may feel a dent, hole, or bump. This often has more to do with the mother's stress than the baby's. For instance, when I find a marking here, I might hear a story from parents about a major move to a new city during the pregnancy.

Birth is at the exact spot where the top of the ear departs from the head. Again, anything unusual here such as a bump or indentation shows that something happened at birth or soon after. If you feel something in this spot, it doesn't mean your child suffered a trauma. Anything out of the ordinary that happened to either baby or mother could have made this a difficult time, because they are still so closely connected in this period that Mom's stress is also the infant's stress. A mark here could also be a reflection of health problems that occurred immediately after birth; for example, maybe the newborn had to spend a few days in an incubator before going home.

If you know for a fact that there were significant difficulties during pregnancy or at birth, yet you don't find any marking at this point on the ear, don't be puzzled. You'll only find something if the experience is still impacting your child's life. If it's no longer a significant influence, you'll find no sign of it. Any information on someone's face can indicate a stressful experience that's still reverberating through his life, *or* it might be pointing out a powerful lesson that was important in making him who he is.

To explore the rest of childhood, look for any changes along the rim of the ear. As you'll see in the map of the ears, each year correlates with approximately a half inch along the edge of this feature. Most ears have a normal rim extending the full perimeter down to where the lobe begins to form. If you observe an area where it becomes thin, for instance, look on the map to see what age it corresponds to. An especially narrow edge is said to indicate a time when the child felt like support was taken away, a time of less safety or stability. A common reason for this mark is a sibling being born, resulting in this child suddenly no longer being the center of attention in the family, or a beloved grandparent dying and causing a sense of loss. You can't determine exactly *what* the stressor is by seeing the mark, only that it happened or will happen.

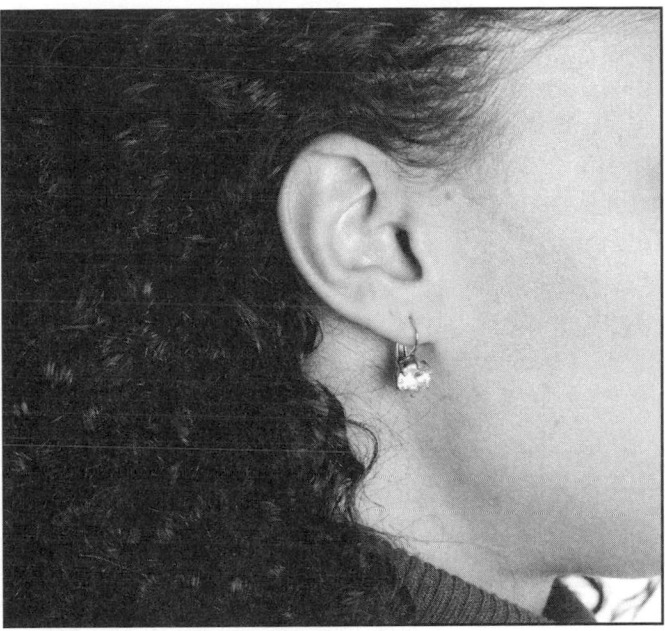

Fig. 99: This ear rim thins out at around age two, marking a time when safety and support were missing.

The amount of time that the difficult situation lasts is revealed by the length of the thinned area. If it extends half an inch, then the event lasted a year or less (please note that measurements are approximate). In addition, sometimes the mark shows up a year or so after the episode actually occurred. For example, you know that your child went through a stressful period at age three, but there's no indication of that until age four. This is usually because the specific stage didn't have as strong of an effect as the changes it caused in the following months or years. One boy's sister was born when he was eight, but evidence of this appeared on his ear in the area representing age nine. In his case, it wasn't until some months after her birth that he started experiencing its impact.

Occasionally, the ear will be marked at a time in *advance* of the actual event that's identified as the stressful time. For example, one couple divorced when their daughter was 11, but a portion of the little girl's ear rim suddenly thinned out when she was 10. During the year leading up to the actual separation, the level of anger and discomfort in the house was high. As many kids are, she was probably highly perceptive and, of course, this affected her deeply.

If the entire rim is unusually thin, this whole phase of childhood was one in which there was a sense of little support. I sometimes see these ears on a child who grew up in poverty, lived in a tumultuous household where parents constantly fought, or had to stay home alone a lot because they were raised by a single parent

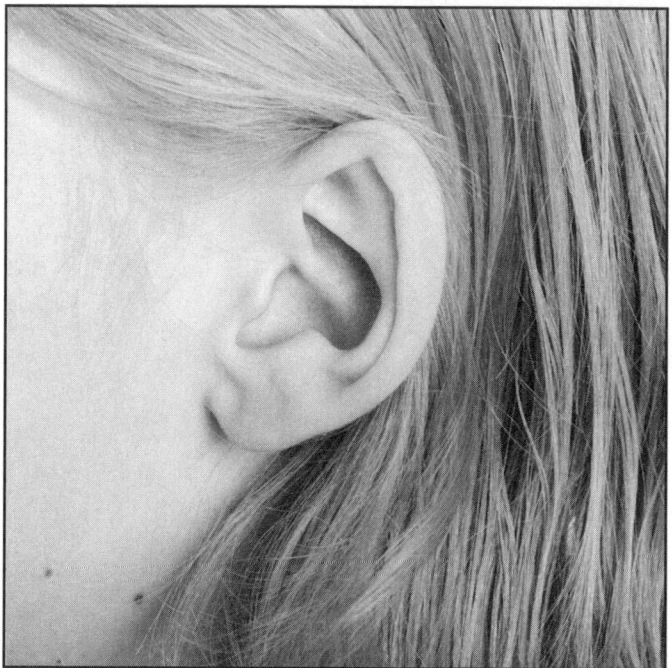

Fig. 100: This boy's ear reflects one single stressful event around age one followed by a time of suppression.

who had to work two jobs. There can be one or several different causes, but the result is the same.

A notch in the helix of the ear is a sign of a one-time occurrence that happened in the year indicated on the map. This may suggest that there was an illness or injury at that point or just a single event that happened suddenly and then was over.

On some ears, a portion of the rim will be pressed down, almost as if it's been ironed flat. You can observe this mark in the previous photo (Figure 100) and see that the rim becomes flattened right after the notch. This indicates a period of suppression during the years this area corresponds with, and, for instance, could suggest that this person grew up in a household with very strict rules. I've seen this marking in the extreme on ears of adults who grew up in religious fundamentalist households and fled at an early age due to parental oppression. No matter what the cause, the result is that the spirit is suppressed, which isn't a good thing.

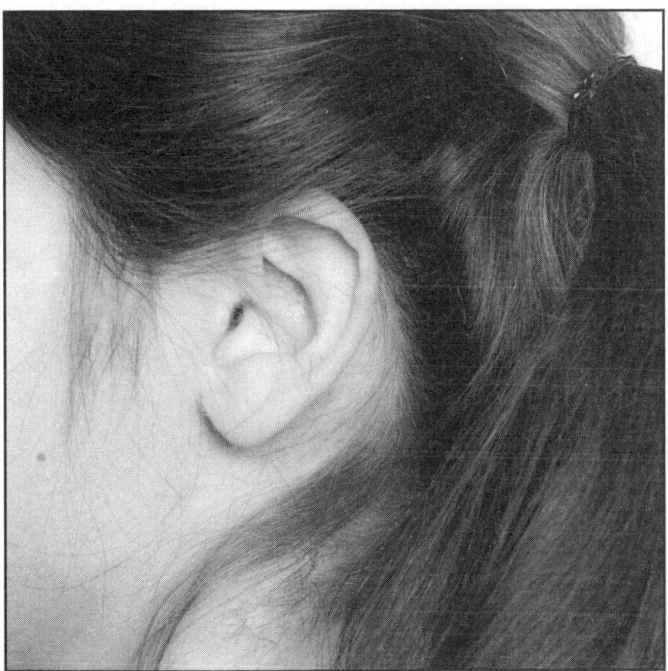

Fig. 101: A bumpy area on the rim is a sign of ups and downs.

If you see this on your child's ears at an age he's already passed, it can be useful to look back and think about what was going on at that time. Identifying the stressor can help you understand him better and see how his past experiences are affecting the choices he's making now.

A bumpy area on the rim of the ear is a sign of ups and downs at that time in life. However, if there's one large bump or an area where the rim gets thicker, this is actually considered to have a positive meaning. Chinese face reading teaches that anything sticking out on the face is a beneficial sign. But this kind of bump on the ear may also indicate that the actual event wasn't all that easy despite its positive impact in the long run. A teenager in one of my workshops had a thick section of her ear corresponding to the years from age 9 to 11. This was right after her little brother was born with Down syndrome, and she felt it genuinely represented both the struggle and the powerful life skills she acquired at this early age.

If you see a dark freckle or flat mole, it means that something significant happened at the age indicated on the ear map. If your child has a natural hole anywhere in the ear (aside from the normal design!), this is said to be the mark of a healer. If the hole is on or near a point on the rim, it also represents major stress at that age.

A mark on the ear can predict an experience, or it can appear after an event has passed to signify its importance. For example, when my son was five, his father and I divorced. We did everything we could to make it as easy for him as possible, but of course, this is completely life changing and difficult for any child. One day when he was nine, I was giving him a haircut. I was always very careful when I did this, but for some bizarre reason, my attention wavered or my hand shook for a split second and I nicked his ear. I was horrified! Fortunately, it was only a tiny cut, but it did leave a small brown mark on his ear—at the point that shows as age five on the map. So there was the sign, an imprint of the year his life changed.

You can imagine how guilty I felt each time I looked at that tiny spot, so you'll understand how relieved I was to notice that it had completely disappeared by the time he was 12. He'd grown emotionally and worked through many of the issues stemming from that experience, and it showed by the change to his ear.

Any indentation, scar, wrinkle, spot, or discoloration on the ear rim is indicative of some type of stress. But what matter most are the more prominent, noticeable marks. Don't worry about feeling the rim trying to find a microscopic dip or bump; just look at what is visible and attracts your immediate attention. I place the most importance on markings I see up to age three, as our earliest experiences often set up our expectations and belief systems that reverberate through the rest of our lives.

If you do see a spot on your child's ear that shows some future stress, this may frighten you, or make you think that something bad will happen. Above all, remember that a mark is probably only indicative of a normal life challenge, not a dramatic event. Also keep in mind that all children encounter difficulties as they grow; it's a part of life. Wouldn't you rather know about something before it happens so you can be sure to prepare for it and be there to support your child through it?

One mother noted that the rim of her eight-year-old son's ear thinned out at the age-ten area and remained that way for about half an inch, indicating stress that could last from a few months to about a year. Instead of viewing this as a dark cloud lurking over their heads, she decided to look at it just like any other challenging stage in her son's life. When her little boy was ten, she got a new job that required a lot of travel. This mother tried the position for six months before realizing that it affected her son and family too much. She e-mailed me to say that the deciding factor was knowing the meaning of that marking on her son's ear, and that it confirmed what she already felt intuitively: that the demands of this job didn't match the level of obligation she had to her son.

Hairline = Adolescence

Life experience during adolescence, age 14 through 17, is reflected in the hairline. Although your children certainly aren't as mature as they'll be in adulthood, they do have a better capacity for dealing with life stress at this age. Therefore, difficulties now don't mark here in the same way they did on the ears.

There are two basic kinds of hairlines you'll tend to see that indicate your child is facing enough stress to merit your attention. The first is an uneven hairline (the hair grows in an irregular line across the forehead) that represents a challenging adolescence, as so many are! This can mean the usual emotional difficulties that most of us go through during this phase, or it can reveal tougher problems—the more uneven the hairline, the greater the troubles. If your child's hairline has an extremely up-and-down shape, this is valuable information, and it's important for you to be there as a support at this time.

Another type of hairline to pay attention to in regard to adolescence is the opposite of an uneven one. If you see a hairline that's nearly a perfect oval shape—possibly with very fine hairs along the border—this is said to be the sign of a heavy "Mother's influence," as discussed in Chapter 6. If you notice this on your child, look for ways to encourage her to break out on her own without worrying too much about pleasing anyone.

Forehead = Late Teens Through 20s

This feature reflects what life will bring as youngsters move toward adulthood and out into the world. The upper forehead shows the late teens, the middle of the forehead reveals the early through mid-20s, and the lower forehead represents the late 20s. This is the first Mountain time on the face, a yang era, when they start taking steps as independent adults. It's often when people first experience the consequences of their choices without the buffer of their parents' help. Most kids in their late teens are very sure of one thing: that they know all about life, and their mothers and fathers are idiots. So what generally happens is that they leave home and encounter quite a few surprises!

When you're surprised, you make a certain facial expression: your eyebrows raise and temporary horizontal wrinkles form on your forehead. When you repeat an expression, even subtly, the lines associated with it begin to carve into that area. So if your child's experiences in this decade are substantially challenging, these wrinkles can appear deeper on his forehead. In fact, the more prominent the creases, the more powerful the incidents. These aren't negative signs, and they represent what young adults have learned as a result of living on their own. The lines are formed as people experience their first real-life issues: a romantic relationship that doesn't work out, a challenging job, or the stress of starting a family. A horizontal crease across the top of the forehead represents a lesson at some point between ages 18 through 20, one across the middle of the forehead shows knowledge gained between the ages of 21 to 23, and one toward the lower part of the forehead is from an experience from 24 to 26 years of age. The deeper the line, the more powerful the lesson learned.

A horizontal wrinkle might develop that extends completely across the forehead without breaks, or one that starts on one side, disappears, and then reappears again on the other side of the forehead. An unbroken line reflects a lesson completed, and a fragmented one indicate that something wasn't resolved in the 20s and will be revisited later in life until the lesson has been fully integrated.

A line can be predictive, showing up in advance of this stage in life, or it may appear after the 20s to mark what lesson has been learned. If you see a horizontal wrinkle on your child's forehead in advance of her late teens, this can mean that she's setting herself up to learn a significant lesson during the age range it indicates. Because the crease is appearing so far ahead of the actual time, it can be helpful to try to establish what's coming so you can assist her in laying the groundwork for dealing with it later on when you may not be nearby.

Our lives don't consist of separate, unconnected stages; rather, they're more like an evolution of interrelated phases, one affecting the next. Therefore, you'll be able to predict aspects of your children's current struggles that may continue into their 20s. As you encourage them with their emotional and spiritual development now, you're having an impact on how they'll handle life in the future.

There's also an experiment you can try, with your youngster's agreement, to see if you can discover the core issue involved in an upcoming lesson . . . and it involves using adhesive tape! Have him put a piece of tape over the wrinkle he's curious about and leave it on for a few hours. Each time he notices the tape pull, it means he's making the expression that's forming the line. At that moment, he should stop and ask himself, *What am I thinking about? What am I feeling?* It may well be that he can discern a repeating pattern of thoughts and feelings that pertain to one particular aspect of his life. If so, he can begin to work on the lesson around this issue now. One 15-year-old boy discovered that each time he felt the tape pull, he was thinking about his stepfather. His mother recognized that this was related to the difficult relationship between her husband and her son, and the revelation resulted in the whole family going to counseling. A year later, the crease in his forehead had faded considerably. Again, it's not that wrinkles are a concern, but more that a line appearing so far in advance of a certain phase suggests that some issues already require attention.

Ages 27 to 29 are reflected in the area right at the eyebrows, and as a result, it's less common for a wrinkle here to extend all the way across the forehead. This is a powerful time of life, with the brow bone and eyebrows usually creating the strongest, most prominent part of the face up to this point. In addition, this area has to do with Wood Element's energy: the ability to think logically, make decisions, and take action. So with this boost, your child may finally be emerging into a more active phase.

The more pronounced the brow bone or eyebrows are, the more your child will make the transition into the next phase of increased power. Significant events and choices often happen at this stage that weren't possible earlier in the decade.

Eyes = 30s

The decade of the 30s is really looking ahead in your children's lives, far beyond the point at which you'll probably have much influence or control over them! The area around the eyes reveals the experiences they'll have during this time. This is a River period, a very yin era, when their job will be to contend with personal growth. Even though they'll be working and living as usual, they'll be drawn inward to deal with emotional issues in some way, and will most likely have experiences that help them focus on their internal world. Creases under the eyes are mostly what will reveal any upcoming lessons in this regard. The more wrinkles that form in the under-eye areas, the more inner struggle that occurs at this stage, whether through their own choosing or being forced to because of life circumstances.

Occasionally, a single, half-moon-shaped wrinkle will form directly under each eye, and these are sometimes called "Lost Loves," indicating that your child is eventually going to lose someone he loves. It doesn't necessarily mean this will occur during his 30s—it could happen before or after. Please be aware that this isn't something that you should feel distressed about or try to get rid of; it's just the sign of a challenge he'll experience as part of his soul's growth and evolution.

Nose = 40s

The Chinese believe that you encounter your most powerful transitions as you move from one decade to another. They consider the turning points at ages 40, 50, 60, and 70 to be the most critical; and call these stages the "Four Gates." The first gate is at the very top of the nose, the point at which people enter their 40s. A horizontal wrinkle here reflects the possibility of a significant life change or break with the past. However, remember that signs on the face can correspond with a certain time of life, an emotional issue, a physical condition, or all three. A sign at the top of the nose might instead indicate a problem with the digestive system and/or a subtle sign of a lack of self-nurturing.

From there your child's nose reveals what the decade of his 40s will bring him. This is a yang, or Mountain, period that's more about experience in the external world, so career success often occurs for the first time during this period or expands. As you remember from Chapter 14, the nose represents the potential for personal power, and it's often not until the 40s that someone begins to achieve this. If this feature is prominent and well formed, this will most likely be a positive decade. Remember that your child's nose will be small until later in childhood, but even if it ends up as a diminutive one, it doesn't mean these years will be bad. It's just that this stage won't be as strong as one that's associated with a larger facial feature.

Any malformations to the nose indicate possible challenges to be dealt with during this time, and you can read when they're likely to arise. The upper part of the nose represents the early 40s, the center relates to the middle of the decade, and the bottom is associated with the years just before the 50s.

Mouth = 50s

The center of the philtrum correlates to age 50 and is the second of the Four Gates. A marking here can signify an important passage at that time, and it also relates to the reproductive system and the expression of personal creativity.

In the mouth, you'll see how your child will move through her 50s, which is yet another River decade. This yin period is about looking inward to see what she needs in order to feel satisfied in life. If you remember from Chapter 12, the mouth correlates with how well you feel nurtured and cared for and if you've been over-giving while not receiving enough. When people enter their 50s, they bump up against this issue and must deal with it.

I believe that men and women cross paths in this decade, going in different directions, but for the same reason. Women, after emphasizing yin behavior—possibly by caring for their families for years—now face the fact that they've put themselves last far too often. The result is that they become more yang and refuse to be everything for everyone any longer! No more making five different meals at dinner to keep everyone happy or being the kids' chauffeur. Instead, they start to make what seem like selfish choices, but ones that actually bring their lives back into balance —for instance, spending more time doing what *they* like to do, going back to school, or letting family members help take care of themselves.

Men, on the other hand, become more yin. For instance, some fathers, after spending all their time at the office, wake up to the fact that they've missed a lot of their kids' childhoods toiling at their jobs, and their personal relationships have suffered as a result. Suddenly, as they move into this decade, they make the choice to turn away from the external and lead more meaningful and gratifying lives. Men and women, for the same reason, make choices that will give them a greater sense of satisfaction.

You can get an idea of what your child's experiences in his 50s will be like by observing his mouth. A large one represents a powerful time, and a small mouth reveals that it may be more difficult to create fulfillment at that time. If any wrinkles or markings develop around the mouth, they will reflect a decline in personal nourishment that needs to be rectified in this period.

Chin = 60s

Your little one's chin shows you what he'll encounter in his 60s. This is a Mountain period, and it's often a very positive time that comes after the adjustments made in the 50s. Remember that the chin doesn't fully develop until puberty, so you won't get a realistic picture of what this decade will be like if you're studying this feature on your child too early. The stronger the chin, the more likely this will be a vital stage. A weaker one doesn't mean that the 60s will be bad, however. It just won't be as powerful as the other decades represented by larger aspects of the face.

The upper area of the chin represents age 60, and it's the Third Gate; a horizontal line here may indicate a major change. Because the chin also represents willpower, a marking here or anywhere on the chin can reveal whether your child's level of will has been negatively affected. All of us go through challenges, difficult times when we're forced to reach down and summon our determination to persevere—and this is a part of life, not something to resist. But when we've successfully emerged on the other side, we then need to rest and refill our reservoir of willpower. If this isn't done, our life force will diminish, eventually evident by a mark on the chin.

Because our culture doesn't value downtime, even children can feel pressured to get right back to work again without recuperation. Or they may be trying to keep up with overloaded calendars consisting of too many sports and after-school activities that drain their reserves. If you see a wrinkle on your child's chin, consider if any of the above makes sense; you might need to help replenish your little one's energy or alter the daily schedule to better suit his individual needs.

Jaw = 70s

The jaw extends to the left and right of the chin and reflects life experiences during the 70s. As with the other features, the general rule is that a large and well-defined jaw means a strong decade. Age 70 is the last of the Four Gates, and a specific new purpose often shows up during this time, as we begin a phase of letting go. This is really about starting to refine our vision for the rest of our lives and discerning what we no longer need. This can literally mean letting go of possessions, moving to a smaller home, or resolving old conflicts. It may also be about finally making it a priority to do only that which serves our self-development from this point forward.

Sides of the Face = 80s and 90s

On women's faces, the 80s correlates to the area that goes up the right edge of the face, and the 90s are on the left side. For men, it's the opposite. This era is a continuation of the refinement and letting-go process that began in the 70s. It begins the inward contraction to the essence of who we are, with less of an importance given to the outside world. There's little to find on children's faces to know what this period will bring them—all of that is determined by their life choices and experiences between now and then.

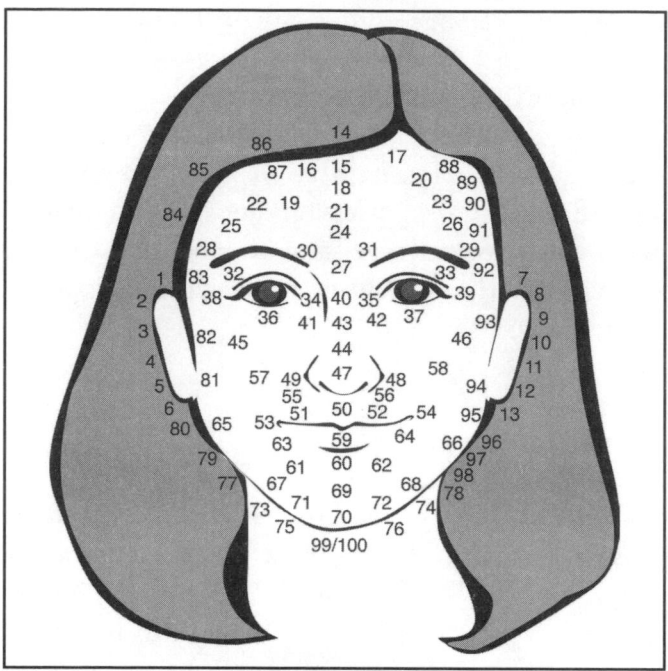

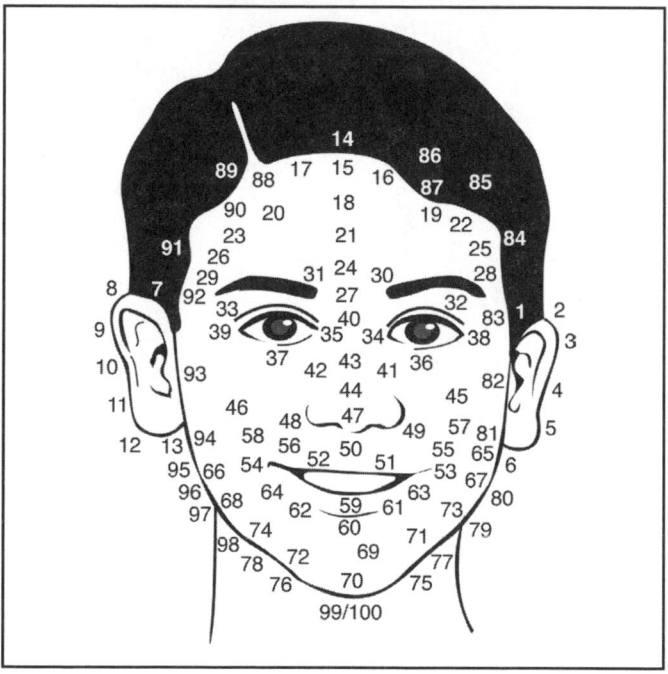

Figures 102 and 103: *Facial Maps:* Every year of life is represented by a point on the face.

Moles, Scars, and Other Marks on the Face

Everything on your child's face means something. It's the map of her journey through life—the past, present, and future—and every lesson, positive or negative, will leave an imprint. The shape and size of her features also reveal her inner nature and its effect on how she chooses to perceive and respond to her experiences. Information about the physical body can be read on the face, too. As you know, the mind and body are interconnected, so any marking can have one, two, or all three of these meanings. It can represent emotional stress or physical conditions, or may be an indication of a significant event. It's far more important to pay attention to the messages that the features reveal compared with what a small spot somewhere on the face suggests. But sometimes the small signs can offer additional insights into your child's inner design and life plan.

Freckles, Spots, and Birthmarks

A face covered in freckles is a sign of some Fire in a child's nature. However, if there are just a few that are permanent and don't come and go depending on sun exposure, Chinese face reading defines these marks—along with spots or flat brown moles—as signifying meaningful life experiences. Consult the facial map to see what year is closest to the freckle or spot, and thus, when the event happened or will happen.

A birthmark is usually a discolored area much larger than a freckle or spot, but the meaning may be the same. It could indicate an important time of life, which can be determined by noticing what years it's nearest to on the facial map. In addition, a birthmark may also suggest a deficiency in the power of the feature it occupies. For example, one on the cheek can suggest trouble with the Metal traits of assuming authority and speaking up. Knowing this information can help you support your child in the best way possible. If a birthmark is removed, that's fine; however, if it leaves a scar, this reflects a slight depletion in the energy of the area where it was. These characteristics are usually judged on a case-by-case basis.

Moles

In Chinese face reading, moles are defined as flesh colored and sticking out from the face; they're not the flat brown spots we think of as moles. In some African and Asian faces, moles that protrude are slightly darker than the skin, and these are still considered moles. But a very dark growth that sticks out is considered to be the same as a spot that is brown and flat; it has the identical meaning as a freckle or a spot.

A true mole is associated with extra Metal in a child's nature and indicates enhanced power for whatever feature it occupies. For instance, a mole right next to the eyebrow indicates extra strength in logic and practicality; and possibly a tendency toward frustration, anger, or aggressiveness. One on the chin will enhance willpower and intuitive ability but also provides a stronger supply of stubbornness.

In addition, moles can signify an especially powerful and beneficial time in life—so you'd consult the facial map to find out when this will occur. If one is removed, this influence is said to disappear; and if the surgery leaves a scar, this further decreases its power.

Scars

There's more than one thing to consider when it comes to scars. First, they can mean diminished strength in whatever personal quality that area represents. For example, a scar on an eyebrow can suggest a lack of confidence, or one on the jaw can reveal a difficulty with decisiveness. This information will be valuable for you to know as a parent so you can give your little ones a boost in whatever areas they're weak in. Interestingly, if you help your child build her confidence, for instance, it's very possible that her eyebrow may grow back and diminish or eliminate the scar. The face is just a hologram of a person's true nature, so inner changes are reflected in the outer form.

But there's another meaning to a scar. It can indicate a life issue that someone is meant to work on that has a sort of "pull date" for that problem to show up again. Let me give you an example: A woman in one of my workshops had a deep scar on her left cheek caused by a household accident when she was 16. At that time, she was the oldest of five children and her mother was dying of cancer. She soon had to drop out of school and abandon her plans for college in order to be the full-time caregiver for her brothers and sisters once her mother died. This was an enormous sacrifice that affected her for the rest of her life.

The facial map indicated that the scar on her cheek was marking age 46. When this woman turned 46, she had long been married with kids of her own, and her oldest daughter had a baby while still in college. The family decided that the mother should quit her job to take care of her grandchild so the daughter could finish school. Once again, she was bumping into the exact same issue she'd experienced as a teenager— having to sacrifice her own needs for the family. This brought back all the anguish and resentment she'd felt before, and after much thought she resolved to find a way to do things differently this time. She created a plan to get help from friends and other family members and altered her work schedule so the baby would be well cared for but she could continue in her fulfilling job.

With a scar, you must first consider what was happening in your child's life at the time he got it. You don't need to remember what occurred on that particular day. Instead, examine the big picture of what was stressing him during that time period, then look on the facial map to see what age the scar is closest to. This will be when the same lesson will reappear to be processed on a different level. If you can identify the origin, you can help your little one work on the issue now and reduce his need to deal with it later. In that case, you may even see the scar diminish, fade, or disappear.

◉ ◉ ◉

"It's like driving a car at night. You never see further than your headlights, but you can make the whole trip that way."

— E. L. DOCTOROW

READING A CHILD'S FACE

Chapter 17

I often warn people who come to my workshops that they'll never look at faces the same way again! You'll certainly look at children's faces with new eyes: spotting the unusual ears on the boy in the shopping cart at the checkout line, the prominent cheeks on your daughter's best friend, and the kid with the pointy nose in day care—and you'll now know what all these features mean. In fact, playing with face reading every day is the very best way to learn it. You can notice a characteristic on someone's face and then see if you observe the behavior that correlates with that aspect. Or maybe try reading faces "backwards"—first notice the behavior and then you may be delighted when you're able to identify the facial feature that's associated with it. The more you practice reading the messages in the faces around you, the better you'll be at recognizing and understanding those in your own child.

Let's Get Started!

If you sit down with your child to try to thoroughly read his or her face, know that there's no one right way to do this. In fact, even before you start, my advice is that you take a few moments to get relaxed, take a couple of deep breaths, and smile! Become aware of any anxieties or expectations you may have about what you're going to discover, and try to empty your mind of them so you can be as clear and present as possible. Sometimes people are surprised to realize that they're afraid of what they're going to see on their child's face. Remember that this isn't about finding out what's "wrong"; in fact, this is about discovering even more ways to love your child.

As I've already mentioned, reading a face is like putting a jigsaw puzzle together, so don't expect to instantaneously see all of the information. You have to start somewhere! One way to begin is to step back for a big-picture look. If you were to observe your child as if for the first time, what feature immediately attracts your eyes? Usually this is the largest or most prominent aspect and will be associated with one of the Five Elements. It's very likely that this means the Element is either the main one or at least important in your child's makeup, and this alone will give you a wealth of information. Look up the significance of that feature in this book, and review the personality characteristics associated with it to see if this resonates with your own understanding of your little one.

Continue on to see if you can determine a second feature that catches your eye and what Element it's associated with. If it's the same one as the first, you may have a child who's mostly one Element, with the other four playing smaller roles. For instance, if the initial thing you notice is a large nose, that means Metal is an influential part of your son's or daughter's nature. Next, if you're drawn to very full upper cheeks, this also indicates Metal, which probably strongly informs your child's inner self. If, however, the second thing that draws your attention is all the freckles dotting his or her face, then you can be pretty sure that Fire affects this personality, too. Look then to see if there's a third and fourth prominent feature. Sometimes there are, and other times there aren't. Of course, you'll see all five Elements represented on your child's face in different amounts, but one will always be the dominant influence.

Observe what traits, if any, seem unusually small or inconsequential. Keeping in mind that your child's face is still growing and changing, consider that this means the Elements those features relate to aren't major aspects of his personality—and this may even reveal new insights about his challenges. For instance, if your son has very weak eyebrows, Wood is not a significant factor in his nature. This can also indicate that his challenges in life may center around feeling confident and assertive enough. These clues empower you, and they can prevent you from thinking that something's wrong if you notice that these traits aren't a part of his natural mind-set. You can also help him find other places inside to draw from to develop a different kind of self-assurance. Fire kids, for example, feel certain that their natural gift of easily relating to others will create positive outcomes, and those with Metal know that their attention to detail will probably ensure a good result.

After evaluating the relative size of your child's features, you can then focus on more details. For example, you may notice that your daughter's earlobes are large, her temples are indented, there's a mole by her right eyebrow, and her upper lip is thin. Even small aspects such as these can give you important messages about who she is and how she can move through life successfully. Don't be overly concerned about any one detail; keep in mind that this is just information that's contributing to the entire design of who's inside.

Remember that one feature can modify the impact of another. That is, if your son has a sharp jaw, this means he's competitive and likes to win. But if he also has a large mouth, there's a good supply of generosity and kindness to balance that quality. So don't jump to conclusions without the full picture.

In addition, consider the right and left sides of the face and what these tell you about the public and private messages your child is sharing, and then observe the horizontal zones to see how decisions are processed. At some point, examine the timeline of your child's journey through life. Start with the ears to read the earliest experiences, and continue on using the facial map as your guide. Remember that markings like scars are much less significant than the meaning of the actual size and shape of the features, but keep in mind that some of these features will grow over time. In other words, if a four-year-old has a small chin, it doesn't mean that his adult chin will be weak. Understand as well that who your child is at this point will transform as he experiences life, and that his face will change correspondingly—not only as he matures physically, but as he makes important choices, grows emotionally, and responds to the lessons he encounters.

It's vital to be aware that a piece of information on someone's face can have anywhere from one to three meanings. It might reveal something to do with the physical body, the emotional nature, and/or a stage of life. For instance, if your child has a mark in the under-eye area, this can reflect an issue with hydration and a lack of rest, an emotional upset, or a life lesson that will emerge in her 30s (since this is the aspect of the face that relates to this decade)—and all of these factors may be true.

Remember, also, that there's no cookie-cutter approach to face reading. The core meaning of the information on the face will always be consistent, but there are myriad ways it can manifest in your child's nature. For example, bushy eyebrows can show one or all of the following characteristics: a logical mind, a reactive temper, an athletic nature, or strong confidence, among other possibilities. The important thing is to understand the energy of bushy eyebrows, which is Wood's dynamic plan and strong push forward. Indented temples can be observed as indicating a potential for compulsive behavior, the ability to concentrate intensely, addictive tendencies, a highly spiritual nature, and possibly more. The essence of this trait is an inner tension, and if you understand that, you'll be able to see how it emerges in your child's life.

But it's easier to demonstrate than explain! Following are some children's faces. Try reading them for yourself before looking at my commentary, and you may be surprised at how much you already know.

Developing Your Face-Reading Skills

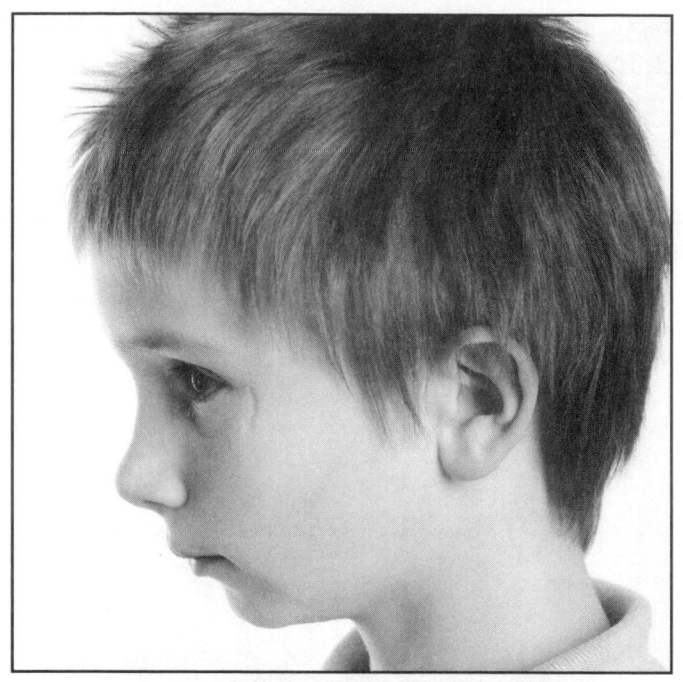

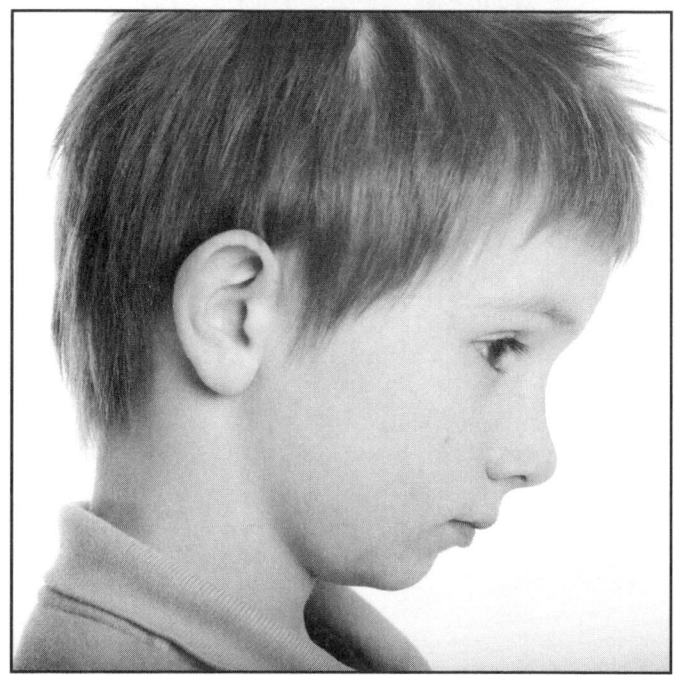

Doesn't your heart just melt the moment you look at this boy's face? You don't even have to read it to feel what a sweet presence he is in the world. One of the wonderful things about my work is that I get to look at all these beautiful children and fall in love with all of them!

The first things that catch my attention when I gaze at him are his spiky hair and large eyes. His hair is red, which is an immediate clue that there's definitely some Fire here. But the spiky cut is also a tip-off. (Although a parent may have decided what kind of haircut he got, this is an example of how someone's Element manifests naturally.) We then turn to this boy's large eyes, and remember that these also relate to Fire and how open one is to communication. His are held wide open; in fact, they verge on being those of an empath—letting in a lot of information from the outside world—and this has the potential to contribute to shyness. And because Fire is always about the heart, these eyes reveal a little guy with a very open heart, meaning that he might be vulnerable as a result. His apparent timidity is most likely also impacted by the delicacy of his heart.

Looking more closely at his eyes, we see how rounded they are. Any roundness on a feature is actually Earth acting on it, so although the eyes aren't associated with this Element, here we see its inherently kind nature affecting how he'll communicate. He cares very much that others have a positive experience with him, and this will add to his Fire-y desire to please and be liked. There's also a subtle half-circle line under each eye, which is a hint of Lost Loves lines developing.

This boy's eyebrows aren't overly strong, but they're not weak either. They give him some healthy Wood energy, but he doesn't have an aggressive nature. The brows grow in a straight line, suggesting that he'll be able to think things through before making a decision or taking action. Here we have an example of what may be a modifying feature. Since Fire reacts so quickly, he could tend to be a little impulsive or not plan carefully enough in certain situations. But his eyebrows help slow him down, so he can consider the consequences of his actions. His eyebrows also don't grow closely together in the middle, indicating that he'll be able to get along with a variety of personality types throughout his life.

This little guy's nose is just starting to grow into maturity, but there's a hint that it may be pointed, which is another sign of Fire. He also has a well-defined philtrum, revealing his creative side. And if we look at his face in profile, we see a rounded forehead, which is a sign of a Watery imagination. Even though this feature may change shape as he grows, the meaning is the same while he exhibits it.

The ends of his mouth are a bit pointed—again, we encounter Fire. His mouth isn't very large, but his lips aren't thin; therefore, we know that while Earth is not his main Element, it's definitely present. The horizontal line on his chin can be an indication of an important life change as he turns 60. Remembering the Four Gates—the four turning points in an individual's life—a horizontal line at any one of these areas can mean a break with the past at that age. But note that any sign on the face can have more than one meaning. This little wrinkle may reveal a physical issue with the body, or much more likely here, a deficiency in what the chin represents emotionally: his willpower and ability to be stubborn. And before we leave the chin, notice the barest hint of a cleft—yet another sign of Fire.

Comparing the right and left sides of his face, we see that his right ear sticks out a tiny bit more than his left. The fact that his ears stick out at all shows some Watery willfulness and independence; and his right ear exhibiting more of this tendency means he's trying to convince the world that he's more determined to have his way than he actually is. The only other significant difference between the right and left sides is that we can see more of the white below the iris in his right eye. Since this photo was taken as he was standing in a room full of strangers, my sense is that this delicate Fire nature may have been temporarily stressed, which isn't a serious concern.

Looking at his ears overall, we see he has good-sized earlobes that detach rather than grow into the sides of his head. This aspect means that he'll be able to plan for the future and save both money and energy. Sizable earlobes also show another touch of Water in his nature, and the fact that they detach suggests that maintaining a strong connection to family won't be a major focus once he's an adult.

Then, starting with his left ear, we read the story of the first half of his childhood. The rim is intact for the entire ear, with no thinning or notches; however, it thickens at the spot closest to age three. This indicates that some stress occurred at this time, but because the rim gets thicker here and not thinner, the implication is that if it wasn't positive (stress can be positive or negative), it was still an experience that benefited him in the long run. When we view his right ear, there are no unusual markings and the rim is normal throughout. For this child, the only significantly stressful experience so far came at three years of age.

Now we look again at this boy's profile. We've already noticed his rounded forehead and won't pay much attention to his nose, as it's not yet fully formed. However, there are two things here to attend to. One is the small scar on his upper cheek near the corner of his eye. If we had him and a parent here, we could find out at what age he got the scar and what was going on in his life at the time. Armed with this information, we'd then look at the facial map to see that this mark is nearest to age 38. During this year, he'll encounter another opportunity to work on whatever was stressing him when he got it.

We also need to consider that this scar reflects a deficiency of some sort in the Element represented by that part of his face. In this case, it's the outer corner of the eye, which is Fire. This area has to do with faithfulness in romantic relationships and possibly reveals the loss of a love. Traditionally, it was said that an indentation or crosshatch wrinkle here indicated an unfaithful partner, the loss of one, or even that he'll be unfaithful. The essence of this meaning is the potential of betrayal: feeling betrayed by life if a spouse dies, for instance, or deceived by a romantic partner who strays. A scar here could represent an inclination to worry about these issues or, at the extreme, have that experience.

However, a scar here can also simply mean an especially vulnerable heart. When we remember all the other signs of Fire in his face, this makes sense. This is a boy who definitely carries the delicate hummingbird energy of Fire, and the scar could mean this sensitivity is amplified, again contributing to shyness and a greater likelihood for his light to be dimmed by harsh treatment.

Finally, in his profile we see that his chin isn't very strong, and that he even seems to hold it in a way that reduces its power. Despite the fact that his mature chin has not yet grown, this, combined with the wrinkle here, seems to suggest that his Watery will is a bit weak and may be deficient overall. This boy doesn't think he's powerful enough to be stubborn, even when he should be. He may be experiencing strict rules at home and feeling oppressed as a result, or he may have arrived in life with an inherent lack of this energy as part of a lesson he needs to learn.

Returning to the scar on his cheek, we see some information that may add to our understanding. It extends down slightly to his cheek as well as the corner of his eye. This feature reveals how well someone can speak up to say what they want, and a scar here might diminish some of that power. So again we observe a sign that he may not easily stand up for himself and resist the influence of others' will upon his own.

This boy's home planet is Fire. It's so important for him to give and receive affection, and he's a sweet guy who's easy to love. Anyone who starts in Fire has a delicate heart, but almost every message we've read on his face shows that this is even more of a significant aspect in his nature. He won't do well with sharp discipline, and he may be much more easily hurt by friends rejecting him or being teased by others. Add to this the fact that he's probably quite empathic, and we have a boy for whom help in developing healthy energetic boundaries on many levels will be enormously beneficial.

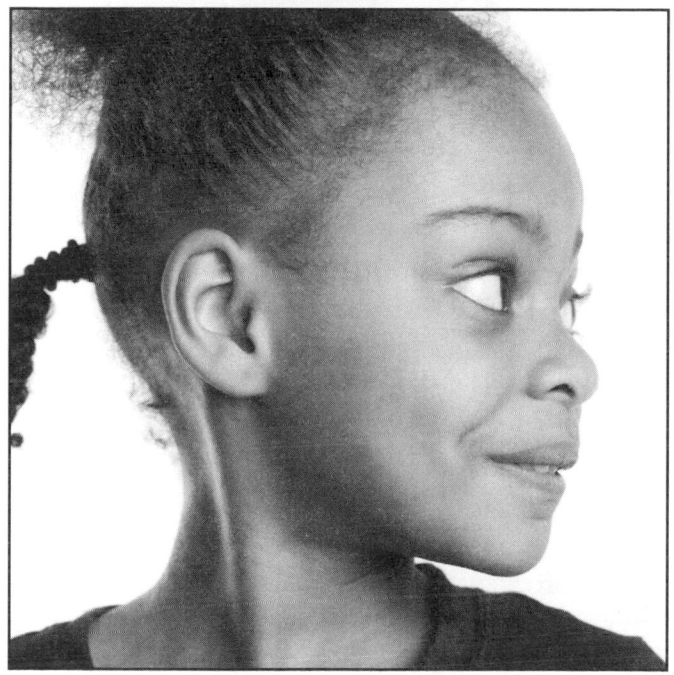

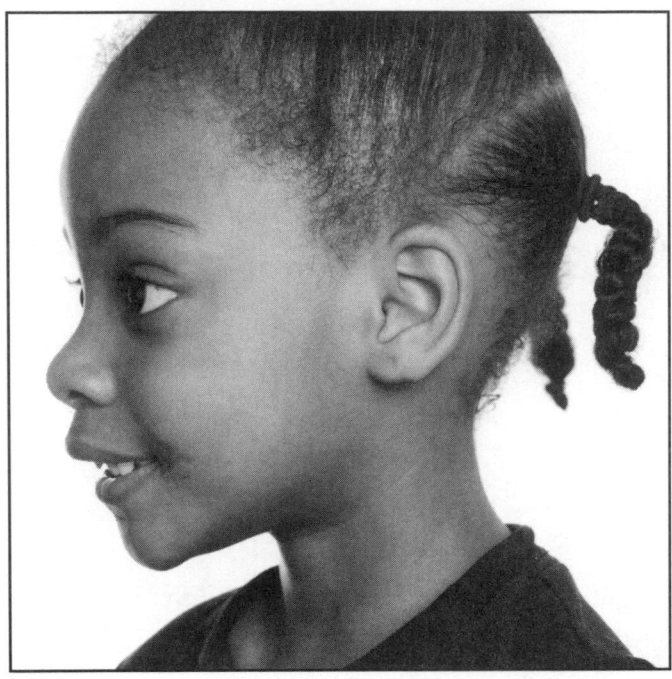

So here we have another little one who just makes your heart break wide open! If we all started our days by gazing into the face of a child, the world would become a very different place.

One of the things that first draws my eye is this girl's very high eyebrows, a sign of Metal sensitivity and, as we know, the "Queen"! She'll have certain preferences for how things should be in her life, and we'll be sure to hear about them. This trait is enhanced by her relatively strong cheeks, and we also see that they're more bony than plump.

This is a girl who will speak up for what she wants or needs without too much beating around the bush. Yet while this can feel like she's ordering you around, understand that as a highly aware Metal person, she'll be much more impacted by little details that are even slightly off. This isn't about her being bossy; it's her attempting to keep things under control so she's comfortable.

Remember that this Element is the sensor, and she can physically sense information from the people and places around her.

This little one also appears to be growing purpose lines at quite an early age, evidenced by the fact that her nasolabial folds are already forming. This is another sign of Metal on the face, so considering how much of this Element we've seen already, it should be no surprise that her features reveal an early focus on living an authentic life.

We notice that her mouth is a good size, which indicates that although she may be the royal figure in the family, she can be kind and caring, and relationships are important to her. Her lips aren't overly full for an African face, so while Earth is part of her nature, it's not a major factor. Our eyes are drawn to her rounded forehead that suggests a strong imagination; and if it stays this way as she matures, it also exhibits an important connection to her lineage, meaning she has inherited traits and talents from her ancestors.

This girl's eyes are large—much like the boy we looked at first—indicating an equally open heart; but because they're more almond shaped and not as open and rounded as his, her heart isn't as vulnerable. Her lower eyelids and eyebrows are rounded, both contributing to the Earthy kindness revealed by her mouth. Combined with her oval eyes, they show a talent for diplomacy that will be enhanced by her Metal graciousness. Giving us one last piece of information, her eyes slant slightly upward. This aspect reveals her positive outlook and ability to see opportunities in any situation.

Her philtrum and chin are strong, and these, along with her rounded forehead, announce that Water is a factor in who she is. Amazingly, here we have a second child in a row with a horizontal wrinkle on the chin. This has the same meaning as discussed previously: that there will be a potentially important transition as she enters the decade of her 60s and/or that she may encounter some difficulties expressing her will in life. However, because her chin is more prominent than the boy's, deficient willpower is less of a factor in defining her life issues—especially considering the fact that her cheeks and eyebrows give her the ability to speak up.

This child's jaw is well defined, so she'll have a firm belief system and may have a tendency to be a bit judgmental and competitive. These characteristics can combine to give her the drive to achieve, and the addition of those subtle dimples gives her the charm to open doors and make that success happen!

In looking at her right ear, which shows the first half of childhood in girls, we see that the rim thickens near the top at around the point relating to approximately age one. This suggests that some stress occurred at this time, but as with the previous example, the long-term effect was positive. For instance, this could have been the birth of a sibling or a move to a new home that at first was difficult but ended up being beneficial.

The rim continues without further markings, but does seem to disappear right around age four to five. This indicates a change in life that was more significant, resulting in her feeling less safe and supported. Her earlobes are quite small and more attached than detached, which suggests her tendency to focus on the present rather than the future, and that she'll maintain a lifelong connection to family, whether positive or negative.

When we turn to look at her left ear that corresponds to life experiences from ages 7 through 13, we see that the rim is pretty even from top to bottom. There's a very slight thickening at the top, around age seven or eight, but what draws our eye most is how the earlobe is slightly malformed. This could have been the result of an earring accidentally being pulled and ripping the lobe, or perhaps she was born with it. The cause isn't so important, as it still has the same meaning; in this case, it shows more significant stress at age 13.

If the marking is a scar as a result of an accident, we'd also consider what was stressing her at the age she got it; and this means she'll have another opportunity to work on this issue when she turns 13. Because children are so closely connected to their parents, it's common for them to be impacted by any stress that their mothers and fathers are dealing with. So in order to determine what the issue was that she'll return to at 13, we'd want to think about what was happening for this child *and* for her parents at the time she got the scar. In any case, knowing what this marking on her ear means is a gift to Mom and Dad, as it empowers them to know that she'll be working on something important during this time so they can be fully available to support her.

In evaluating the Elements and what her home base is, Metal is first because of her high eyebrows and strong cheeks. Water seems to come on as a secondary influence, with her rounded forehead, strong philtrum, and prominent chin. Wood and Earth factor in, too, based on her large mouth and defined jaw and eyebrows; and Fire reveals itself in a minor way with her dimples and large, up-slanted eyes.

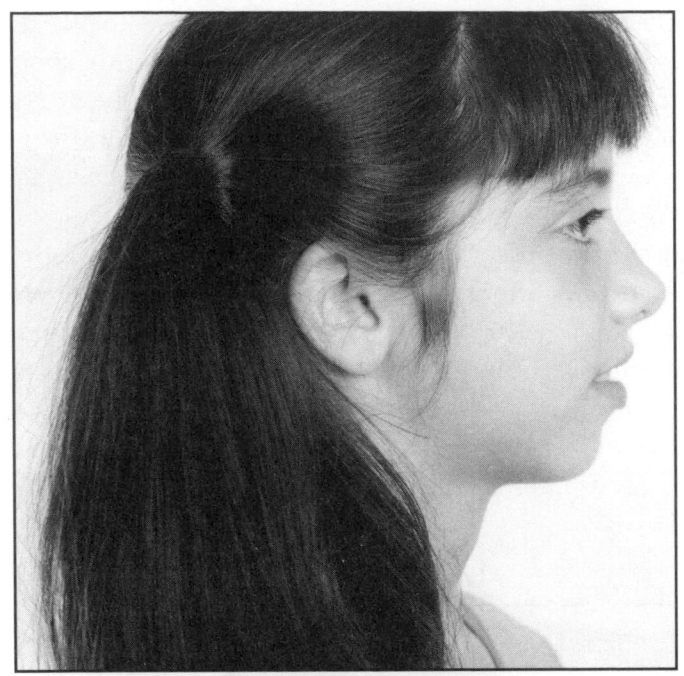

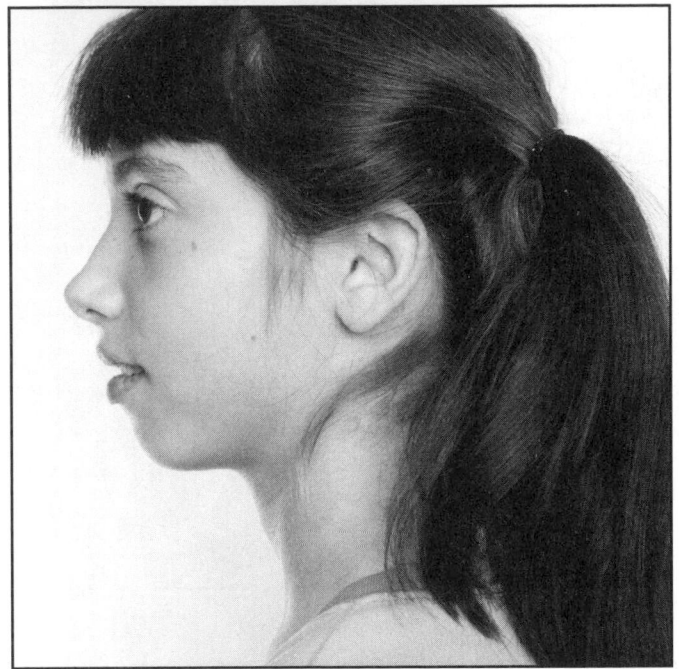

What a gorgeous, soulful-looking girl! One thing we first notice are her beautiful eyes. The most important thing about this feature is that we can see so much of her upper eyelids. They indicate Metal overall, and specifically exhibit her deep sensitivity. This is amplified by her relatively wide cheek area, which is another sign of this Element.

But Metal is modified by Wood revealing itself nearby in her strong eyebrows, which make her less likely to be overly sensitive. Instead, she has a good potential for confidence and assertiveness, and will probably be able to cope with a structured learning environment and lessons that require logic and reasoning. This girl will be practical, have good common sense, and can be well organized. These qualities are enhanced by her almond-shaped eyes, which also contribute to her logical nature.

The fact that her brows are slightly rounded lends some Earth kindness to her nature, and her rounded lower eyelids and full lips reinforce that. In fact, we can home in on one more tiny detail: the inner canthus (corner) of her eyes. Here we see that they're rounded rather than pointed, indicating a tendency toward kindness and tact in her communications—more corroboration of the information already noted.

There are some very faint wrinkles under her eyes, which reveal that her 30s will likely be a decade in which she experiences some personal growth, as is appropriate during this River period. These are very subtle wrinkles and nothing to be concerned about, but the fact that they're showing up so far in advance makes me want to watch for any emotional issues surfacing now that should be worked on, in case they're already building momentum.

There appears to be a tiny cleft right under the tip of her nose. It's usually the tips of features that indicate Fire issues associated with vulnerability of the heart, but because this is so close to the tip, I'd suggest that her parents take this into consideration. Her hooded upper eyelids, the wrinkles under her eyes, and the tiny mark near the tip of her nose all add up to a child who has quite a complex emotional core. This little girl may be dealing with feelings that most kids don't tackle at such a young age.

She has a defined philtrum, showing Watery creativity, and the wrinkles in the under-eye areas lend some energy of this Element as well. Her jaw is defined but narrow, suggesting some more Wood in her personality. But while she'll have good integrity and values, this characteristic shows us that she'll be flexible in her judgments and not so likely to size others up and reject or accept them in the first few moments of meeting. This little one may have some issues with indecisiveness or being easily influenced because this jaw shows she's like the bamboo, which can sway a bit too much in the breeze.

We also notice that although this girl wears bangs, her forehead seems relatively short. This indicates that she probably prefers to learn by doing rather than studying. But the lower third of her face is the largest in terms of comparing the three zones (Analytical, Practical, and Intuitive), so while she has a practical mind, intuition will be a part of her learning style and how she processes decisions—she should definitely trust her gut instincts. While the lower third of her face is strong, her chin is not overly prominent, so we know that she won't be too stubborn.

Her earlobes are a good size and detached, revealing that she'll be able to separate from her family and have a lifelong ability to focus on long-term planning. The rim on her right ear looks normal, so we can assume that any stress that occurred in the first half of her childhood wasn't significant. However, when we look at her left ear, we see a bumpy area on the rim, affecting approximately ages 7 through 10. It's not a dramatic marking, but it does indicate a time of ups and downs. After age 10, things resolve and we don't see any other challenges in this stage.

She has a very small mark on her left cheek nearest to age 39 on the facial map. This means that something of significance will happen in her life at that age, but it doesn't have the same meaning as a scar; in other words, it won't connect back to a stressful experience in the past. Instead, this signifies a lesson, challenge, or change that will be present at this point in her life.

It appears that this girl's main Element is Wood, but then she moves right into Metal as a strong influence as well. A good supply of Earth is seen in her lips and other small details; Water plays a minor role; and there isn't much Fire in her nature, as a very slight point on her nose is its only visible sign.

• • •

Fig. 113: The twin on the left reveals a more yin personality.

Fig. 114: The twin on the left reveals a more yin personality.

Sometimes people have asked me how to read identical twins. Even with twins, no two faces are ever the same, and you can discover valuable information from little details that reveal how their dispositions differ. In general, Chinese face reading considers one twin to be the yin version and the other to be the yang expression of their particular personality. For instance, even beginners at face reading may observe how one twin's energy seems to go outward, and the other stays more inside. Every parent I've worked with has quickly acknowledged that indeed one twin is yang and the other yin. In each of these photos, the twin on the left is more yin. As you look more closely, you can begin to see small aspects that differ between them—and use this book to determine their meanings!

◉ ◉ ◉

"The most important thing a father can do
for his children is to love their mother."

— THEODORE M. HESBURGH

Chapter
18

THE FAMILY

The I Ching is an ancient Chinese book of wisdom that predates historical memory and is considered one of the most important texts in the world. Both Lao-tzu and Confucius drew from it in the development of their own philosophies, and it still informs the essence of Chinese culture today. This work offers a profound understanding of life as an evolution of connected events in process, and it teaches how to live in accordance with this flow of constant change. Aside from studying it to better comprehend their world, people consult the I Ching for guidance with major life decisions. In China, it's still greatly revered, and someone may only turn to it once in his life for help with a momentous decision—it's not treated lightly.

When I first began writing this book, I consulted the I Ching to ask what would be important to include. I received Hexagram 37, "The Family." How appropriate! At first this might seem obvious, but it's a vital concept below the surface. In this chapter, the I Ching talks about "the influence that goes out from within the family [and] influence working from within outward." On one level, the meaning is that if the family is in balance, then society at large will be as well. But it also makes us look at the influence coming from within each parent outward to affect their child. Who you are, your personal energy, will influence your children far more than you may realize.

Certainly the information in this book is devoted to helping you understand your children better by discovering who they really are and give you insights into their responses and reactions to you and life in general. Its purpose is to assist you in raising them in alignment with their true nature so they grow into their authentic selves. But remember that in any relationship, there's an energetic exchange between the people involved. Your own personal patterns will have an impact on how your children perceive you, react to you, and, most important, how they feel about themselves.

Humans as Tuning Forks

There's a growing body of knowledge about just how powerfully we're affected by the people and places around us. Research has shown that aside from our minds immediately creating the same emotion shown on the face we're viewing (as discussed in Chapter 3), there are mirroring neurons in the brain that light up in response to what we're seeing. When we watch someone take an action, the part of our brains that controls that behavior activates. Research by the Institute of Heartmath even shows that the *feelings* we have inside radiate out to physically and emotionally influence the people around us. This is also central to many energy healing techniques; even in Western medicine, a practitioner's compassionate state of mind is known to have a significant impact on the patient. The personal energy of those we interact with affects us emotionally and physiologically, and vice versa. And the more time we spend together, the more pervasive and deeper the response.

The scientific concept of *entrainment* can be important to understand here. Entrainment is when two or more systems come into synchronization and begin to operate at the same frequency. This happens naturally in the world and is an example of how deeply interconnected everything is. For instance, if you strike a tuning fork and hold it near a second tuning fork of the same frequency, that one will also begin to vibrate and produce the tone. Or if you put several grandfather clocks in a room together with each pendulum swinging in a different way, they'll eventually end up in sync. Entrainment is also the reason why when women live together, their menstrual cycles come to mirror each other. It's even been found that people tend to chew to the rhythm of the background music played in restaurants. This might not seem so remarkable, except that if there's no music, people will still chew at the same speed as those around them!

One of the most astonishing studies was with a group of American, Canadian, and German college students that looked at how we're all affected by the background hum of electricity in our environment. In North America, the electrical system operates at 60 hertz, or cycles per second. If this frequency is translated to the musical scale, it relates to the tone B-natural. In Europe, the system operates at 50 hertz, which translates to G-sharp. In the experiment, each student was asked to spontaneously hum any tone that came to them naturally. The Americans and Canadians hummed B-natural and the Germans hit G-sharp! We're all involved in a dance with the energy around us, whether it's from our environment or other people. Human beings are like tuning forks that synchronize to the frequencies we encounter, and the more time we spend in a place or with the same people, the more we'll vibrate in alignment with them.

In other words, consciousness is contagious. No matter what your child's true nature is, your own personal energy has an enormous influence on how she constructs her reality. Just as important as what you *do* with your child is who you *are* as a person—that is, how in balance you are within yourself and the quality of your relationships.

John Gottman is a renowned psychologist in the field of marriage and family counseling whose early work showed that you can predict the likelihood of divorce simply by viewing the husband's and wife's facial expressions during a conversation. He now states that he knows the quality of a marriage simply by taking a urine sample from the couple's child to measure the level of stress in her system.

When people live together, they're immersed in each other's energy and are affected by each other's positive and negative states, and they naturally take on each other's stress. When you're living a balanced life, managing your emotions in a healthy way, this helps your children do the same. The more out of harmony you are, the greater the likelihood is that your children will struggle with learning to self-regulate and manage stress overall.

As you've been reading this book, you may have recognized aspects of yourself in each of the Elements, and as a result gained some new insights into your own nature. I'd also recommend reading my first book, *The Wisdom of Your Face,* to learn more about applying this knowledge to yourself. When you're able to feel more understanding and self-acceptance for who you are, the change in your own energy gets transmitted to your children and benefits them enormously. Conscious parenting means a willingness to always do your own inner work and become aware of the life story you've been creating all these years . . . and whether or not that's what you want to pass on to your children.

Energy in Motion

It's said that each person has about 60,000 thoughts every day. The problem is that they have pretty much the same 60,000 thoughts the *next* day! Who you are is the story you're telling yourself over and over again about what your life is like and what the future will bring you. It can grow into a belief system that keeps you quite stuck. Every time you have a negative thought or feeling, it creates a moment of tension that, if repeated over time, can send your system out of balance, affect your physiology and emotional health, and even stifle your natural intuition.

But the beauty of understanding the Five Elements and these archetypes that everyone carries is that you're now empowered to react in a very different way. Rather than taking every emotion that rises inside you so personally and seriously, you can now identify it as part of a natural cycle of energy, a process of "e-motion" (energy in motion) that's passing through. This isn't about staying in perfect balance at all times; rather, it's about dancing effortlessly with whatever comes your way. To align with your own personal choreography, you must not resist, deny, or suppress a feeling; but allow it, feel it, and let it go. The only "bad" emotion is a stuck emotion—one that remains in your system to stagnate and cause harm.

When a feeling begins to form inside of you, there's an instant before it floods your body and sweeps you away. This is the moment when you have an awareness of the emotion rising but before you're lost in it. If you can expand that into a more conscious moment, you're empowered to choose how you relate to it and not get knocked off balance. There's a visualization I use in workshops that can be helpful for you as a parent, as well as to share with your child, that involves balloons. Imagine that when you experience an emotion, a balloon starts to float up that has a label on it defining which emotion it is—anxiety, for instance. So up comes the balloon with ANXIETY written on it that you'd normally grab and off you go, carried away by that feeling. You say to yourself, *I'm anxious!* when in actuality, *you* aren't anxiety; it's just what rose within you. If instead you could think, *This feeling is anxiety,* that would have an entirely different influence on your system.

If you can observe that balloon rising up and say to yourself, *Hmm, that's anxiety,* you'll be less likely to latch on to its string and get swept away. What will happen, of course, is that a second one will come up right behind it with ANXIETY on it, and you'll predictably grab *that* one and off you go! But with a little practice, you can expand that conscious moment of choice so you don't get lost in the emotion and then have to find your way back to your center. This doesn't mean the feelings won't stop coming, but you'll soon be able to stand there still in balance, watching the balloons float by.

We've all probably heard this before: "Don't believe everything you think!" We tend to take our thoughts and feelings too seriously, and as we do so, they return again and again to further cement that old story of who we are, ensuring that we'll continue to create a future based on our past.

The exciting news that Western science now offers is of the plasticity of the mind: Researchers have discovered that your brain can change much more quickly than was previously believed. Each time you think or feel a certain way, it strengthens the neural connection associated with it; but if you choose to have a different thought or feeling, that connection weakens and another one begins to form. If you continue to favor that new choice, the new link gets stronger and the old one soon ceases to exist. It doesn't take long before the less healthy pattern ends and a better one is established; you can change much more easily than you might have imagined. The saying in neurology is "Neurons that fire together, wire together."

• • •

I often talk about Chinese face reading opening a new doorway to compassion in life. The Dalai Lama has said that in Tibetan (in fact, in all Buddhist countries in Asia) the meaning of the word for *compassion* includes feeling it both for yourself and others. Most of us can usually respond to others in this way, but it's not so simple when it comes to ourselves. We tend to be so ingrained in patterns of self-blame that it can be very hard to extend this kindness toward our own spirits. But this is the most important place to start, especially if we want to raise our children to love themselves. As we feel compassion toward ourselves, we'll model this for our children, too.

My wonderful friend Louise Hay suggests looking in the mirror, staring deeply into your own eyes, and saying, "I love you." Try it out and, if you're like most people, it won't be as easy as you might assume. Hopefully, some of what you've learned in this book will help you move to a new place of compassion for yourself as well as others.

⊙ ⊙ ⊙

"A human being is a part of the whole called by us universe, a part limited in time and space. We experience ourselves, our thoughts and feelings as something separated from the rest . . . restricting us to our personal desires and to affection for a few persons nearest to us. Our task must be to free ourselves from this prison by widening our circle of compassion to embrace all living creatures and the whole of nature in its beauty."

— ALBERT EINSTEIN

Chapter 19

FIVE-ELEMENT PARENTING

Our children's deepest wish is to be loved and accepted for who they are. If we trust and honor their true nature, we have an infinite source of wisdom—their personal map of the Five Elements—that empowers us to give them this gift. The guidance of the Five Elements can carry us through even the most difficult times in our sacred role as mothers and fathers.

Water

Don't fear the mystery of that not-knowing place you so frequently find yourself in as a parent. Our culture trains us to always be in a rush to arrive at a solution and fix what we judge as a problem, but it's only by trusting the process that we can truly find our way.

Remember that you're not alone; you carry the inherited wisdom and strength of all your ancestors. Imagine your parents standing behind you, their parents standing behind them, and your great-grandparents behind them. Going back just 20 generations, you may have over a million ancestors behind you, beaming blessings and support.

Wood

Desire for change is the booster rocket that gets you going toward your goals. Help your children define the vision for their lives, but in the same way that the rocket falls away from the space capsule after liftoff, let go of your attachment to what their destinations need to be. Remember that they arrived with an inner plan for their life goals that may be even more powerful than you can imagine. Be flexible as they grow, guide but don't push, and let them do it.

Fire

The truly fearless heart is almost unimaginable to us, since most of us are so lost in resisting our life experience and judging others through the filter of our own personalities. This kind of heart opens to whomever it encounters with total love and acceptance.

The practice of being a parent can be used to break your own heart wide open, but your soul must stay centered in this process. When feelings of anxiety make your energy scatter, call your spirit back. It can help if you gaze into your children's eyes and feel love for who they are in every moment. Start each day by allowing yourself to fill your heart with that kind of joy.

Earth

Bring in the essence of the divine feminine to create harmony, compassion, and community. Remember that the strength of the Earth goddess is not only in her ability to give, but in her receptive nature. Accept aid and comfort from others and ask for assistance when you need it. The African proverb is true: "It takes a village to raise a child." Stay grounded in the support of family and friends who help to provide your children with a stable and loving foundation. Recognize that being of service is very different from being a servant. Like the powerful Mother, don't lose your boundaries; extend the same nurturing care to yourself as you do to your child.

Metal

Stay in the present moment with your children, yet retain your awareness of the bigger picture of the road ahead. Allow yourself to feel the preciousness of each breath you share with them, knowing it means that your time together continues to slip away—and let that feeling be okay. Project yourself a thousand years into future generations of your family, and feel your essence in who they are. Who you are and the choices you make now will reverberate onward through your lineage. Maintain your connection to the divine as a way to not get so lost in your personal emotions of the moment, and remember that being true to your own authentic nature will clear the way for your children to do the same.

⊙ ⊙ ⊙

AFTERWORD

Being a parent has been the most important, difficult, magical, grueling, transformational, and beautiful experience of my life. It changed me forever, and even now continues to reach down deep to make me grow further into my strength. I did the best I could, but sometimes feel as if my son is the incredible man he is *in spite* of me, not because of me. As I write this, he has just graduated from college and stands poised to move into the next phase of his life. And I'm even more in awe than I was the day I brought him home from the hospital.

I send you all my love and support in your own special journey as a parent. Remember that no matter what you encounter along the way, your main purpose is to give your children love and receive their love in return. Let the wisdom of their faces be the guiding light to show you the way.

⊙ ⊙ ⊙

ACKNOWLEDGMENTS

Well, this is just ridiculous. If I included everyone I should probably acknowledge, too many trees would be wasted and you wouldn't be able to lift this book . . . so I'll try to be succinct.

Thank you to my mother, Phyllis, for showing me the world through the eyes of an artist and for still being such a bright spirit at 92. Thank you to my father, Wendall, for modeling how deeply someone can care; and to my sister Diane for carrying on this tradition. Thank you to my son, Jeffrey, for filling my heart and for being such an amazing presence in the world. Thank you to the Taoist and Buddhist teachers over the years who opened my eyes to the incredible beauty and truth of our lives.

Thank you as well to: Louise Hay, my soul sister, who moves through the world surrounded by a sheen of pure love from the millions of people she's helped to heal; Lorie Eve Dechar, author of *Five Spirits,* alchemical acupuncturist and Five Element teacher, who's been a brilliant guide for me; and Jessie Shaw, an insightful Five Element acupuncturist, whose advice for this book was invaluable.

Thank you also to: Rhonda Dicksion, for her genius in design, true-blue heart, and the best sense of humor in this or any nearby galaxy. Stephanie McWilliams, my long-lost Fire twin, who was such an amazing help with the photos and illustrations in this book. Brian Hartman, for his great photography. Carl Buchheit, for his masterful work with the magic of Family Constellations and who helped to find a new home for me in the sunlight; and to Gita Gendloff, who made it real. My great-aunt Bertha, who held the space; and to the other ancestors by whose blessings I am so honored.

Shan-Tung Hsu; Lillian Bridges; Jon Sandifer; and Charles, May, and Bokmon Dong for teaching me so much. Hay House editors Jill Kramer and Patrick Gabrysiak, for their thoughtful work in refining the material in this book. Roselle Kovitz, for modeling the purity of the open heart that does quiet and continuous work in the world. Susan Atchison, lifelong friend, who is now a remarkable healer. David Illig, who many years ago helped me find my courage and call my baby in.

Gratitude as well for the warm waters of the Pacific Ocean that swirl around my legs, and the gentle breezes of Southern California that feel like miracles in every moment.

And a heartfelt thank-you to the *beautiful* children who generously offered their faces for this book to help us all understand how to love more completely—and also to their parents for sharing them with us. And most of all, I thank those who have allowed me to work with them over the years; I've learned so much from the beauty, courage, and divinity revealed in their faces. I look forward with honor and gratitude to those yet to ask me to be present with them on this spirit level. Chinese culture represents the *shen* as being like wild birds of heaven coming to nest in the branches of the heart. And there is so much birdsong in mine that I walk around each day enthralled.

◎ ◎ ◎

BIBLIOGRAPHY

Brazelton, T. Berry, M.D., and Stanley I. Greenspan, M.D. *The Irreducible Needs of Children: What Every Child Must Have to Grow, Learn, and Flourish.* New York, NY: Perseus Publishing, 2000.

Cleary, Thomas. *The Taoist Classics, Vol. 1–4.* Boston, MA: Shambhala Publications, Inc., 1994.

Dechar, Lorie Eve. *Five Spirits: Alchemical Acupuncture for Psychological and Spiritual Healing.* New York, NY: Lantern Books, 2006.

Ekman, Paul. *Emotional Awareness: Overcoming the Obstacles to Psychological Balance and Compassion.* New York, NY: Times Books, 2008.

Eliot, Lise, Ph.D. *What's Going On in There? How the Brain and Mind Develop in the First Five Years of Life.* New York, NY: Bantam Books, 1999.

Gottman, John, Ph.D., with Joan DeClaire. *The Heart of Parenting: How to Raise an Emotionally Intelligent Child.* New York, NY: Simon & Schuster, 1997.

Gurian, Michael. *Nurture the Nature: Understanding and Supporting Your Child's Unique Core Personality.* San Francisco, CA: Jossey-Bass, 2007.

Hallowell, Edward M., M.D. *The Childhood Roots of Adult Happiness: Five Steps to Help Kids Create and Sustain Lifelong Joy.* New York, NY: Ballantine Publishing Group, 2002.

Hicks, Angela, John Hicks, and Peter Mole. *Five Element Constitutional Acupuncture.* London, England: Churchill Livingstone Elsevier, 2004.

Kagen, Jeremy. *An Argument for Mind.* New Haven, CT: Yale University Press, 2006.

Kutscher, Martin L., M.D. *ADHD—Living Without Brakes.* London, England: Jessica Kingsley Publishers, 2008.

Liebmann-Smith, Joan, Ph.D., and Jacqueline Nardi Egan. *Body Signs: How to Be Your Own Diagnostic Detective.* New York, NY: Bantam Dell, 2008.

Marrin, Stephen, M.F.T, and Victoria Costello, with Linda L. Simmons, Psy.D. *The Everything Parent's Guide to Children with OCD.* Avon, MA: F&W Publications, 2008.

Mayes, Linda C., M.D., and Donald J. Cohen, M.D. *The Yale Child Study Center Guide to Understanding Your Child.* New Haven, CT: Yale University Press, 2002.

McCurry, Christopher. *Parenting Your Anxious Child with Mindfulness and Acceptance.* Oakland, CA: New Harbinger Publications, Inc., 2009.

Medina, John. *Brain Rules: 12 Principles for Surviving and Thriving at Work, Home and School.* Seattle, WA: Pear Press, 2008.

National Geographic. *Body, The Complete Human.* Washington, DC: National Geographic Society, 2007.

Newton, Ruth P. *The Attachment Connection.* Oakland, CA: New Harbinger Publications, Inc. 2008.

Polis, Ben. *Only a Mother Could Love Him.* New York, NY: Ballantine Books, 2001.

Rossi, Elisa. *Shen: Psycho-Emotional Aspects of Chinese Medicine.* London, England: Churchill Livingstone Elsevier, 2007.

Schoenwolf, Gary C., Ph.D., Steven B. Bleyl, M.D., Ph.D., Philip R. Brauer, Ph.D., Philippa H. Francis-West, Ph.D. *Larsen's Human Embryology.* Philadelphia, PA: Churchill Livingstone, 2009.

Sohn, Alan, Ed.D, and Cathy Grayson, M.A. *Parenting Your Asperger Child: Individualized Solutions for Teaching Your Child Practical Skills.* New York, NY: Penguin Group, 2005.

Stux, Gabriel, Brian Berman, and Bruce Pomeranz. *Basics of Acupuncture.* Berlin, Germany: Springer-Verlag, 2003.

Taylor, Shelley E. *Tending Instinct: How Nurturing Is Essential for Who We Are and How We Live.* New York, NY: Times Books, 2002.

Veith, Ilza, transl. *Huang Ti Nei Ching Su Wen: The Yellow Emperor's Classic of Internal Medicine.* Berkeley, CA: University of California Press, 1972.

Walker, Richard. *Encyclopedia of the Human Body.* New York, NY: DK Publishing, Inc., 2002.

Williams, Tom, Ph.D. *The Complete Illustrated Guide to Chinese Medicine: A Comprehensive System for Health and Fitness.* London, England: Thorsons, 2000.

⊙ ⊙ ⊙

ABOUT THE AUTHOR

Jean Haner is an internationally recognized teacher, consultant, and author of the book *The Wisdom of Your Face: Change Your Life with Chinese Face Reading!* She uses ancient principles of Taoism and Chinese medicine to "read" people's inner nature, with an emphasis on compassionate and affirming ways for them to live in alignment with their own true selves.

Jean married into a Chinese family in the late 1970s and first learned face reading from her very traditional mother-in-law. It wasn't until years later that she discovered how tolerant her mother-in-law had been; since she had no "moneybags" on her face, she wasn't considered to be a lucky match for her husband!

She went on to study the deeper foundations of face reading with many teachers over the years, and learned that it has nothing to do with luck and everything to do with living an authentic life. With her nearly 30 years of experience, Jean is well known for providing grounded, practical information that can be put to immediate use in your life, presenting workshops from introductory to professional-practitioner levels, as well as corporate training seminars and private consultations. More information is available through her Website: **www.wisdomofyourface.com**.

◉ ◉ ◉

NOTES

NOTES

NOTES

NOTES

NOTES

NOTES

NOTES

We hope you enjoyed this Hay House book. If you'd like to receive our online catalog featuring additional information on Hay House books and products, or if you'd like to find out more about the Hay Foundation, please contact:

Hay House, Inc., P.O. Box 5100, Carlsbad, CA 92018-5100

(760) 431-7695 or **(800) 654-5126**
(760) 431-6948 (fax) or **(800) 650-5115 (fax)**
www.hayhouse.com® • **www.hayfoundation.org**

• • •

Published and distributed in Australia by: Hay House Australia Pty. Ltd., 18/36 Ralph St., Alexandria NSW 2015 • *Phone:* 612-9669-4299 *Fax:* 612-9669-4144 • www.hayhouse.com.au

Published and distributed in the United Kingdom by: Hay House UK, Ltd., 292B Kensal Rd., London W10 5BE • *Phone:* 44-20-8962-1230 *Fax:* 44-20-8962-1239 • www.hayhouse.co.uk

Published and distributed in the Republic of South Africa by: Hay House SA (Pty), Ltd., P.O. Box 990, Witkoppen 2068 • *Phone/Fax:* 27-11-467-8904 • info@hayhouse.co.za • www.hayhouse.co.za

Published in India by: Hay House Publishers India, Muskaan Complex, Plot No. 3, B-2, Vasant Kunj, New Delhi 110 070 • *Phone:* 91-11-4176-1620 • *Fax:* 91-11-4176-1630 • www.hayhouse.co.in

Distributed in Canada by:
Raincoast, 9050 Shaughnessy St., Vancouver, B.C. V6P 6E5 *Phone:* (604) 323-7100 • *Fax:* (604) 323-2600 • www.raincoast.com

• • •

Take Your Soul on a Vacation

Visit **www.HealYourLife.com®** to regroup, recharge, and reconnect with your own magnificence. Featuring blogs, mind-body-spirit news, and life-changing wisdom from Louise Hay and friends.

Visit **www.HealYourLife.com** today!

Mind Your Body,
Mend Your Spirit

Hay House is the ultimate resource for inspirational and health-conscious books, audio programs, movies, events, e-newsletters, member communities, and much more.

Visit **www.hayhouse.com**® today and nourish your soul.

UPLIFTING EVENTS

Join your favorite authors at live events in a city near you or log on to **www.hayhouse.com** to visit with Hay House authors online during live, interactive Web events.

INSPIRATIONAL RADIO

Daily inspiration while you're at work or at home. Enjoy radio programs featuring your favorite authors, streaming live on the Internet 24/7 at **HayHouseRadio.com**®. Tune in and tune up your spirit!

VIP STATUS

Join the Hay House VIP membership program today and enjoy exclusive discounts on books, CDs, calendars, card decks, and more. You'll also receive 10% off all event reservations (excluding cruises). Visit **www.hayhouse.com/wisdom** to join the Hay House Wisdom Community™.

Visit **www.hayhouse.com** and enter priority code 2723 during checkout for special savings!
(One coupon per customer.)

OKANAGAN REGIONAL
3 3132 03049 6634

HEAL YOUR LIFE ♥

Take Your Soul on a Vacation

Get your daily dose of inspiration today at **www.HealYourLife.com®**. Brimming with all of the necessary elements to ease your mind and educate your soul, this Website will become the foundation from which you'll start each day. This essential site delivers the latest in mind, body, and spirit news and real-time content from your favorite Hay House authors.

Make It Your Home Page Today!

www.HealYourLife.com®

HAY HOUSE

www.hayhouse.com®